Student-Centered Teaching
in the Secondary School

Robert B. Sund

Leslie W. Trowbridge

University of Northern Colorado

Charles E. Merrill Publishing Company
A Bell & Howell Company
Columbus, Ohio

Photographs by W. Lee Youngblood

Published by
Charles E. Merrill Publishing Co.
A Bell & Howell Co.
Columbus, Ohio

Copyright © 1974 by Bell & Howell Co. All rights reserved. No part of this book may be reproduced in any form, electronic or mechanical, including photocopy, recording or any information storage and retrieval system, without permission in writing from the publisher.

International Standard Book Number: 0-675-08846-1

Library of Congress Catalog Card Number: 73-93272

1 2 3 4 5 6 7 8 9 10—77 76 75 74

Printed in the United States of America

Preface

The field of education changes rapidly, reflecting the accelerated modifications in society and the explosion of knowledge. Information related to how humans function, develop cognitively and affectively, learn, love, and become eventually fully functioning human beings is constantly unfolding. Revelations about these areas are further complemented by discoveries in subject matter, creating libraries of material reported in numerous journals. All this information must be sifted for its relevance to teaching.

This book (a portion of which is taken from our 1973 edition of *Teaching Science by Inquiry in the Secondary School*—Merrill) assists the prospective as well as the experienced educator in the filtering process by relating modern educational and psychological theory and teaching practices to instruction in the middle and secondary schools. Research has indicated the desirability of student-centered instruction. Therefore, we have followed John Dewey's dictum, "the student learns by doing," in selecting methods and designing activities for you to use. Because of this viewpoint, you are often invited to act and react to the text material. We offer examples outlining how to prepare various investigative lessons, and we suggest that you use these models to prepare activities for your particular instructional needs. For example, the Hilda Taba inductive-deductive method is briefly explained, and we encourage you to produce lessons for your subject area using this teaching strategy. By preparing these as well as other lessons, you not only learn how to use a method, but also apply your creative abilities. It is by integrating lessons and techniques that this text becomes a practical source for planning and improving your teaching.

Considerable attention is given in several chapters to students' cognitive abilities as determined by Piaget and other scholars. Why do some students understand and easily grasp complex verbal explanations, ratios, probability, etc., while others experience difficulties? Suggestions are outlined indicating how to react to and help individuals experiencing such problems. In several sections, we stress examples for improving inquiry oriented question abilities so that teachers may better develop students' critical and creative thinking and other valuable human talents.

There is disagreement among educators as to the desirability and role of behavioral objectives in instruction. We present the opposing views and outline examples and suggestions for writing cognitive, affective, and psychomotor objectives for those who want to become more proficient in their use. Furthermore, because the area of affectivity is becoming more important in today's schools, a chapter is devoted to this topic plus others related to it, such as the multiple-talent approach espoused by Taylor and the value clarification techniques elaborated by Simon, Kohlberg, Shavier, Oliver, and others.

We have also devoted considerable attention to evaluation, outlining how to determine achievement using not only tests but also other measures such as observation and self-evaluational inventories. Related to evaluation is the work of the National Assessment of Educational Progress Project the purpose of which is to inform teachers about the achievement of certain objectives on a national level. We discuss the results and the implications of their first assessment.

Other areas of practical concern covered in this text are discipline problems, student teaching, professional growth and development, the advantages and disadvantages of numerous experimental teacher-training approaches, and problems in inner-city schools.

It is our hope that this text facilitates the development of your human potential and professional capabilities. Teaching is a challenging profession, demanding the best of individuals. Preparing and enriching yourself for this career is a fascinating human endeavor worthy of your best efforts. The rewards, in terms of satisfactions gained in aiding youth to develop into more viable, mentally healthy humans, will contribute immeasurably to your growth as a person and enhance your professional competence.

Contents

1	Building Your Instructional Theory	1
2	What Are Adolescents Mentally Capable of Doing?	16
3	Investigative Teaching	39
4	Questioning and Listening as Aids to Excellent Teaching	56
5	Establishing What Is Important in Teaching	81
6	The Affective Domain	105
7	Teaching and Learning Methods	122
8	Teaching in the Inner City	164
9	Adjusting Instruction for Individual Variation	173
10	Creativity—The Way to "Being" More Human	204
11	Evaluation	242
12	The National Assessment of Educational Progress	281
13	Competency-Based Teacher Training	299
14	A Positive Approach to Discipline	309

15	Student Teaching	326
16	The Professional Educator	347
Appendix 1	Self-Evaluation Inventory for Teachers	361
Appendix 2	An Analysis and Checklist on the Problem-Solving Objective	367
Index		377

1 Building Your Instructional Theory

The function of education, the goal of education—the human goal so far as human beings are concerned—is ultimately the "self-actualization" of a person, the becoming fully human, the development of the fullest height that the human species can stand up to or that the particular individual can come to.[1]

Changes in society during the past decade have necessitated revisions in materials and methods . . . .[2]

The Learning Process Is Complex Because People Are Complex

Prospective teachers initially tend to assume that the educational process is relatively simple, often perceiving a teacher's role as mainly imparting knowledge to the young. Such a simplistic view of education has advantages. For example, any failure in having students learn can be easily justified: "I covered the *information* but the students didn't learn. I covered the information but the students were slow. I covered the information but the students didn't listen. I gave assignments but the students didn't read them." By using this rationale some teachers maintain their own egos regardless of what the students learn. Other

---

[1] Abraham H. Maslow, *The Farther Reaches of Human Nature* (New York: The Viking Press, 1971), p. 168.
[2] A statement made by the Biological Sciences Curriculum Study Writing Team to explain why they were rewriting and modifying their materials for the secondary school.

instructors, however, see their role differently and, because of their orientation, they interact successfully with students who were failing under the "covering" type of instructor. Why? How do they view teaching?

Instructors are hired to insure that students learn. If materials, methods, or teaching strategies are not working, teachers must draw upon their capabilities as professionals to diagnose and prescribe a new mode of operation to insure learning. Clearly because of the complexity of a human's genetics, background, experience, emotional orientation, and personality; the conception of teaching as imparting information is not likely to be totally effective.

This is not to say that successful instructors do not use subject matter as a means in attaining educational goals, but they are more likely to focus on the individual student as a person "becoming" and not limit their teaching to covering material. They are "person" instead of "information" oriented—they do not rush through activities for the sake of coverage but pace the learning process so students have time to ascertain and assimilate in their minds the significance of what is being studied. In asking questions, for example, they may wait several seconds for students to reason and create replies instead of immediately calling on someone for an instant and often insignificant response. By giving students time to think, they provide opportunities for them to express themselves as humans. The thinking process and the growth of human expression becomes more central to the teaching process. Teachers who operate in this way do not look upon students as sponges soaking up knowledge, but rather as individuals in the process of evolving toward the greater manifestation of their human potential. A sponge can only give back what it has absorbed, but an individual whose talents have been developed is capable of utilizing his learning and applying it to new situations. He thereby is more likely to interact uniquely and innovatively with his environment.

You as a teacher will be involved with helping people *become*. Hopefully, students under your care will become more beautiful and mentally healthy, effective persons. Your ability to insure this end requires increasing professional competence by your continual growth in the knowledge of human behavior, the educational process, and subject matter. Since there is no end to the limit in how knowledgeable you can become with these areas, the task of becoming truly a great teacher never terminates.

Whatever we do to improve ourselves as teachers simultaneously improves our richness as individuals. The reverse is also true. Whatever we do to improve ourselves as persons also contributes to our effectiveness as teachers. This is truly one of the great fringe benefits of teaching.

Building Your Instructional Theory

Increasingly, the critics of American schools have attacked the dehumanizaing aspects of our educational institutions. Schools to some extent reflect our society which has evolved into an industrial, technological, impersonal, and, by and large, urban complex—far removed from the agrarian society of our forefathers. Youth, until comparatively recently, played valuable roles in society. They performed the chores on the farm, assisted in the harvesting, baked cakes, canned food, and prepared meals. They were needed, they were wanted, they had purpose and developed "self-esteem" as a result. *They were somebody; they had identity.* Contrast this with many adolescents today who are often an economic drain on the family. Many have never worked nor contributed much to the maintenance of their families, and thus they coast along striving to affirm their value.

Schools have not always helped to lessen this personal loss of value. This is so because they have often increased in size and adopted many of the techniques of the industrial, technological complex. It has been reasoned that because mass production techniques work for industry, they should function equally well for education. National curriculum projects funded by millions of dollars from our government have been established to "modernize" the subject matter in the same manner as in redesigning a new car. Students have been grouped and regrouped into large classes, large lectures, small groups, open laboratories, and have been given programmed learning, instructional modules, etc., with little regard for their particular psychological and personal needs, inclinations, interests, or desires. Just as in industry where the corporation produces a product and then spends millions telling people they can't live without it, so have educators produced products and then spent much time and energy trying to convince the student, the consumer, that he needs it.

It's interesting to note that workers feel insignificant in overly mechanized industries where there is little opportunity for them to build their "self-esteem" or their value as persons. As a result, labor unrest is kindled and the workers often produce products of inferior quality, necessitating costly quality control checks. So too in public schools and universities adolescents and young adults have often revolted against the dehumanizing characteristics of these institutions. Students want to be consulted and respected, as well as obtain opportunities to grow in important and relevant ways as noble, valuable individuals. They have given notice that educational institutions and their personnel must treat then humanely. What this means is that the teachers and administrators must help the young discover, manifest, and develop as much as possible their unique human capabilities. As a teacher, how will you insure that you constantly are fulfilling this function?

The Need For a Theory

Many prospective teachers do not understand the role of an instructional theory. A theory is a fantastic intellectual instrument economizing the chores of the mind. It becomes a guide in directing your behavior so that you operate more effectively and affectively in the classroom. By knowing relatively little—a theory—the mind knows much, for it is through theoretical understanding that it is capable of interpreting volumes of information. This is so because a theory provides three fundamental functions for the mind. It:

1. Enables prediction and therefore provides direction.
2. Explains phenomena and human situations.
3. Provides organizational structure.

Think for a moment of the implications of knowing the theory of evolution. Given a strata with some fossils, you can predict the types of fossils you will find above and below the layer of exploration. You can explain why the fossils change. And, if you bring fossils up from different layers and somehow become confused as to what fossils came from the lowest strata, you know how to reorganize your findings and put the fossils in the proper order. This would all be impossible without a theory.

Disraeli said, "A man without a theory is doomed to make the same mistake twice!" Just as the task of a scientist is to formulate and evolve theories, so must teachers build through their teaching life span an instructional theory which helps them to predict, explain, and organize learning. Beginning teachers start with but a few fibers entwined into a weak theoretical structure, but as they progress through an infinitude of experiences, awarenesses, and learning about human behavior, teaching strategies, and the structure of knowledge, they slowly fashion an instructional theory that works best for them. A teacher's instructional theory is never complete because as he grows and gains insights into human behavior, he evaluates, modifies, and rebuilds his own theoretical framework.

Foundation for Instructional Theory

What are the origins for an instructional theoretical construct? Much of them must come from what is known about the behavioral sciences plus what the teacher discovers in a pragmatic way in his own classroom —what works for him with his students is what counts. Just as the physical and natural sciences have their scientific principles so have psychology and sociology established certain principles.

Building Your Instructional Theory 5

Education applies the principles revealed by psychology and sociology to the field of learning. An effective teacher is aware of these disciplines. Teachers have taken courses in educational psychology to learn principles of human behavior and theories of learning, but this knowledge is of value only if it can be translated into action in the classroom. It is then that the teacher is truly evaluated, not by his professors but by his students.

The following sections discuss both principles of learning and teaching. As you read these, think of how you would use them as guidelines in your teaching. Imagine your own class, your students, class episodes, and how you would operate as an effective teacher. To memorize a psychological principle takes little intelligence, but a principle can be applied well only by a truly intelligent and gifted person. From the day you start teaching to the day you retire, you will be trying to apply principles of learning successfully in your instruction.

In the following sections no attempt has been made to present an exhaustive catalogue of principles but only a helpful list for the prospective teacher.

What principles of learning are being applied here?

Principles of Learning

1. *Students learn best by being actively involved.* If they are involved in activities themselves rather than just reading about them, they learn better. This is particularly true if students have to reason and work out the meaning of something or establish attitudes and values for themselves.

2. *Positive, or reward, reinforcement is more likely to result in students' learning than negative reinforcement.* A teacher who accepts an answer as indicative of a student striving to learn even though it is incorrect, and compliments and encourages students is more likely to obtain higher achievement than one who tells them their work is poor or derides them for poor achievement. *Threat, punishment, or demeaning may cause avoidance tendencies* in the student and prevent learning. Failure can best be tolerated by providing a backlog of successful experiences.

3. *Stimulating experiences are kinds of rewards enhancing learning.*

4. *Learning is transferred to the extent the learner sees possibilities for transfer and has opportunities to apply his knowledge.*

5. *Meaningful material is easiest learned and best retained.*

6. *Learning is enhanced by a wide variety of experiences organized around purposes accepted by the students.* Teach in depth. Don't try to cover the book; cover what you do well, giving opportunities for students to have many experiences with the subject.

7. *The learner is always learning things other than what a teacher thinks he is teaching.* A teacher may have a student heat a chemical solution to get a precipitate. The teacher is teaching a chemical process, but the student is also learning laboratory skills and how to organize the equipment, be efficient in the laboratory, and work with others. None of these is likely to be tested in an examination.

8. *Learning is increased in a rich and varied environment.* The richer the classroom, laboratory, and school surroundings in offering opportunities for learning, the greater the level of achievement. A bare, uninteresting room offers little stimulation for learning.

9. *Detail must be placed into a structured pattern or it is rapidly forgotten.*

Building Your Instructional Theory 7

What is this student learning other than what the teacher might evaluate?

10. *Learning from reading is increased if time is spent on recalling what has been read rather than on rereading.*

Teaching Principles

1. *Planning and establishing the learning environment results in more learning than does haphazard instruction.*
2. *Students tend to achieve in ways they are evaluated.* If you test only for facts, they tend only to memorize facts.
3. *Students learn more effectively if they know and have opportunities to determine the objectives.* Teachers, for example, should spend time determining student interest and discussing the purposes of doing activities and the processes used in solving problems.
4. *The teacher's function in the learning process is one of facilitating learning.*

5. *Pupils learn from one another.* Working in groups on activities enhances learning.
6. *When the understanding of a detail of any theory or apparatus is determined by understanding the whole, then the comprehension of that part must wait until the whole is understood.*

In interacting with students, teachers must constantly endeavor to apply these principles in their classrooms. It is easy for a teacher to know a principle, for example, "The greater the student involvement, the greater the learning" and then turn around and ignore it by lecturing, in which there is little student involvement. These principles should be drawn upon and included in your general theoretical construct. One theoretical frame of reference in which they may be entwined has been outlined by the Association for Supervision and Curriculum Development book entitled *Perceiving, Behaving, and Becoming: A New Focus for Education.* It states a general theoretical structure for becoming a fully functioning person and describes the implications of this view for teaching. The book was authored by Earl C. Kelley, Carl R. Rogers, A.H. Maslow, Arthur W. Combs, plus many others, and is mainly concerned with providing teachers a humanistic theory of instruction. This view of psychology looks at individuals as functioning organisms each in the process of striving to build his "self-concept." The humanistic approach centers on the individual teacher as a person rather than a giver of knowledge. The way the individual teacher views "self," others, and the teaching task is the foundation by which the instructional theory is constructed. The teacher's perceptions, beliefs, and values guide his interaction with students and influence his selection of curriculum materials and organization within the classroom. Some of the main tenets of this theory are:

1. The perceptions an individual has at any given moment determine his behavior.
2. Perceptions about self are more important than other existing perceptions.
3. Man is always engaged in a continuous striving for self-fulfillment.[3]

---

[3]Arthur W. Combs, *The Professional Education of Teachers* (Boston: Allyn and Bacon, Inc., 1965).

Building Your Instructional Theory

The Path to Building "Self-Esteem"

Teacher Builds Trust and Acceptance→	Student Becomes Creatively Involved→	Good Mental Health
		Success→ Self-Esteem→ More Likely to Take Risks Again and Be Creative

The role of a teacher under this theoretical framework is to help students build their "self-esteem." This means the teacher involves students in the learning process so that they have successful experiences, feel accepted, are liked, respected, admired, etc. The theory stresses the necessity of perceiving well the individual student on the way to his becoming a person and personalizing the learning environment. This means the instructor must treat every person as an individual with particular needs at a specific place in time on his path to "becoming." The teacher helps him *become* by being open and non-threatening, by accepting and liking him, by reducing fear and helping him discover his identity by developing his talents. As the student becomes more secure through acceptance and successes, he is more willing to take risks and be creative. Being creative is truly a valuable human characteristic contributing to a person's self-esteem and thereby improving his mental health. In these times when so many of our students have problems with their identity and self-concepts, the humanistic approach offers a psychological mode for helping them resolve these problems. Maslow has said: "Every person is, in part, his own project and makes himself."[4] What we as teachers have to do is assist students in this effort and facilitate their development to the best of our abilities.

Outstanding Teachers Relate Well with Students

Evidence to support the importance of interacting in the manner outlined above comes from students. When given the opportunity to define the characteristics of outstanding teachers, they seldom list

---

[4]A.H. Maslow, "Some Basic Propositions of Growth and Self-Actualization Psychology," *Perceiving, Behaving, Becoming: A New Focus for Education* (Washington, D.C.: Association for Supervision and Curriculum Development, Yearbook 1962), Chapter 4.

as paramount in importance subject matter competence. Students believe it is more important that an instructor relate well and interact in an enthusiastic manner with them. This holds true from elementary level to graduate school, regardless of the students' socioeconomic background as indicated below:

Selected Choices in Order of Importance

Popula-tions	A Suburb	B Urban Upward Bound	C Gifted	D University Lab School	E Graduate Students	F Sixth Grade
	2	2	4	2	4	2
	4	4	2	4	2	4
	3	3	1	1	1	1
	1	1	3	3	3	5
Low	5	5	5	5	5	3

General Categories of Teaching Importance
1. Knowledge and organization of subject matter.
2. Adequacy of relations with students in class.
3. Adequacy of plans and procedures in class.
4. Enthusiasm in working with students.
5. Teaching methods.[5]

Note that all of the groups sampled, whether from elementary, secondary, or the university level, chose items belonging to the categories "adequacy of relations with students in class" or "enthusiasm in working with students" as being more important than knowledge, methods, or plans. This is not to say that these latter categories are not valuable, but if you do not interact with students in a warm and human way they perceive you as not being an excellent teacher. Their perception undoubtedly affects how they function in class.

The Multiple-Talent Approach

How is the teacher to convey to students his interest in them as individuals and help them build their self-concepts? Guilford, Taylor, and others have shown that a person is a composite of over 120 talents.[6]

---
[5]The above was modified from unpublished research data provided by Rodger Bybee, Laboratory School, University of Northern Colorado, 1970. No title.

[6]Calvin W. Taylor, "Multiple Talent Approach Teaching Scheme in Which Most Students Can Be Above Average," *The Instructor* (April 28, 1968): 27.

Building Your Instructional Theory

If they are to develop their self-concepts they must have teachers helping them manifest those talents in which they are particularly gifted.

Dr. Taylor states that because individuals are a collection of talents, e.g., academic, creative, planning, organizing, social, forecasting, communicating, decision making, etc., a multi-talent approach in teaching is required. By this he means that teachers should attempt to develop all the talents of their students rather than just the academic ones. To evaluate a student solely on the basis of academic talent is to insult him as a person.

To perceive students as talent pools broadens the vision of the teacher and insures better interaction between him and students, for if you view students through a multiple-talent perceptual framework, they are then all above average in some ways. Dr. Taylor states:[7]

> If we restrict ourself to cultivating only one talent, we will merely find the top 10 percent to be highly gifted, but if we will seek for the highly gifted in each of several different talents, the number found to be gifted will increase tremendously. In fact, if we cultivate three talents instead of only one, the percent found to be gifted will more than double (will be over 20 percent). Furthermore, if we work in six talent areas, the percent who are highly gifted will triple (will be about 30 percent).

Dr. Taylor further points out that for any one talent only 50 percent of the students will be above average. However, if you combine six talents to group students, over 90 percent will be above average. Teachers have traditionally thought that academic talent correlated well with other talents. Taylor has shown this is not true. In fact, some of the most creative individuals may be the poorest academically. No longer can a teacher presume he's a good instructor if he limits himself to just developing academic ability.

Understanding the complexity of striving to manifest all human talent may be frightening. But think for a moment of the beauty of the idea—no student is below average in all talents. Fifty percent of the students may be below average academically. However, if you find a way to bring out the outstanding talents of the academically poor students, they will experience feelings of success. This will affect positively their "self-esteem" and contribute to their expectancy level so that they will eventually believe "I can learn and be rewarded for my talents in school." As a result, their academic achievement will likely improve.

---

[7]Calvin Taylor, "Accent on Talent," *An NEA Service to the Schools of the Nation*, Vol. 2, No. 2 (January, 1968).

Taylor's Multiple-Talent Approach

	Academic Talents	Creative Talents	Communication Talents	Planning Talents	Forecasting Talents	Decision-Making Talents	Other Types of Talents
Language Arts	X						
Social Studies	X						
Humanities	X						
Arts	X						
Biological Sciences	X						
Physical Sciences	X						
Mathematics	X						
Other Subjects	X						

How many talents of those shown on the chart may have been involved in producing these items?

A MODERN INSTRUCTIONAL THEORY

> BETTER MENTAL HEALTH
> Resulting in
> SELF-CONCEPT OF THE PERSON
> Builds the
> MULTI-TALENT DEVELOPMENT
> Contributes to
> LEARNING BY INQUIRY

It seems reasonable, therefore, that a modern instructional theory should have at its foundation a commitment to build the self-concepts of students. Abraham Maslow has said that the goal of education is to provide an environment so that the student ultimately becomes "self-actualized" in a beautiful human way. To become "self-actualized" a person has to be involved in activities contributing to his self-esteem and satisfying his needs as a person. Through such involvement the individual experiences success and thereby comes to the realization that "*I can* do something of value," e.g., "I can think, I can create, I can organize, I can plan, I can get along well with people and motivate them," etc. This "I canness" indicates to the student "he is somebody," helping him to develop his identity and gain a positive realistic view of his "self" image. Because of our discovery of the importance of self-esteem and multiple talents, there is a need for teachers to shift from what has often been the myopic view of the student as an academic producer to a broader, a holistic one encompassing multi-talents, emotions, feelings and attitudes. Research indicates, for example, that students' achievement is affected by attitudes and emotions toward subject matter.[8] For students to become more involved in using their talents, instruction must become more investigatively oriented rather than teacher dominated. The instructor no longer should do all the planning, organizing, decision making, etc., because to do so robs the students of the opportunities to develop these talents.

We believe that the foundation of a modern theory of instruction should, therefore, include as its basis a self-concept—multi-talent—investigative approach. The teacher acts as a facilitator of learning by providing helpful guidance in the learning process, rewarding talents, and enjoying watching students grow into competent persons characterized by high self-esteem and mental well being.

[8] D.R. Green, *et al. Measurement and Piaget* (New York: McGraw-Hill Book Company, 1971), p. 88.

This is not to say that the above components complete the instructional theory. As you evolve through life and continue on your path to self-actualization, you will develop many of your own talents, humanistic capabilities, methods, and procedures through success in your teaching. As a consequence, *you will slowly modify, mold, and reshape your personal instructional theory.* It will have special meaning because you constructed and grew with it.

By now, in your life, you have committed yourself through teaching to the valuable humane pursuit of helping others become exciting, dynamic individuals. Because your ability and sophistication at accomplishing this feat can always be improved, the task of evolving your instructional theory will never cease. This is a beautiful realization because it means you will always have the fun of becoming a better person and teacher. The only hazard is in stopping the process. By so doing, you will become bored and begin to die as a professional and as a fascinating human being.

A Self-Evaluation

Listed below are some general questions to help you evaluate yourself as a person and teacher. Rate yourself now on these and repeat your evaluations periodically to see how and where you might improve.

Rate 1-9

1. How well do I accept individuals and students as they are? Do I try to put *myself in their place and feel* with them?
2. Do I in my struggle for self-esteem, feeling better about myself, help students feel better about themselves?
3. Do I accept attitudes of people I disagree with and strive to appreciate their views and feelings?
4. Do I help make growing up easier for students, especially for the ones I don't care much about?
5. Do I take joy in students' being different or do I say "wrong" because they are different?
6. Do I strive to look at students from different perspectives—e.g., multi-talent; being, becoming through "self-actualization," etc.?

Building Your Instructional Theory

7. Do I endeavor to give as much of myself as I might or do I avoid situations that require me to give and grow as a person?
8. Am I approachable? Do people seek me out in times of emotional stress or intellectual conflict?

Summary

Teachers as they interact in the learning environment evolve theories of instruction that they modify throughout their careers. The principles of psychology and sociology provide the sinews for the theory and practical experience, the web.

Fundamental to a modern instructional theory is helping students build their self-esteem. The achievement of this depends upon the instructor "reading well," perceiving the needs, inadequacies, and potential of his students. Important to this perception is a holistic view of the person and the realization that each student is a composite of over 120 talents, e.g., academic, creative, communicative, planning, forecasting, and decision making, etc. Note, academic talent is only one of these. An instructor restricting his goals solely to the manifestations of academic talent limits the horizons of learning. The facilitation of multi-talent development should be the aim of every teacher, for it is through development of talents that the individual gains insights into his "person," builds his self-concept, and acquires a feeling of identity and a belief in his significance as an individual. If a teacher looks upon his class from a multi-talent perspective, he sees every student as being above average in several respects. By interacting with students through this philosophical framework, he is more likely to respond in a positive manner and be considered a good instructor by his students.

A teacher constantly has to improve his perceptions of students. Where are their "heads"? Why are they having difficulty with a problem? What is wrong with their thinking processes? How can this be corrected? How can they improve their thinking facilities? What emotional or attitudinal problems seem to be interfering with the learning process? Fortunately, there is a wealth of research providing assistance to instructors in answering these questions. The other chapters in this text endeavor to provide a base for answers to these questions and assist you further in building a foundation for a modern instructional theory.

2 What Are Adolescents Mentally Capable of Doing?

Application of Piaget's Theory of Cognitive Development

> A friend of mine has said that every time you teach a child something, you keep him from reinventing it.—Piaget[1]

An adolescent is different from an adult—we even have a word to describe and demarcate this period of human development. Yet junior and senior high school instructors often interact with their students as though they were mentally like adults. The teacher who thinks logically, in hypothetical-deductive ways, often assumes that his students can easily follow and perform this type of thinking process. Research done by Dr. Jean Piaget and his colleagues has indicated that this may be far from true. Adolescent minds are not adult minds, and many students in this period of mental development do not reason like adults.

For approximately fifty years Dr. Jean Piaget and his co-workers at the Genetic and Epistemology Institute in Geneva, Switzerland, have studied how the human mind develops. A baby clearly comes into the world with an unfinished mind and as he grows and matures he slowly evolves through the years into a mature adult capable of performing fantastic mental, computer-like operations. What is the sequence of mental development? How does the mind evolve from the babblings of a child to the creative intellectualizing of a fully functioning adult?

---

[1]Frank G. Jennings, "Jean Piaget: Notes on Learning," *Saturday Review* (May 20, 1967): 81.

What Are Adolescents Mentally Capable of Doing? 17

Piaget says individuals pass through four stages of mental development. They are:

Piaget's Stages

Sensori-motor	0-2 years
Pre-operational	2-7 years
Concrete Operational	7-11 years
Formal Operational	11-14 years

It would appear from the above age levels that all high school students would perform mental tasks similar to adults after fourteen years. However, these categorizations refer to the majority of individuals. There may be a considerable number of students in any one class who have not attained the level indicated. In fact, we have evaluated students in suburban and inner-city high schools and in the university and found many did not perform well on formal operational tasks. If a teacher tried to get these students to do assignments requiring mental operations at this level, he was bound to experience difficulty. It must be remembered also that there are degrees of mastery of cognitive mental abilities—a person never ends his facility to use his mind more efficiently and effectively except perhaps in the waning years of life.

Most middle and high school teachers have students in their classes who have difficulty in thinking on the formal level. This is particularly apparent in the lower grades of middle school. However, even in the senior class there will be many students who do not perform well on the formal level. Middle school and high school teachers need, therefore, to become aware of Piaget's theory, particularly the concrete and formal levels, so they can better diagnose thinking problems and respond more wisely to students. For this reason a brief synopsis of each of the stages follows:

The Sensori-motor Stage: 0-2 Years
A Period of Discriminating and Labeling.

A. *Stimulus Bound*
The sensori-motor stage is so named because the child mainly interacts with the environment with his senses and muscles and is directed by sensations from without. He develops his ability to perceive, touch, move, etc., during this stage. Most of his body motions are in a sense an experiment with the environment. As the child interacts with his surroundings, he slowly learns to handle it better. For example, he eventually perceives depth, whereas in the early part of the stage he only sees things as flat.

B. *Order and Organization Begins*
As a child develops he is faced with the challenge of taking information in and then organizing it so that he can call upon it later and better interact with his environment. By so doing, he gains both physical and cognitive experience. Piaget believes that the origin of cognitive mental structures is physical action. By this he means that when a child perceives or moves an object, he is forcing his mind to construct mental programs to handle it. In a sense, this activity is analogous to a computer programmer constructing a program. When a child acts upon information in his mind, he may classify it or file it away in an appropriate niche in the cerebral tissue. By so doing, he has mental experience —he is learning to program his computer, his mind. He thereby establishes a foundation of cognitive skills so important for the manifestation of the other stages of development in later years. The better the experiences, the better mentality he will have in the future.

The rudiments of cognitive activity he builds are organized progressively into more elaborate schemes as he develops. He begins by adapting his innate reflexes to the objects around him and proceeds to coordinate the various actions that are possible with each one thus learning the object's properties. Later he may use these properties in solving practical problems. As he develops and uses his mind he is finally able to recall mentally the properties of objects without having to test them each time he confronts them.

C. *Simultaneous Physical and Mental Operations*
At this stage of development the child cannot perform any mental operations without actually doing the operation physically at the same time. He has no imagination for objects or acts. What is not in sight is out of mind. He cannot add, subtract, or even classify unless he is acting with real objects. These thought processes only become meaningful to him in later stages of mental development. Even the most rudimentary sense of direction and purpose does not develop until well into this stage. He is, for example, unable to detour or remove an obstacle without forgetting where he is going.

D. *Ability to Label Develops*
At the end of this period he is able to imagine. The child can call to mind certain people, animals, objects and activities. By age two, he has "names" for many objects and activities enabling him to elaborate his concepts in the next stage. Space is limited to the area in which he acts, and time is limited to the duration of his actions. Progress de-

What Are Adolescents Mentally Capable of Doing?

velops as he becomes more involved with activities concerning space and time.

Pre-Operational (2-7 years)
The Intuitive Stage

The second stage of mental development (years 2-7) is pre-operational. It is called pre-operational because the child is *not* yet capable of carrying on any mental *operations*. Piaget's examples of mental operations include the following.

Logical Operations

ADDING	$+$	COMBINING
SUBTRACTING	$-$	TAKING AWAY
MULTIPLYING	$\times$	REPEATING
DIVIDING	$\div$	REPEATING SUBTRACTION
CORRESPONDENCE (ONE TO ONE)	$\sim$	ALIGNING ONE ROW WITH ANOTHER ROW
PLACING IN ORDER	$>$	THIS GREATER THAN —OR THIS LESS THAN
SUBSTITUTING	$=$	REPLACING SOMETHING WITH ANOTHER ENTITY
REVERSIBILITY	$\rightleftarrows$	SUBCLASSES BELONG TO A CLASS—A CLASS HAS SUBCLASSES

In addition to these, the pre-operational child also is not able to perform certain infralogical operations. The word *Infra* in Greek means below. Infralogical operations then are considered by Piaget to be mental processes below operations in the degree of mental sophistication required. Most of these logical and infralogical operations are not demonstrated by the child until after the age of seven when he reaches the concrete operational level of mental development.

During this period the child continues to perform many actions, but actions become internalized in the mind. For instance the child thinks of moving an object (a mental action) before he moves it. Infralogical operations include the following:

Infralogical Operations

OBSERVING	LOOKING AT SOMETHING CRITICALLY
MEASUREMENT	HOW LONG, HIGH, WHAT VOLUME, ETC.
QUANTITY	HOW MUCH
TIME	NOW, FUTURE, PAST
CLASSIFYING	GROUPING ACCORDING TO SIMILARITIES
SPACE	ROOM, HOME, COMMUNITY, COUNTRY, CONTINENT, WORLD, UNIVERSE
INTERPERSONAL REACTIONS	GETTING ALONG WITH OTHERS—NOTING THE EFFECTS OF ONE'S BEHAVIOR ON OTHERS
VALUES	ESTABLISHING VALUES

A. *Stimulus Limited*

The child in this stage no longer operates just on stimuli from the environment. He operates on a plane of representation—he can use language. However, his mental images or representations are limited to what he has experienced, and he may use the images he has formed in his mind incorrectly. He may in the early part of this stage, for example, call all men "Daddy." The pre-operational stage is said to be intuitive because as the child develops he begins to sense mentally the difference between such things as an individual item and its class, singular and plurals, some and many, man and men, and "Daddy" and other men.

B. *Centers, Does Not Decenter Attention*

The pre-operational child centers his attention usually on the surface of the problem. He may see only the superficial features stimulating him the most. For example, if you take a ball of putty and roll it out, the child will notice that it is longer; he centers on length. However, he will not notice that the putty is also thinner; he has not decentered his attention to include width. If you ask him whether the rolled out putty weighs more, less, or the same as the ball of putty from which it was made, he will usually say the rolled out putty weighs more even though you may roll it back into the ball once again in front of him. He

What Are Adolescents Mentally Capable of Doing?

doesn't conserve substance, or realize changing the form or distribution of something doesn't affect its amount, until late in the period.

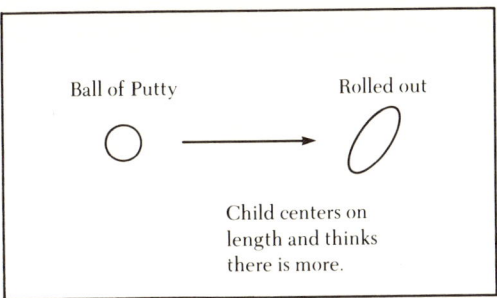

C. *Focuses on States, Not Transformations*
A pre-operational child cannot combine a series of events to show how the changes they have undergone unify them. For example, if a child is shown a series of pictures of a pencil falling and asked to order them in the manner the pencil fell, he can't do it. He focuses on the state of the pencil before and after it has fallen, and will probably place the first and last picture in order but be confused about the others. He wouldn't, for example, be able to tell you when an apple would no longer be an apple as you chopped it up to make applesauce.

D. *Thought Processes Not Reversible: A → B, but doesn't think of A ← B*
A child at this stage doesn't reverse his thought processes. For example, if he is asked: "What is a chicken?" he will say, "It is a bird." Then if asked: "What would happen if all the birds were killed? Would there be any chickens left?" he will probably reply, "Yes." If forced into giving some other answer he will usually state an irrational one such as: "There are chickens left because they run away." The child doesn't realize that the subclass *chicken* belongs to the class *bird*. If the class is destroyed then the subclass is also destroyed. For him to grasp this point he would have to have a good idea of class and subclass plus be able to reverse his mental process to go from subclass to class.

E. *No Understanding of Chance and Probability*
The understanding of chance and probability is absent. Children in the pre-operational stage have difficulty forming genuine ideas of chance and probability.

F. *Animistic Artificialistic Explanations Common*
The child of this period is animistic and artificialistic in his view of the world. He may believe that anything that moves is alive, an animistic view. If you ask him how a crater was formed, he is likely to say that it was formed by a giant. He is artificialistic because he believes mountains, lakes, etc., are made by men or men-like creatures such as giants. He has names for all kinds of objects and thinks the name is inherently a part of the subject and comes with it. Furthermore, he believes all things have a purpose. The moon and sun move because they want to, etc. The why questions these children constantly ask are an effort to find simple purpose.

G. *Play and Reality Confused*
The pre-operational child can't discriminate play from reality. This is because he hasn't developed sufficient rational structures since most of his beliefs are relatively arbitrary and have not been derived from reason.

H. *Egocentric*
It is difficult for a child of this period to understand views other than his own. He talks, for example, with little attention given to whether he is being understood or even listened to. He thinks the way he sees things is the way all people view them. It is futile to expect him to follow the rules of a game until at least age 4, for the rules are his rules. This egocentricity changes in time largely by being confronted in social interaction with other individuals' various opinions.

I. *Time and Space Concept Now Expanded*
His impression of time has changed from the immediate present to where he can think of future and past. His understanding of time, however, doesn't extend very far beyond the present and the time on a clock has little meaning for him. His conceptualization of space has enlarged to include an understanding of his house and neighborhood.

Concrete Operations (7-11 years)

A. *Thoughts Stimulus Related*
During the concrete operational stage a child slowly becomes proficient in developing his ability to perform all of the logical and infralogical

What Are Adolescents Mentally Capable of Doing?

operations listed previously. Thought, however, is mainly limited to thinking about things rather than doing propositional or hypothetical-deductive thinking.

B. *Class, Relation Concepts Devised*
One of the main outcomes of this stage of development is that the student constructs class and relation concepts in which he can more effectively order what he encounters in his environment. He conceptually organizes his environment into cognitive structures—ideas. Each new encounter with nature does not require extensive examination but can be classified according to properties, structure, and function, which allows for much more efficient responses. He can go beyond things and think of groups. Since the concrete operational person can do reversible thinking, he is able late in the stage to classify things in an ascending as well as descending manner. He realizes ducks are birds—ascending, and if birds are destroyed there will be no ducks. In this case he descends from birds to ducks in his thought processes and thereby reverses his thinking. This ability to form classes and groups enables the child to expand his mental activity greatly.

ASCENDING AND DESCENDING HIERARCHY

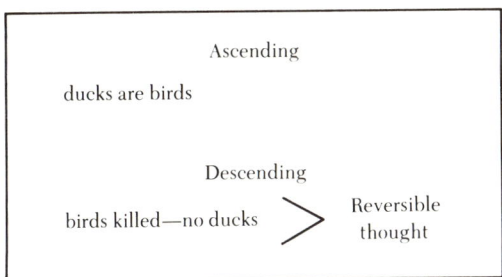

C. *Limited Hypotheses Possible*
A child of this period is capable of noting what happens if you add something to the volume of a container, both to the object receiving the liquid and the one being depleted of it. However, in trying to resolve problems, he is usually limited to making only one hypothesis and this involves only one variable. Furthermore, he is better able to solve problems if he is concretely acting on them, e.g., in volume problems he needs to see actual containers before him. It is still difficult for him to hold a problem in his mind, act upon it, and to come up with an answer.

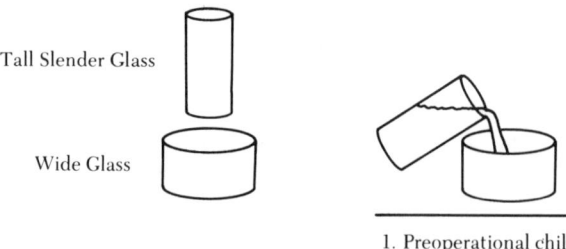

1. Preoperational child thinks there is less in wide glass.
2. Concrete child conserves.

D. *Understanding of Space and Time Greatly Expanded*
The concrete operational child's understanding increases significantly over the previous period. He now has some notions of geographical space, town, city, county, state, nation, hemisphere, and historical time, e.g., age of Egyptians, Romans, Washington, Napoleon, etc.

E. *Action Representation Occurs*
The child of this period begins to represent actions in his mind. His mental action takes the place of performing some real act on an object. For example, if an instructor pours water from a wide flat jar to a slender one, the water level in the slender jar will be higher. The preoperational child typically thinks the wider glass will have less water in it than the tall one even though he has seen all the water poured into the wide container. The concrete operational child realizes they both contain the same amount. Mentally he may perform the following operations: "All of the water was poured from the tall jar to the short wide jar. No water was added or taken away. Therefore, the wide jar has the same amount." Furthermore, he realizes that if the water in the wide jar were poured back in the same jar (reversing the mental operation) it would be at the same level as it was previously. Because a concrete operational child can perform these mental operations, he is able to conserve. In this situation he conserves substance. He realizes changing the container size doesn't affect the amount of liquid. This mental activity of replacing the water in the tall jar substitutes for the actual refilling of the water in order to come to the same conclusion. Dr. Elkind, a specialist on Piaget, has said that this process of mentally performing operations is analogous to a child's doing math in his head instead of counting on his fingers.

What Are Adolescents Mentally Capable of Doing?

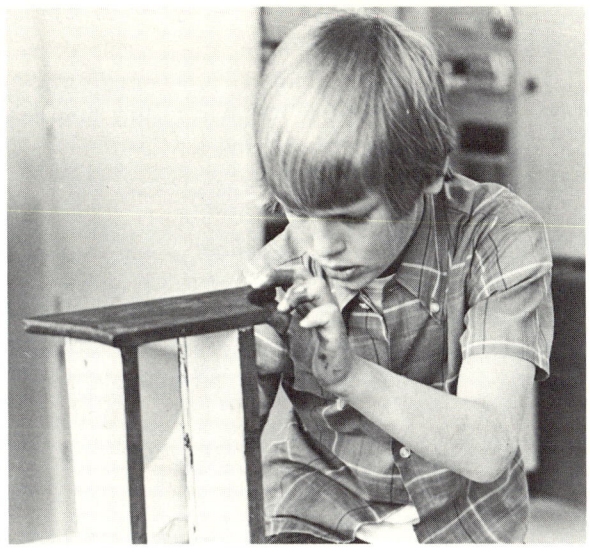

How is this young student building his mind?

Formal Operations (12-15 years)
Development of Abstract Reflexive Thinking

The majority of high school students should attain this level by the time they reach graduation. Piaget initially believed that most adolescents reached formal operational thinking by age 15. Recently, however, he has come to question this because other investigators have found that many students even on the university level do not do well on formal tasks.[2] Research done at our university has further substantiated that many students in senior high and in the university don't function well formalistically. You as an instructor, therefore, can expect to have students in your classes who are concrete operational, in transition to formal, or are formal operational thinkers. The age category above should therefore only be thought of as a rough indication of the cognitive level of a group of students. You will, in interacting with students in your class, have to determine whether they have difficulty in grasping certain ideas because they are at a concrete stage of their thinking.

---

[2]Jean Piaget, "Intellectual Evolution from Adolescence to Adulthood," 3rd International Convention and Awarding of Foneme Prizes, Foneme Institution for Studies in Human Formation, Milan, Italy, May 9-10, 1970, pp. 160-165.

A. *External Stimulus Unnecessary*
The formal student becomes stimulus free in that he doesn't need an external stimulus to activate his thinking processes. In this sense he is liberated from immediate stimulation in directing his behavior. He originates many of his own ideas enabling him particularly to broaden his creative enterprise.

B. *Reflexive Thinking Processes Begin*
One of the main characteristics of this stage is the student's ability to do reflexive thinking. He is now capable of thinking back over a series of mental operations, reflecting on them. In other words, he can think about his thinking. In the process of doing this he represents his own mental operations by symbols. In science, for example, a student, asked after finishing an experiment how he could improve his results, would reflect and evaluate everything he has done in order to come up with better data.

"If I were going to do this again, how would I improve it?"

C. *Probability Becomes Understandable*
The formal operational student thinks in terms of many possibilities rather than being limited to the facts before him. He can think of ideals as opposed to realities, and he is capable of understanding probability theory.

What Are Adolescents Mentally Capable of Doing?

D. *Thinking Processes More Hypothetical-Deductive*

The formal adolescent is capable of doing hypothetical-deductive "If . . . then" thinking. He formulates hypotheses as testable ideas in his mind and does not necessarily regard them as realities. He is more likely to demonstrate deductive patterns of thought than at previous stages of mental development. For example, he might perform the following operations:

John really is well liked.

He has long hair and nice clothes.

How can I become well liked? (Formulates a problem)

If I had long hair *then* . . . (Makes a hypothesis)

No, it is not his long hair, but his interest in people. (Rejects hypothesis)

If I were to relate better to people then I would be well liked, etc. (Makes a conclusion)

The formal student establishes a problem, e.g., "How can I become well liked?" and then mentally acts on it making hypotheses, that is, "If I had long hair then . . . ." He either accepts or rejects them. It is this ability of being able to hold a considerable amount of information and then mentally act upon it that distinguishes the formal student from those of an earlier stage.

E. *Propositional Thinking*

Formal operational students may further demonstrate propositional thinking and reasoning as follows:

It is this or that.

It is this and that.

It is this, but not that.

It is neither this nor that.

Or, he might perform the following logical propositions:

1. If A then B.
   If it is raining (A) then the sidewalks are wet (B).
2. If B then A.
   If the sidewalks are wet, then it is raining.
3. Not A then not B.
   If it is not raining then the sidewalks are not wet.
4. Not B then not A.
   If the sidewalks are not wet then it is not raining.

He may maintain these propositions in his mind and by reasoning eliminate the non-appropriate ones. Or, he may hold one factor constant while varying the others. Doing this type of "If" thinking easily characterizes the formal child from those in the other stages.

F. *Accepts Contrary to Fact Assumptions*

Formal students accept contrary to fact assumptions for the sake of discussion. For example, they will accept coal being white, ducks not having wings, dinosaurs existing today, a different ending to a play or story from the traditional. Because of their increased rational ability, these students comprehend the double meaning of a statement, allegory, and psychological, ethical, etc., implications of literature and plays. *Gulliver's Travels* no longer is just a single story. They also can accept the idea of a utopian society and discuss its constitution in relatively sophisticated ways.

G. *Controlling Variables*

In science they are capable of *controlling one variable* at a time in order to isolate the one affecting a situation. For instance to ascertain whether it's the weight, length of string, or height from which a weight is released which affects the frequency, they control all but one variable at a time to find the answer. For example, they may keep the weight and the height from which it is released the same, but change the length of a string. On the other hand, concrete operational children doing this experiment may change the weight and length of the string at the same time; they seem to become confused in identifying and controlling variables.

H. *Accepts Decisions and Rules by Consensus*

Piaget as well as other authors has shown that children's values and ethics vary with development. Piaget found that children progress generally through three stages. Infants tend to believe the way they see things is the way they are, up to about age four. From four up to the late concrete stage they tend to accept authority, e.g., father, mother, teacher, etc.

In the formal stage teenagers tend to rebel against authority since they now know that there is no sanctity in authoritative dictums. They know that rules and ethics may be arrived at by consensus and thereby expect to be consulted in determining rules governing their behavior. An instructor or parent who doesn't realize the significance of this development manifestation and continues to exert authoritative pressure well into a child's adolescence will find rebellious behavior likely to surface.

I. *Abstraction Processes More Developed*

The student of this period generally is more capable of thinking abstractly, e.g., in performing complex mathematical tasks. Dr. Flavel summarizes the achievement of the formal stage as follows:

> In brief, the adolescent can deal effectively not only with the reality before him . . . but also the world of pure possibility, the world of abstract, propositional statements, the world of "as if." This kind of cognition is adult thought in the sense that these are the structures within which adults operate when they are at their cognitive best, i.e., when they are thinking logically and abstractly. [3]

The above summary of the intellectual development of children is admittedly very brief, but it should give you a viewpoint that will be of considerable assistance in teaching. Interest in the cognitive development of children has been accelerating among psychologists and educators over the last decade. As a consequence, many modern curriculum projects have been designed to give greater attention to the child's cognitive developments. This has been particularly so on the elementary levels, including such projects as The Illinois Studies in Inquiry Training, The Science Curriculum Improvement Study at the University of California, the Elementary Science Study, the Madison Project, the American Association for the Advancement of Science, Science A Process Approach, the Biological Sciences Curriculum Study, and Human Sciences, plus many others in science, social studies, and mathematics. The middle and secondary school curriculum revisions have been related to Piaget's work in that they stress critical thinking through learning. The subject matter is used, therefore, to enhance cognitive development.

A word of caution is necessary about the age grouping in the model of child development presented in the previous pages. The age periods demarcating cognitive development should be used only as a guide. Individuals vary considerably. Many individuals in junior high and senior high will probably be in a state of transition between concrete and formal operations. This means they behave as concrete thinkers on some activities but respond formally on others. Furthermore, Piaget's work comes from research studies of children as they are and not as they might be. If enriched and well-designed experiences are provided, the chronological age at which these different steps develop might presumably vary while the sequence would undoubtedly remain the same.

There is a question among curriculum developers as to whether or not the cognitive development of the child can or should be accelerated. Whether it can or not does not seem as important as providing experiences for developing good rational thinking at each of the cognitive stages. Piaget believes it is important to involve students in rich experi-

---

[3] John H. Flavel, *The Developmental Psychology of Jean Piaget* (Princeton, N.J.: D. Van Nostrand Company, Inc., 1963), pp. 86-87.

ences at their levels of development because to do this is more likely to provide a better foundation for later stages of cognitive growth. To Piaget the quality of experiences at each level is most important.

The paramount concern of teachers, therefore, should be to design experiences for students that will insure that they have opportunities to perform desirable mental operations at their stages of development. For example, if students are to become good problem-solving adults, they must have opportunities to solve various types of problems throughout their school lives. An awareness of the cognitive development of the child and a translation of this awareness into teaching practices provide great challenge. Meeting this challenge can make the difference between teaching as a professional or as a technician.

Suggestions for Facilitating Logical Thinking

The following suggestions for facilitating the development of rational thought seem warranted after studying Piaget's work:

1. Piaget believes only the individual builds his own mind. Teachers can, however, facilitate and enhance mental growth by providing activities in which the student mentally acts on what is being learned. Clearly then, if the purpose of the teacher is to help students build their rational processes, he must have materials and design activities whereby the student becomes involved mentally and acts or does something with what is being learned. This means there must be a shift from the traditional approach of the teacher being the teller and the student the receiver to the teacher being the facilitator and the student the actor and doer. In planning lessons the teacher should strive to get the students involved as much as possible in acting on what is being learned rather than simply listening to a lecture. You may, for example, have them read or create something and then share in small groups their views on what each individual thinks is the most important, best, creative idea. The groups then should decide what they agree on as being good and report these to the class as a whole for further discussion and evaluation.

2. Encourage students and give them freedom to choose some of their learning activities. This allows them to use their minds to evaluate what should be studied and learn to contribute more to their commitment toward their studies.

3. Attempt to determine the cognitive levels of your students and accept and interact with them at their levels.

4. Realize that most classes you teach will have students in the concrete operational, in transition to formal, and in formal operation-

What Are Adolescents Mentally Capable of Doing?

*Summary of the Characteristics of
Piaget's Stages of Mental Development*

SENSORI-MOTOR Birth - 2
1. Mainly directed by stimuli outside the mind
2. Pre-verbal—no language
3. Thought proceeds from actions
4. Learns to perceive and identify objects
5. By end of period distinguishes parents, animals, and knows names
6. Rudimentary sense of direction and purpose appears late in stage
7. Time—present
8. Space—immediate

PRE-OPERATIONAL 2-7
1. Can't perform operations but language develops
2. Can't do abstract thinking
3. Egocentric
4. Non-reversible thinking
5. Mainly acts on perceptive impulses
6. Static thinker—doesn't think of series of operations
7. Time—thinks of present, future, past but limited to short duration
8. Space—house, yard, neighborhood

CONCRETE OPERATIONS 7-11
1. Performs operations: combining, separating, ordering, seriating, multiplying or repeating, dividing, substituting
2. *Reversible* thinking
3. Can do correspondence by end of period
4. Analyzes, aware of variables, classifies, measures

FORMAL OPERATIONS 11-15
1. Performs hypothetical and propositional thought
2. Reflexive thinker—evaluates his thinking processes
3. Synthesizes
4. Imagines
5. Does abstract non-concrete conceptual thinking
6. Understands probability
7. Questions ethics
8. Does ratios, proportions, and combinatorial logic

al stages. When explaining things to a class where there are a considerable number of concrete operational individuals, it is best to involve them in concrete activities or explain things using objects, diagrams, pictures and other aids, as much as possible. Avoid using complex verbalizations of abstractions with these students.

5. In interacting with individual students ask questions so as to determine how they think. For instance, you might wish to determine whether a student has achieved formal thought by asking him to perform reflexive thinking processes; for example, in mathematics he might be asked to describe the steps he went through in resolving a problem. In English literature he might summarize what he believes were the significant forces molding a character in a story. If students do not perform well with problems of this nature, it is indicative that they have not yet achieved the formal level of cognitive development.

6. Students who are on the formal level should be encouraged to perform the following types of operations:

Formal Operational Processes

1. Hypothetical-Deductive Thinking
2. Propositional Thinking
3. Evaluating Information
4. Originating Problems
5. Reflexive Thinking

Examples of how teachers and students might be involved in each of these are outlined below:

A. *Hypothetical-Deductive Thinking*
In this approach the teacher invites the students to formulate hypotheses (guesses) and then deduce what their effects would be in a situation. The teacher-student interaction would approximate the following:

The teacher proposes a problem requiring students to make hypotheses.	How would your learning to play a musical instrument affect your social life?
The students formulate hypotheses.	Students might think any of the following: 1. If I played an instrument, people would think me more capable. 2. If I played an instrument, I would have to practice a lot and, therefore, have less time to develop myself socially.

What Are Adolescents Mentally Capable of Doing?

	3. If I played an instrument, I would "turn on other people" and meet exciting persons, etc.
The student rejects some hypotheses but accepts one, and then makes certain deductions.	Yes, I think playing an instrument would be socially desirable since I would have something more to share with other people and after all music is a form of communication, etc.

B. *Propositional Thinking*

Example: It is this or that, neither this nor that. It is both of them. It is that but not this.

Teacher proposes a problem involving several factors all, some, or none of which can be related.	A car ran into a ditch. There were no other cars on the road that night. The weather bureau stated there was a 70 percent chance of rain. There was an empty can of beer found in the car. What kind of evidence do you see to determine the cause of the accident? For example, how would you determine whether the road had been wet at that time in that area and whether it contributed to the accident, etc.
The student proposes propositions.	Student might conclude the following: If it rained the roads and the shoulder would be wet and mud would collect on the fender. But, mud could collect even if it were not wet. If there were no rain then there would be no mud. But, if there were little rain there still could be no mud, etc.

C. *Evaluating Information*

Teacher asks: Which of these poems, plays, stories, articles, recipes, games, experiments, laws, resolutions to the problem do you think is the best and why?

Student establishes criteria in his mind and uses these as a basis in evaluating each poem, etc., to come to an answer.

D. *Originating Problems*

Teacher asks question related to a topic in which student has some information sufficient to formulate problem.	1. What do you think are the main problems with morale in this class, school, club, team, etc. 2. What can we do about pollution, racial tension, esthetics, etc., in our community?

Student suggests problems.	3. What other problems do you think should be investigated? One problem is that....
E. *Reflexive Thinking*	
Teacher presents a problem asking students to reflect on their thinking and reasoning.	1. What steps did you go through in solving this problem? 2. If you were going to do this experiment again, how would you get better data? 3. How did you move to block that last tackle? 4. What was wrong with your last dive? 5. How should you rewrite your theme, etc.? 6. What kind of problem is this? What was known, what was unknown, what steps were necessary to solve it?

7. Since the adolescent mind is capable of determining and synthesizing general properties, theories, values and ethics, students should be given many opportunities to discuss ethical questions, devise and discover general laws, principles, rules and laws in science, art, math, music, athletics, interior design, etc.

8. Students should be encouraged to think formally in areas where they have great interest and background because it has been found that their level of thinking is better and they become more involved.

9. Involve students in work or work-like activities. It is characteristic of formal operational adolescents to believe that what is rationally right should be so in reality. They suffer from "egocentric idealism." The world of work confronts them with reality and tempers this idealism so that they can better accept and interact with their environment

10. Students of this age are able to make correlations and deal with proportionality. A teacher should be aware of this fact and should provide the necessary guidance to help students comprehend problems of this nature. Many students, however, may have considerable difficulty in accommodating these ideas until they have had wide experiences with them.

Above all, allow students as many opportunities as possible to think and use their minds. They may do this by organizing how they are going to perform a task, motivating other students to work with them on a project, interacting with other students about a problem, collecting and interpreting data, deciding on some class presentation they are going to give, creating something for the class, etc.

Summary

Dr. Jean Piaget has researched for over fifty years on how the minds of children develop. He says individuals pass through four stages of cognitive development as they mature: the sensori-motor, 0-2 years; the pre-operational, 2-7 years; the concrete operational, 7-11 years; and the formal operational, 11-15 years.

Piaget's work centers upon an individual being able to perform operations. Operations include such mental processes as adding, subtracting, multiplying, dividing, performing correspondence, ordering, substituting, and reversing. Sensori-motor and pre-operational students are unable to perform these, whereas during the concrete operational period, individuals slowly develop these rational skills. Formal operational students, in addition, can perform hypothetical-deductive thought and propositional reasoning as well as do reflexive thinking.

Although the ages given for the periods above indicate that by the time of high school, individuals should be formal operational, in fact, many are not. Frequently, in middle and secondary schools instructors have within the same class individuals at varying mental stages including many in transition from one period to another. Teachers should adjust their teaching accordingly. For example, concrete operational students do not perform well verbally. Teachers should, therefore, provide experiences in which they can learn more effectively by being involved in activities, laboratory or pictorial types of lessons.

Further Investigation and Study

1. Take the following Self-Evaluation Inventory to see how well you have learned the information contained in this chapter compared to other students in the class.

   How Well Have You Learned the Material of This Chapter?

   Directions: Listed below are some objectives relating to the Piaget theory you have been studying. Read each and rate it on the scale TWICE: first indicating what you knew or felt about it *before* studying this area and second *after* having finished this portion of your study. Circle the appropriate number and mark B for Before and E for End next to the number as indicated below.

Example: Objective	Student Evaluation Low Moderate High
1. Distinguish important Piaget mental operations.	Content 1 2B 3 4 5E 6 Interest 1 2B 3 4E 5 6
Objectives	Student Evaluation Low Moderate High
1. State the four stages of Piaget's developmental theory.	Content 1 2 3 4 5 6 Interest 1 2 3 4 5 6
2. Identify three characteristics of each of the stages.	Content 1 2 3 4 5 6 Interest 1 2 3 4 5 6
3. Give two ways of identifying concrete and formal operational thinking.	Content 1 2 3 4 5 6 Interest 1 2 3 4 5 6
4. State four specific ways to ask questions that will help students develop cognitively.	Content 1 2 3 4 5 6 Interest 1 2 3 4 5 6
5. Define a. Logical operations	Content 1 2 3 4 5 6 Interest 1 2 3 4 5 6

What Are Adolescents Mentally Capable of Doing?

	Objective		Student Evaluation Low Moderate High
b.	Transformation	Content	1 2 3 4 5 6
		Interest	1 2 3 4 5 6
c.	Reversible	Content	1 2 3 4 5 6
		Interest	1 2 3 4 5 6
d.	Egocentric	Content	1 2 3 4 5 6
		Interest	1 2 3 4 5 6
e.	Establishing a class hierarchy	Content	1 2 3 4 5 6
		Interest	1 2 3 4 5 6
f.	Propositional thought	Content	1 2 3 4 5 6
		Interest	1 2 3 4 5 6
g.	Reflective thought	Content	1 2 3 4 5 6
		Interest	1 2 3 4 5 6
h.	Cognitive development	Content	1 2 3 4 5 6
		Interest	1 2 3 4 5 6
6.	List five types of operations.	Content	1 2 3 4 5 6
		Interest	1 2 3 4 5 6
7.	Name five educational implications of Piaget's theory.	Content	1 2 3 4 5 6
		Interest	1 2 3 4 5 6
8.	Give a reason suggested by this chapter for having students learn by inquiry.	Content	1 2 3 4 5 6
		Interest	1 2 3 4 5 6
9.	State whether this chapter has been valuable and has helped alter the way you shall look at students.	Content	1 2 3 4 5 6
		Interest	1 2 3 4 5 6
10.	Indicate whether you would like to learn more about Piaget's work.	Content	1 2 3 4 5 6
		Interest	1 2 3 4 5 6

Review the above form and where your evaluation indicates weakness do some additional study until you can answer the questions more positively.

After having completed the above, compare your results with another student in the class. Discuss with him any significant variations between your two evaluations.
2. Read: David Elkind, *Children and Adolescents, Interpretive Essays of Jean Piaget,* Oxford University Press, 1970, and devise some simple tests to determine the mental thinking of students in a class.
3. List five things that had the greatest impact for you in this chapter.
4. What do you think about the use of the above self-evaluational inventory to determine how well you learned the material?

3 Investigative Teaching

Of only one thing I am convinced. I have never seen anybody improve in the art and technique of inquiry by any means other than engaging in inquiry.[1]

Most of the programs over the last ten years funded by the United States Government for developing modern instruction for the elementary and secondary schools have stressed student involvement in discovery or inquiry oriented activities. Millions of dollars have gone into constructing science, mathematics, social studies, English, etc., curriculums for this purpose.

What is discovery or inquiry? Many educators use these terms interchangeably while others prefer to differentiate their meanings. In this book the terms are used differently. To us, *discovery occurs when an individual is mainly involved in using his mental thinking processes to mediate* (or discover) *some concept or principle.* For example, the student may discover what a cell is, that is, form a concept of a cell, or later on he may discover a scientific principle: cells only come from cells. A discovery activity is a lesson designed in such a way that a student, through his own mental processes, discovers concepts and principles.

For a student to make discoveries he has to perform certain mental processes such as observing, classifying, measuring, predicting, describing, inferring, etc. Many modern elementary school curriculum

---

[1] Jerome Bruner, *Harvard Educational Review,* XXXI (Winter, 1961): 32.

Concepts	momentum	democracy	comedy
	nucleus	right triangle	tense
	parallel	design	harmony
	culture	noun	texture
	society	tragedy	

Principles	(1) The environment affects living things.
	(2) Sound is produced by vibrating matter.
	(3) Evolution takes enormous amounts of time for its operation.
	(4) A sentence usually contains a complete idea.
	(5) Every culture has its own mores.
	(6) A right triangle contains one 90° angle and the sum of the angles is 180°.

project materials are mainly designed to involve children in discovery activities.

Starting in the middle school and becoming increasingly more sophisticated as students progress through the high school, materials are designed to stress inquiry. Inquiry teaching, however, is built on and includes discovery, because a student must use his discovery capabilities plus many more. *In true inquiry the individual tends to act more like a maturing adult.* An adult behaves in a number of ways in order to unravel the hidden relationships relative to a problem. He originates problems, formulates hypotheses, designs experiments, etc. He performs certain relatively sophisticated mental processes, as indicated in the chart on page 41.

DISCOVERY

Discovery— The mental process of assimilating concepts and principles in the mind.

Discovery Cognitive Processes— Observing, classifying, measuring, predicting, describing, inferring.

The elementary child may observe mealworms and discover they are photosensitive to light. A secondary student may be asked to choose and investigate an organism and report research he has done on it. If he originates his own problem, designs experiments, and collects data, etc., he is behaving in an inquiry manner. Refer to the charts on Discovery and Inquiry. How do their processes differ? How would you design a discovery-oriented lesson in your subject field? How would you design an inquiry lesson?

INQUIRY

Originates problems
Formulates hypotheses
Designs investigative approaches
Tests out his ideas, e.g., carries out experiments
Synthesizes knowledge
Develops certain attitudes
    e.g., Objective
           Curious
           Open-minded
           Desires and respects theoretical models
           Responsible
           Suspends judgment until he obtains sufficient data
           Checks his results, etc.

Because secondary teachers often do not have a clear distinction in their minds between discovery and inquiry, they tend to overemphasize discovery activities. Remember, however, Piaget indicates adolescents are in the process of developing formal thought and should, therefore, have opportunities to use this type of thinking. Hypothetical-deductive and reflexive thinking are two characteristics of this period. Formulating hypotheses, designing investigations, evaluating data, and looking back over an investigation, play, essay, math problem, etc., to determine how it can be improved (reflecting) require these mental operations. Middle and secondary instruction should, therefore, not only include discovery, but an increasing number of inquiry activities.

Clearly, one develops his discovery and inquiry thinking abilities only by being involved in activities requiring the performance of the above types of mental tasks. Since an individual never really masters any of these in the complete sense, there is only a degree to which one becomes proficient in learning how to discover and inquire. Even the most sophisticated Nobel Prize scientist, author, painter, mathematician, or sociologist is still moving forward in developing these skills. The task of the school system is to construct its curriculum so students manifest these human investigative abilities.

Advantages of Discovery and Inquiry Teaching?

Already you are probably beginning to see some of the reasons discovery and inquiry teaching are permeating learning in the schools. Jerome Bruner, an eminent Harvard University psychology professor, has been instrumental in leading the movement toward discovery teaching.

He has outlined four reasons for using this approach, as indicated in the chart below:

Bruner's Reasons for Discovery

1. Intellectual Potency
2. Intrinsic Rather Than Extrinsic Motives
3. Learning the Heuristics of Discovery
4. Conservation of Memory

By intellectual potency Bruner means an individual only learns and develops his mind by using it to think. In his second point he believes that as a consequence of succeeding at discovery the student receives a satisfying intellectual thrill—an intrinsic reward. Teachers often give extrinsic rewards (A's for example), but if they want students to learn for the fun of it, they have to devise instructional systems enabling students to obtain intrinsic satisfaction. In Bruner's third point, he emphasizes that the only way a person learns the techniques of making discoveries is to have opportunities to discover. Through discovering, a student slowly learns how to organize and carry out investigations. Bruner argues in his fourth point that one of the greatest benefits of the discovery approach is that it aids in better memory retention. Think for a moment of something you have thought out yourself and compare it with information you were told in a freshman course. The material you reasoned and came to some conclusion about probably is still fresh in your mind even though you may have learned it years ago. On the other hand, concepts you were told often escape recall.

Although these four justifications have been outlined for discovery teaching, they also have relevance for inquiry. This is so because the teaching strategies for the two approaches are similar in that they stress the importance of the students' using their cognitive mental processes to work out meaning of things they encounter in their environment.

Although Bruner has suggested the salient justifications for modern teaching, there are additional reasons for using student investigative approaches, including the following:

1. *Instruction becomes student-centered.* One of the basic psychological principles of learning states the greater the student involvement, the greater the learning.[2] Usually when teachers generally think

---

[2] Watson, Goodwin, "What Psychology Can We Feel Sure About?", *Education Digest* (May, 1960): 19.

Investigative Teaching

about learning, they have in mind that the student is assimilating some information. This is a very limited view of learning as was pointed out in Chapter 1. Learning involves those total aspects that contribute to the individual becoming a fully functioning person. For example, in inquiry situations students learn not only concepts and principles, but self-direction, responsibility, social communication, etc. In teacher-centered instruction on the other hand, much of the opportunities for developing these talents are denied to the student by the instructor. He or she provides the self-direction, retains the responsibility, etc. If you look at instruction as enabling a "person" to become more than he is in all the facets that make up a human, it is difficult to justify a mainly teacher-centered learning environment.

What are all the ways you can think of to make instruction more student-centered? How has this teacher done it?

2. *Inquiry learning builds the "self-concept" of the student.* Each of us, as pointed out in Chapter 1, has a "self-concept." If our "self-concept" is good we feel psychologically secure, are open to new experiences, willing to take chances and explore, tolerate minor failures relatively well, are more creative, generally have good mental health, and eventually become fully functioning individuals. Part of the task of becoming a better person is to build one's self-concept. We can only

do this by *being involved* because through involvement we manifest our potential and gain insights into "self." Inquiry teaching provides opportunities for greater involvement, thereby giving students more chances to gain insights and better develop their "self-concepts."

How are these students building their self-concepts?

3. *Expectancy level increases.* Part of a person's self-concept is his expectancy level. This means that the student believes or expects he is able to accomplish a task on his own. He has learned from previous discovery and inquiry experiences that he can "think autonomously." In other words, from having had many successful experiences in using his investigative talents, he learned, "I can solve a problem on my own without the help of teacher, parent, or anyone else." As a consequence, he learns "I canness."

4. *Inquiry learning develops talents.* Humans are a collection of more than 120 talents. Academic talent is related to only a few of these. The more freedom we have to use these, the more opportunities we have to develop our talents other than academic, such as creative, social, organizing, etc.

5. *Inquiry methods avoid learning only at the verbal level.* Some years ago we saw Dr. Richard Salinger, a renowned educator, play a game with some prospective Peace Corps teachers to show them how

Investigative Teaching

easy it is for an instructor to mistake verbal play for real learning. He placed the following on the board:

            Arks > Gorks
            Gorks > Grons
            Grons > Smoes

He then asked the students in rapid sequence: "What is an Ark to a Gork? What's a Gork to a Smoe? A Smoe to an Ark? An Ark to a Gron?, etc." The students soon became facile at playing the game. Dr. Salinger then erased the board and continued the game, and although the students had difficulty, they could still play it relatively well.

He then stopped and asked: "Haven't I taught you something? Haven't you learned something?" The students looked perplexed. Dr. Salinger said, "Come on, don't you know an Ark is greater than a Smoe? Couldn't I give you a test: An Ark is greater than _____? and couldn't you complete the test?" He then asked: "How often do teachers play Ark games?"

When you learned the definitions for words such as osmosis, photosynthesis, communism, logarithm, counterpoint, etc., did you play Ark and Gork games, or did you work out the meaning in your mind and really understand what you were learning? Could you define these terms operationally or were you only able to give memorized definitions? Inquiry teaching, since it involves students working out the meaning of their work, tends to avoid "Ark and Gork" teaching.

6. *Inquiry learning permits time for students to mentally assimilate and accommodate information.* Teachers often rush learning, resulting in students playing Ark games. Students need time to think and use their minds to reason out and gain insights into the concepts, principles, and investigative techniques they are involved in. It takes time for such information to become a part of the mind in a meaningful way. Dr. Jean Piaget believes there is no true learning unless the student mentally acts upon information and in the process assimilates or accommodates what he encounters in his environment. Unless this occurs, the teacher and student are involved only in pseudo-learning (i.e., Arking) the retention of which soon fades into useless oblivion.

Guided Versus Free Inquiry

How much structure should be provided in inquiry situations? There should be enough to insure that the student has success in coming to understand the important implications of his studies.

If students have not had experience in learning through inquiry they should initially be given considerable structure in their lessons. After they have gained some experience on how to carry out an investigation, the structure should then be lessened. In this text a general term *investigative* is used to include both discovery and inquiry teaching approaches. The term *guided discovery and inquiry* is used where there is considerable structure given and *free discovery and inquiry* indicates there is little guidance provided by the instructor. Shown below is an example of part of a science guided inquiry lesson. Note that much of the planning is outlined by the teacher. The students, for example, do not originate the problem, and considerable guidance on how to set up and record the data is provided. In a free type lesson, the students may originate the problem and determine how to resolve it.

HOW LONG CAN YOU BOIL WATER IN A PAPER CUP?
Junior High Level

Teachers' note: Sections I through III are for the teacher only and Sections IV and V are to be duplicated for the student.

I. *Concepts*

   A flame is a source of radiant heat

   Water, when heated, expands and gives off water vapors

   Water can absorb a considerable amount of heat

   Before a substance will burn, its kindling temperature must be reached

   The kindling temperature is the temperature at which a substance will first start to burn

II. *Materials*

   Non-waxed paper cup

   Bunsen burner, propane torch, or alcohol burner

   Ring stand

   Ring clamp

   Wire screen

Investigative Teaching 47

III. *Pre-laboratory Discussion*
   Processes:

   Hypothesizing 1. What do you think will happen to a paper cup when you try to boil water in it?

   Hypothesizing 2. What do you think will happen first, the water boiling or the cup burning?

   Hypothesizing 3. How do you think you could get a paper cup containing water to burn?

   Designing An Investigation 4. What should you do to find out?

IV. *Pupil Discovery Activity*
   Processes:

   Collecting Material 1. Obtain the following equipment: a non-waxed paper cup, torch or burner, ring stand, ring clamp and screen.

   Designing an Investigation What ways could you use this equipment to find out if you can boil water in a paper cup?

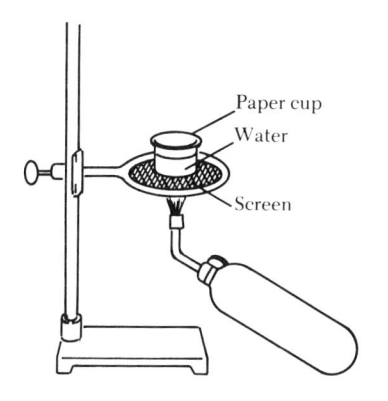

Paper cup
Water
Screen

An alcohol burner may also be used.

Teachers' note: The students should place the paper cup, containing not more than 5 cc. of water, on the wire screen as indicated in the diagram and heat it from below with the burner.

Following Directions	2. If you can think of no other ways to test your hypothesis, set up the equipment as indicated by a diagram your teacher has.
Observing	What happens when you try to heat the water in the cup?
Inferring	What do you think the ring clamp and screen do to the heat from the flame?
Inferring	What can you say about the heat energy entering and leaving the water as you try to heat it to the boiling point?
Inferring	Why does the water level in the cup change?
Inferring	What effect does water in the cup have on its temperature as it is being heated?
	3. Keep heating the cup until all the water is evaporated.
Inferring	Record your observations and conclusions.

V. *Open-Ended Questions*

Processes:

Hypothesizing	1. If you took paper, cloth, wood, and charcoal and heated them, in what order would they start to burn? Why?
Criticizing	2. If you were going to repeat the above experiment, what would you do to obtain better data?
Hypothesizing	3. How would the results of the above experiment differ if you used a Styrofoam cup?
Hypothesizing	4. How would varying the amount of heat energy applied to the cup change the results?
Hypothesizing	5. How would the results vary if there were a different liquid in the cup such as Coca Cola, syrup, etc.?
Hypothesizing	6. In what way would the results vary if the cup were supported by the top instead of being supported by a ring clamp and screen?
Designing an Investigation	7. What other experiments does this investigation suggest to you?

Investigative Teaching

Modified Free Inquiry

In a modified inquiry approach the instructor provides the problem and encourages students to work out the procedures to resolve it. Examples of problems teachers might give to involve students in this type of process are listed below.

1. What ways is algebra used in our community?
2. Given the story up to this point, how would you end it?
3. How would you write a poem to indicate your feeling about seeing the ocean?
4. What do you think about intermarriage?
5. How could you make a better salad dressing?
6. Here are some snails. Find out as much as possible about them.
7. Here is a pond and some apparatus. Find out as much as possible about how this pond changes over a year.
8. How could we make poetry more popular in our school?
9. A new highway is built through the jungles of Brazil and passes by an Indian village that has had little contact with modern civilization. What will happen?
10. Here is some apparatus for studying motion. Set these up in any way you choose to study the movement of an object.
11. How does using a different language change a person's perceptions of other cultures?
12. Here is some apparatus for studying circuits. Do what you must to find out as much as possible about circuits.
13. With this salt do whatever you want to determine its physical and chemical properties.
14. What should be done to improve the environment of our school?
15. Here is some water that is supposed to be polluted. How will you prove that it is?
16. If you were going to produce a piece of art to show contentment, what would you do and why?

In a modified inquiry plan students are encouraged to attack problems similar to those above on their own or in groups. The teacher is available as a resource person giving only enough aid to insure that the students do not become too frustrated or experience failure. The assistance the teacher gives, however, should be in the form of questions he asks to help students think about possible investigative procedures. Ask students questions giving them direction rather than telling them what to do. For example, in the problem about intermarriage, if the students do not think of the genetic consequences, an instructor might ask: "What happens genetically when people marry? What good genetic characteristics do various races have? How would you find out?" Questions like these, given at the right time, may provide just the needed stimulus to cause the students to become more involved in creative investigation. Contrast this with a teacher who says, "Study races and find out their characteristics." In the second instance the teacher has robbed the students of many opportunities for thought and creativeness.

Free Inquiry

After students have studied and learned how to attack a problem, gained sufficient knowledge about the subject, and performed modified free inquiry, the instructor might invite them to become involved in free inquiry. This differs from the modified approach in that the students identify what it is they would like to study. The following questions are suggested as a basis for this type of class activity.

1. If you were the teacher of this class and you were going to select the most exciting things to investigate this term, what would they be?
2. What are some problems related to our community that you would like to study?
3. Now that you have studied, for example, salts, algae, light, heat, radiation, animal behaviors, etc., what problems can you come up with that you would like to investigate individually or in teams?
4. Now that you have finished this experiment, for example in population, what other experiments can you think of and which of them would you like to do?
5. When you see problems in the community, such as pollution, or some problem related to science that you would like to discuss, bring it to our attention in class.
6. What types of mathematical investigations would you like to carry out, e.g., determining the acceleration of a skier, race car driver?

7. What authors would you like to read?
8. What biographies would you like to write or read?
9. What kind of play would you like to write, read, or produce?

Present Research Findings about Using Investigative Teaching Approaches

Although the research findings still need further investigation, particularly concerning how students vary in feelings about the different approaches (affectivity) and the development of more than just subject matter achievement differences, i.e., "multi-talents," "self-concept," etc., they do indicate that the investigative approaches have been successful. Dr. Shulman, as a result of a Conference on Learning by Discovery, summarizes the research in discovery as follows:

> In the published studies, guided discovery treatments generally have done well both at the level of immediate learning and later transfer.[3]

Similar conclusions have been found by the Biological Sciences Curriculum Study for inquiry approaches in biology,[4] by William Day[5] and Omar T. Henkel for physics,[6] and by John Montean for general chemistry and general science,[7] plus many more. BSCS, for example, did a study to determine how well students would do on the BSCS Comprehensive Biology Test at the time they enrolled in college biology. Of the 3062 students in the sample, 39.1 percent had taken one of the BSCS courses in high school. At the .01 level of significance, BSCS students were superior both on inquiry and recall items than were those students enrolled in other types of biology courses.[8] Carl Rogers has written the popular education book *Freedom to Learn*

---

[3] Lee S. Shulman, "Psychological Controversies in the Teaching of Science and Mathematics," *Science Teacher* (September, 1968): 90.

[4] BSCS, "Evaluation," *BSCS Newsletter*, No. 24 (January, 1965).

[5] William Worthy Day, IV, "Physics and Critical Thinking: An Experimental Evaluation of PSSC and Traditional Physics in Six Areas of Critical Thinking While Controlling for Intelligence, Achievement, Course Background and Mobility by Analysis of Covariance" (unpublished Ed.D. dissertation, The University of Nebraska Teachers College, 1964), cited in *Dissertation Abstracts* XXV (1964): 4197.

[6] Omar Thomas Henkel, "A Study of Changes in Critical Thinking Ability: A Result of Instruction in Physics" (unpublished Ph.D. dissertation, The University of Toledo, 1965), cited in *Dissertation Abstracts*, XXVI (1965): 5291.

[7] John J. Montean, "An Experimental Study of Discussion Groups in General Chemistry and General Science as a Means of Group Growth in Critical Thinking" (unpublished Ph.D. dissertation, Syracuse University, 1959), XX (1959): 3666-67.

[8] Jack Carter and Alan R. Nakosteen, *BSCS Newsletter*, No. 42, (February, 1971): 6-8.

[9] Carl Rogers, *Freedom to Learn*, (Columbus, Ohio: Charles E. Merrill Publishing Co., 1969).

in which he reports case studies of several instructors who have used the investigative approach with much success [9] in both the public schools and on the university level.

One of the best studies done on inquiry teaching has been a three year longitudinal one to determine what differences this type of teaching made on the learning behavior of students. Investigators at Carnegie-Mellon University found an inquiry oriented social studies curriculum significantly increased students' abilities to inquire about human affairs compared to those studying non-inquiry materials.[10] This study is important because it shows that inquiry teaching over a

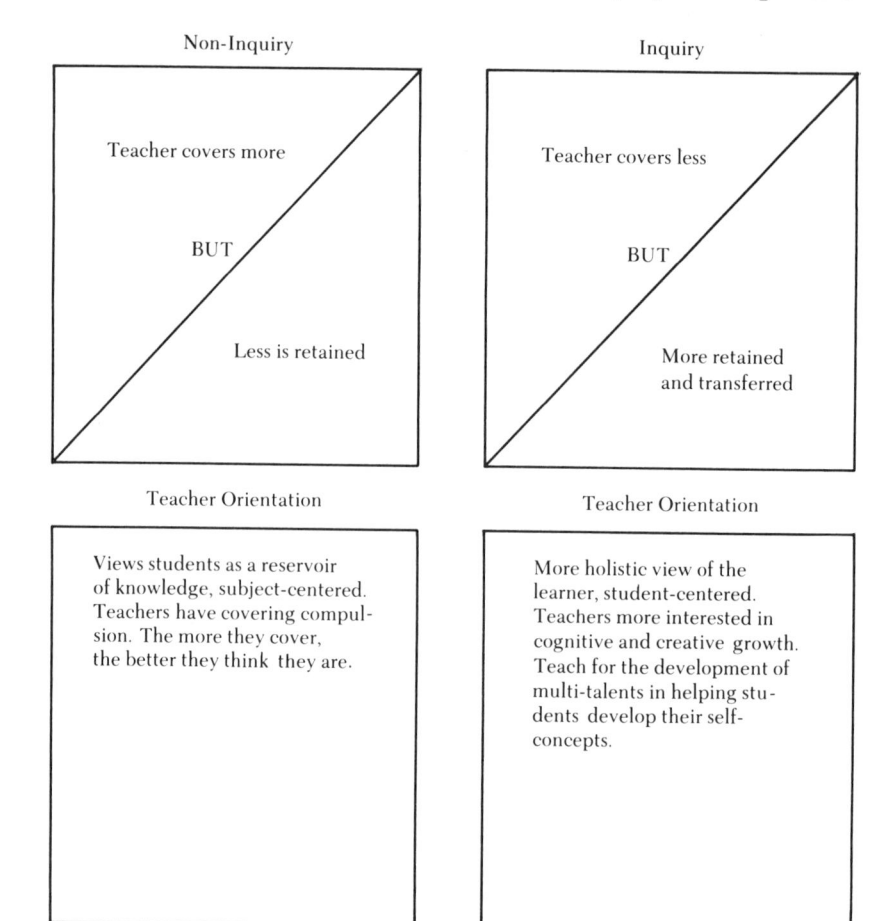

Non-Inquiry

Teacher covers more

BUT

Less is retained

Teacher Orientation

Views students as a reservoir of knowledge, subject-centered. Teachers have covering compulsion. The more they cover, the better they think they are.

Inquiry

Teacher covers less

BUT

More retained and transferred

Teacher Orientation

More holistic view of the learner, student-centered. Teachers more interested in cognitive and creative growth. Teach for the development of multi-talents in helping students develop their self-concepts.

---

[10] John M. Good, John U. Forley, and Edwin Fenton, "Developing Inquiry Skills With an Experimental Social Studies Curriculum," *The Journal of Educational Research*, Vol. 63, No. 1 (September 1969): 35.

prolonged period (three years) does cause individuals to become better investigators. Often teachers when they first begin to use this approach become frustrated and think they are not making sufficient progress. These instructors suffer from a "covering" compulsion; they feel better as teachers if they cover something because they have a mistaken idea of the function of teaching. They are surprised to learn that often students don't learn well what was covered by lecture, and, as a result, teachers rationalize that the students are dumb because they didn't learn, or the class is a slow one. This saves the teachers' egos, but the sad consequence of such a compulsion and rationalization is that they don't look for alternatives in instruction. Because a teacher covers something is little assurance students learn it. You can prove this to yourself by covering a topic in a lecture, giving a test over it, and then repeat the test three weeks later. You will probably find out that retention is very low. If this is so, what was taught and what was learned? If you teach well, students learn and *retain* what they have studied over a prolonged period of time.

It takes time for students to learn to be inquirers and rational creative beings on the road to "self-actualization." Being an inquirer contributes to an individual's becoming a thoughtful insightful person, thereby increasing his self-concept. However, since inquiry requires more time, not as much is covered but more is learned. It is better to allow students time to manifest their human capabilities such as thinking and creating by studying some topic in depth than to have them rush through several varied units. Recall once again the psychological principle, *the greater the student involvement, the more the learning*, and use it as a fundamental guide for devising your instruction. Dr. Jean Piaget has said: "There is no learning without experience." What do you think he means by this statement?

Summary

Many of the modern curriculum materials for the middle and secondary school are discovery and inquiry oriented. In discovery teaching, a student uses his mind to gain insights into some concept or principle. In the process of discovering, an individual performs such mental operations as measuring, predicting, observing, inferring, classifying, etc. In inquiry, an individual may use all of the discovery mental processes plus those characterizing a mature adult such as formulating problems, hypothesizing, designing experiments, synthesizing knowledge and demonstrating such attitudes as objectivity, curiosity, open-mindedness, and respect for theoretical models, values, attitudes. Discovery and inquiry teaching may vary from a relatively structured approach where considerable guidance is provided by the instructor to free investigation where the students originate problems.

Why teach using these investigative approaches? The philosophical and psychological advantages appear to be many. These methods increase intellectual potency; cause a shift from extrinsic to intrinsic rewards; help students learn how to learn in investigative ways; increase memory retention; make instruction student-centered, thereby contributing better to a person's "self-concept"; increase expectancy levels; develop multiple not just academic talents; avoid learning only on the verbal level; and allow more needed time for students to assimilate and accommodate information.

Although there is a need to further assess the value of these approaches, particularly relative to attitudes, values, and self-concept attainment, there is considerable evidence indicating students taught by these methods perform significantly better on cognitive tasks involving critical thinking than those taught by traditional instruction.

Teachers often suffer from a covering syndrome. If they cover the material they feel their responsibility as a teacher has been met. Because a teacher covers something is little assurance students learned it. Student-centered instruction, because it often requires more time, results in covering less than traditional teaching. The retention and critical thinking ability of students in investigative oriented classes, however, has been found to be greater.

Further Investigation and Study

1. In some creative way, utilize what you have learned from this chapter and share this and how you feel about it with other members of the class.
2. List five words conveying the meaning of this chapter to you.
3. What are the advantages and disadvantages of investigative types of teaching?
4. How would you define the difference between discovery and inquiry teaching? Give an example of each.
5. How can the investigative approach contribute to building students' "self-concepts"?
6. What are "expectancy levels" and how might they be changed?
7. Give an example of an instructor doing "Ark and Gork" type of teaching, and state how it should be altered to make it more meaningful.
8. In what ways will you try to develop student talents?
9. How does guided differ from free inquiry? How would you prepare students for each?
10. For your subject area, outline a lesson for both guided and free inquiry. What problems do you see in trying to carry these out?
11. List five examples of your own for free inquiry teaching.
12. What does the present research indicate about investigative teaching?
13. Write a brief essay expressing your feelings about investigative teaching now, compared to the way you felt before coming into this class.
14. What one idea did you get out of this chapter that you think is the most significant?
15. Write a simile for inquiry teaching: "Inquiry teaching is like _____."

4 Questioning and Listening as Aids to Excellent Teaching

The essence of discovery-inquiry teaching is arranging the learning environment to facilitate student-centered instruction and giving sufficient guidance to insure direction and success in discovering concepts and principles. One way a teacher helps a student obtain a sense of direction and use his mind is through questioning. The art of being a good conversationalist requires listening and insightful questions, and a good inquiry oriented teacher is an excellent conversationalist. He listens well and asks appropriate questions, assisting individuals in organizing their thoughts and gaining insights. He seldom tells but often questions. This is so because by asking questions the teacher assists the student to use his mind. A properly given question is a hint. For example, in a mathematics or science class a student is given considerable data related to a pendulum and asked to analyze it. He hasn't discovered, as yet, that its frequency is related to its length. The instructor moves about the class and notices the student seems to be having difficulty. He goes to him and asks a series of questions. Listed below on the left margin are the questions he asks. On the right side of the page is an analyses of what the instructor is doing.

An Inquiry Discussion

1. What have you found out about the pendulum?

1. This is an excellent question because it is very divergent. It allows for a number of responses. The student will

Questioning and Listening as Aids to Excellent Teaching

			have found out something and being able to tell this to the instructor will help his "self-concept."
2.	What seems to affect the frequency, the number of times it swings a second?	2.	This is a more convergent question. It helps the student to *center* on frequency. He had not thought of this before. The student replies that he doesn't know.
3.	What things do you think would affect your data if you wanted to find out if there is a relationship?	3.	The teacher then leaves and moves on to another student requiring some assistance. Later the teacher returns.
4.	What have you done to find out about the frequency?	4.	Here again the instructor is asking a relatively divergent question since the student may have done many things. The student replies that he looked at the data to determine the effect of different weights.
5.	How did the different weights affect the frequency?	5.	The instructor is asking the student to interpret data. The student, however, still hasn't discovered that the length of the string affects the frequency.
6.	What do you think the length of the string would have to do with frequency?	6.	This question is fairly directive-convergent. The instructor is helping the student to center on a particular variable.
7.	How would you accurately find this out?	7.	This asks the student to analyze further data or devise an experimental procedure.

Notice the instructor did aid the student through artful questions to make his own discoveries and to use his mind. He further allowed him considerable time to use his mind in resolving an answer. The teacher did not steal the thrill of discovery from the student, but he did facilitate it.

Proper questioning is a sophisticated teaching art. To practice it, a teacher must perceive where the thoughts of a student are and be continually open so that he perceives well. By doing this, the instructor must switch from the classical concept of teaching—telling—to listening and questioning. After perceiving the student's difficulty, he has to formulate a question so as to challenge yet give guidance to the student. In order to do this, the instructor must know what it is he is trying to teach in a conceptual and humanistic way and adapt his question so it is appropriate to the student's cognitive level. As the teacher moves about the class, he constantly has to adapt this procedure from student to student, requiring fantastic awareness and ability on his part. No wonder so many teachers fall back into the classical mold of teaching. But to help students in this manner is to truly individualize instruction, teach for the "person," and, if done constantly in a positive setting, humanize instruction.

Where Questioning Is Involved in Instruction

Good questioning practices are involved in all areas of instruction as indicated in the chart below:

1. Discussion
2. Laboratory Exercises
3. Demonstrations
4. Student Worksheets
5. Using Audio-Visual Aids
6. Evaluations

Types of Questions

Questions may be pre-planned before class or allowed to arise spontaneously because of student interaction. It is always wise to plan a series of questions before you enter an inquiry oriented class. The mere fact that you have done this contributes better to your questioning ability. Having thought about them gives you a sense of security and direction contributing better to your ability to carry on a discussion.

An inquiry oriented teacher must remain constantly flexible. Even though he has planned a series of questions, he must be willing to deviate from them and formulate new ones as he interacts with students. These unplanned spontaneous questions may be difficult to create at first, but by attempting to develop good questioning techniques and truly becoming involved with students in facilitating the learning process, an instructor becomes more sophisticated at devising them and is more likely to interact appropriately with students.

Questioning and Listening as Aids to Excellent Teaching

What Must Be Considered before Questioning?

Before you devise your questions you should decide the following:

> 1. What talents are you going to try to develop?
> 2. What critical thinking processes will you try to nurture?
> 3. What subject matter objectives do you want to develop?
> 4. What types of answers will you accept?

How Well Do You Recognize Good Questions?

Read the questions below and mark them according to whether they are poor, fair, good, or excellent:

		Poor	Fair	Good	Excellent
1.	Given these characteristics, which of these tribes would you expect to live on the plains and why?				
2.	Who was Pasteur?				
3.	What significant things did Michelangelo do?				
4.	Why weren't the Indians able to compete with the white man?				
5.	Are all members of equal value?				
6.	Which is the right triangle?				
7.	What do you notice about the shapes of the different diagrams?				
8.	Are there more squares than circles?				
9.	What would happen if 10 people were isolated on an unpopulated island because of an airplane crash?				
10.	If you wanted to produce leaders for a society, how would you do it?				

		Poor	Fair	Good	Excellent
11.	Are there more big than little trees?				
12.	How does the vegetation vary in this picture?				
13.	How would you communicate fear?				
14.	Which of these masks had more work done on it?				
15.	If you were in charge of starting a new government, what would you do?				
16.	What would you do to a room to contribute to a feeling of serenity when in it?				
17.	How did that . . . make you feel?				
18.	Is this art good?				
19.	What function do you think the religion of these people serves?				
20.	How would you design . . . e.g. a fountain, an experiment, etc.?				

Self-Analysis of Types of Questions

Below are several questions related to the questions asked above. Read each and attempt to answer it. Keep your answers and refer to them again after completing this chapter to see how well you did.

1. What three questions above do you think are the best to ask? Why?
2. Which questions require the student to analyze?
3. Which questions require the student to evaluate?
4. Which questions are convergent?

5. Which questions are divergent?
6. Which questions require students to reason quantitatively and what are they required to do?
7. Which questions require creative responses?
8. Which questions require the student to formulate an operational definition?
9. Which questions require a student to mainly observe?
10. Which questions require a student to mainly classify?
11. Which questions require a student to demonstrate experimental procedure?
12. Which questions require a student to hypothesize?
13. Which question would an authoritarian personality type most likely guess.at if he didn't know the answer?
14. It has been said that "how" questions do not lead to experimentation. Comment on this.
15. How would you classify most of the questions on this sheet?

After completing the above, compare and discuss your answers with other students in the class to determine your points of agreement.

Levels of Educational Objectives

In 1948 a group of college examiners attending the American Psychological Association Convention in Boston, Massachusetts, met and discussed the possibility of preparing a framework to assist test constructors. They agreed that this could probably be devised by developing a classificational system of educational objectives. Their system, established primarily for writing test questions, was entitled *Taxonomy of Educational Objectives, Handbook I Cognitive Domain;* a second book came out several years later: *Handbook II Affective Domain.* Today this classificational system is often referred to as Bloom's taxonomy, after the name of one of the authors. More will be said about this later.

Just as objectives can be classified by this taxonomy so can questions. Refer to the questions asked above and classify them according to the taxonomy. After doing this, list five of the best questions and decide why you believe they are good. Bloom's abbreviated taxonomy is given below to help you, and an example of how you might use it is shown as a guide.

USING BLOOM'S TAXONOMY TO CLASSIFY QUESTIONS

COGNITIVE DOMAIN	AFFECTIVE DOMAIN
Evaluation	Receiving
Synthesis	Responding
Analysis	Valuing
Application	Organizing
Comprehension	Generalized Set
Knowledge	

CLASSIFYING QUESTIONS

Classification	
Knowledge	1. How many states produce oil?
Synthesis	2. What hypotheses would you make about this problem?
Application	3. Knowing what you do about heat, how would you get a lid off a jar that won't unscrew easily?
Analysis	4. What things do Blacks and Chicanos have in common?
Comprehension	5. Define democracy operationally.
Evaluation	6. If you were going to redo the experiment, play, song, game, math problem, furniture, etc., how would you do it better?
Valuing	7. What is your interest in this course now, compared to when you began it?
Valuing	8. What do you feel about this film?

CRITICAL THINKING PROCESSES

1. Classifying
2. Assuming
3. Hypothesizing
4. Inferring and making conclusions
5. Measuring
6. Designing an investigation to solve a problem
7. Observing
8. Graphing
9. Reducing experimental error, etc.
10. Evaluating
11. Analyzing

Questions requiring responses from the higher levels of Bloom's hierarchy are more desirable because answering them involves more critical and creative thinking and indicates a better understanding of the concepts.

Another way to classify questions is to do so by using critical thinking processes. This approach endeavors to insure that the basic structures of critical thinking are taught. More about using this system is illustrated in a later chapter.

Classifying Using Critical Thinking Processes

Shown below is a guide of how you might classify questions using critical thinking processes:

Classification

Observing	1. What do you observe about the landscape?
Hypothesizing	2. What do you think will happen if the population of our town were to double in the next five years?
Designing an investigation	3. How would you determine the absorption of the different wavelengths of light in water?
Graphing	4. How would you graph this data?
Reducing experimental error	5. How many measurements should be made in order to report accurate data?
Inferring	6. What conclusions can you make from the data?

Convergent and Divergent Questions

Another way to classify questions is to determine whether or not they provide for the possibility of many answers or just a few. Questions allowing for a limited number of responses and moving toward closure or a conclusion are called *convergent*. Questions allowing for a number of answers are called *divergent*; they provide for wider responses plus more creative critical thinking answers. In an inquiry discussion it is generally desirable to start with very divergent questions and move toward more convergent ones. Avoid using restrictive or limiting words in your questions. For example, instead of saying "Who was the dynamic character in the play?" say "What do you think about the characters in the play?" The first statement requires the students to "guess what is in your head" while the second allows them more freedom to use their minds. Read the questions below and classify them as divergent or convergent.

CLASSIFICATION	DIVERGENT/CONVERGENT QUESTIONS
	1. What do you think I am going to do with this material?
	2. What conclusions can you make from the data?
	3. Can anything else be done to improve the design?
	4. Is baking powder an important factor in the quality of the cake?
	5. Do you think the police were right?
	6. Which of these paintings would you choose and why?
	7. What can you tell me about pollution of this area from the picture?
	8. Would you say you have sufficient data?
	9. What ways can you make the lights burn with the wire, switch, and power supply?
	10. What things can you tell me about a good plot for a detective story?

Which questions above are the most convergent? What answers are possible for these questions? What words start these sentences? How would you change the sentences to make them more divergent? Compare your answers with another student's in the class and then with those given at the end of the "Further Investigation and Study" section at the end of the chapter.

Generally speaking, convergent questions, particularly those requiring only a yes or no answer, should be avoided because they allow for few possible responses, thereby giving students little opportunities to think critically. The fundamental purposes of using the inquiry approach is to stimulate and develop critical thinking, creative behavior, and multiple talents. Convergent questions certainly do little to achieve this end. In an inquiry investigation getting the right answer is not as important as giving the student a chance to use his mind so that

Questioning and Listening as Aids to Excellent Teaching

he may *become* more of a person. Learning to think rationally and creatively does much to increase our self-concepts. Many teachers are so concerned with getting the right answer that they prevent students from using their minds. Even though a student may come up with wrong conclusions he still has had a mental experience in thinking about it. To have this experience probably is more important than a right answer. We as teachers would, of course, like for him to use his mind and obtain the correct answer as well. However, consider for a moment a mathematics teacher who only accepts the correct answer to a problem. The student may have used very good thinking procedures to obtain the answer only to have misplaced the decimal point. Is the teacher justified in saying that the student hasn't learned because he hasn't the right answer? The student will probably never have the problem again but he undoubtedly will have many situations requiring him to use similar logical strategies. It is the thinking that is most important! The teacher who doesn't remember this may stifle students.

Teleological and Anthropomorphic Types of Questions

Teleological (Greek: *teleos*—an end) questions are those implying natural phenomena has an end or purpose. The word anthropomorphic comes from two Greek words: *anthropos*—meaning man, and *morphos*—meaning form. An anthropomorphic question implies some natural phenomenon has the characteristics of man. Listed below are some examples of these two types of questions. With these definitions in mind, classify the following questions.

CLASSIFICATION	TELEOLOGICAL/ANTHROPOMORPHIC QUESTIONS
	1. How do you think bacteria feel when ultraviolet light is shined on them?
	2. Why does water seek its own level?
	3. Why do plants want to grow toward the light?
	4. Why will a body in motion continue to want to stay in motion?
	5. Why is the end of evolution to become increasingly more complex?

Why do you think these questions should be avoided? What do they do as far as developing critical thinking, leading to further investigation, and how do they contribute to misconceptions? The answers to these questions should be obvious to you and need no discussion here. Refer to the "Further Investigation and Study" section to check your answers.

Questioning for Multi-Talent

Although the procedures thus far have mainly emphasized the importance of cognitive questions, this is not to say other types are not important. Teachers should also spend a considerable amount of time formulating talent-oriented questions so as to come to know their students.

You should not only determine talent but help to manifest it. This means that you reward students for all types of talent. Some teachers and administrators may argue that the only function of a teacher is to develop subject matter knowledge. It is our view this awareness will occur to a higher degree if a student has opportunities to manifest his best talents, thereby building his self-concept and developing more positive feelings about the subject. Some examples of talent-oriented questions are shown on the following page.

Teachers should also ask questions to ascertain students' interests, attitudes and values. Determining these helps the instructor to plan more relevant lessons. Questioning individuals about what they like, particularly in personal conversations, helps to convey to the students your interest in them as persons.

Piaget has pointed out that proper questioning gives insights into a student's thoughts patterns. In order to do this, the instructor must hypothesize how the student thinks and then pose questions to see if he actually is thinking this way. When the student responds, this hypothesis may be reinforced or need further investigation. The instructor as a result may have to formulate a new hypothesis about the student's cognitive processes and construct questions to determine its validity. This type of questioning is particularly necessary when students seem to be having difficulty in discovering or conceptualizing. Excellent mathematics, physics, chemistry, social studies, and English instructors use this approach to diagnose student difficulties in resolving problems.

QUESTIONING TO DISCOVER TALENT

QUESTION	QUESTIONING FOR:
1. Who would be willing to draw for extra credit a mural to be hung in our room?	Artistic Talent
2. Who wants to help organize the field trip?	Organizing Talent
3. Who would write a short article for the school paper about the science fair?	Communicating Talent
4. What ways should we produce something to convey to the rest of the school how exciting this topic or subject is?	Creative Talent
5. Who would like to be on the welcoming committee and welcome our guests?	Social Talent
6. Who would like to be in charge of planning our investigations in the community throughout the term?	Planning Talent

Wait-Time Affects the Quality of the Responses

Mary Budd Rowe[1] and her collaborators have done an extensive study of the questioning behavior of teachers. In their analysis of taped classroom discussions, they discovered that teachers on an average wait less than a second for students to reply to their questions. Further investigations revealed, however, that some instructors waited on an average of three seconds for students to answer questions. An analysis of student responses revealed that teachers with longer wait-times, three seconds or more, obtained greater speculation, conversation, and argument than those with shorter wait-times. Dr. Rowe further found that when teachers were trained to wait more than three seconds, on the average, for a response the following occurred:

---

[1] Mary Budd Rowe, "Wait-Time and Rewards As Instructional Variables: Influence on Inquiry and Sense of Fate Control," in *New Science in the Inner City*, Teacher College, Columbia University, New York, New York, September, 1970.

WHAT HAPPENS WHEN LONGER WAIT-TIME OCCURS

1. The length of student response increases.
2. The number of unsolicited but appropriate responses increases.
3. Failure to respond decreases.
4. Confidence of students increases.
5. The incidence of speculative creative thinking increases.
6. Teacher-centered teaching decreases and student-centered interaction increases.
7. Students give more evidence before and after inference statements.
8. The number of questions asked by students increases.
9. The number of activities proposed by the students increases.
10. Slow students contribute more.
11. The variety of types of responses increases. There is more reacting to each other, structuring of procedures, and soliciting.

Dr. Rowe also found that teachers trained to prolong their wait-time also changed in their classroom behavior as indicated below:

INSTRUCTOR CHANGES

1. They exhibit more flexible types of responses.
2. The number and kind of teacher questions change.
3. Teacher expectations for student performance are modified. They are less likely to expect only the brighter students to reply and view their class as having fewer academically slower students.[2]

For students to become more involved in inquiring into a subject, instructors need to increase their wait-time tolerance so that their learners have more opportunities to think, create and demonstrate more fully their human potential.

Good Discussions are Student-Centered

Most teachers when they are involved in a class discussion dominate it to a considerable extent, but an inquiry class should be student-centered. This means that teacher talk should be at a minimum. Note the two maps of the discussion interaction in a class.

---

[2]For more detailed analysis see: Mary Budd Rowe, "Wait-Time and Rewards As Instructional Variables: Their Influence on Language, Logic and Fate Control," unpublished paper, University of Florida, Gainsville, Florida 32601, 1972.

LOW LEVEL INQUIRY

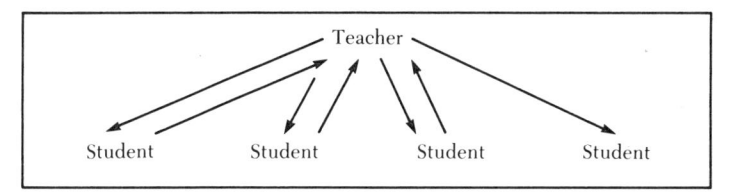

```
        Teacher
   ↙  ↗ ↑ ↓ ↖  ↘
Student  Student  Student  Student
```

HIGHER LEVEL STUDENT INQUIRY

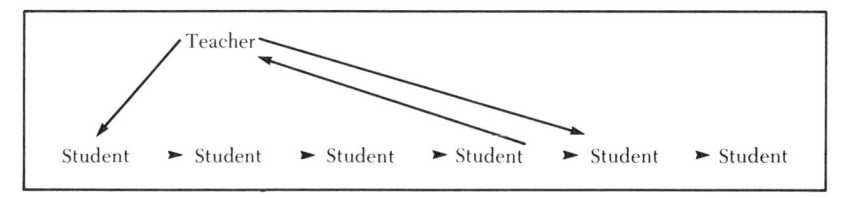

```
   Teacher
  ↙      ↘
Student → Student → Student → Student → Student → Student
```

It is no easy task to develop techniques so that the second type of interaction operates. How would you as a teacher get this pattern to operate in your classes?

Halting Time

Halting time is related to wait-time in that an instructor halts and waits for students to think, but unlike wait-time the student doesn't answer questions. For example, a mathematics instructor is carrying out the derivation of a rather complex formula on the board. He goes through a couple steps and stops so that students have time to see what he has done and think about it before going on to the rest of the problem. While stopping, he visually checks the class to see whether they are with him. If he obtains positive indications that they are following his explanation, he continues on with the problem. If he does not, he may have to ask questions or retrace the work. Philosophers when speaking often demonstrate this technique. They make a statement, pause a few seconds for students to digest it, and then continue on to the next point.

Avoiding Multiple Questions

Avoid asking multiple questions without giving students opportunities to respond. To do this usually is to ignore the principle of allowing for wait-time. For example:

> What causes do you think might have contributed to the accident? What physical as well as psychological ones were acting? Which of these were important?

These questions in themselves are not bad, but when a teacher runs them together he hinders the thinking processes of the students.

Rewarding Responses

When a student gives the correct answer do not prevent the possibility of others continuing their thinking by saying "That is correct." In leading a discussion the *primary aim should be to allow students to use their minds,* to be creative critical thinkers. To say that an answer is correct as soon as it is given prohibits the thinking processes of other students from continuing. It's better to recognize an answer by saying something that is noncommital but indicates acceptance of the student and his ideas such as:

"That is interesting."
"That is your view—I see", etc.

and then allow other students to give their responses. Later after several students have had a chance to participate you can then refocus the class's attention on the correct answer and continue the discussion from there. The indication of acceptance should be immediate rather than delayed. It may be verbal such as above or nonverbal such as a nod of the head or a smile.

Avoiding Over-reacting

Avoid over-reacting to replies. For example: "That is terrific—fantastic thinking, George. Wow, what an answer."

This type of reaction may act as a constricting force because many students might think that their ideas are incapable of being so highly valued by the instructor.

Breaking Constrictive Thinking

Sometimes students become fixed on one aspect of a problem. The instructor then has to devise questions that will break them out of their limited perceptual field. He might do this by asking the following:

What other factors might be contributing to . . . ?
What other information are we given in this . . . ?
What other interpretations are possible?
What alternatives are there?

Questioning and Listening as Aids to Excellent Teaching

Clarifying Material

A student may present a prolonged reply or offer material that is not easily understood by the other members of the class. The instructor may help to clarify this by saying:

> You said it was similar. Similar in what respect?
> Please give a specific example to show where this is operating?
> What other examples are there?
> What do you mean when you say . . .?

Guarding Against Over-generalizations

When students make over-generalizations, focus the class's attention on these by asking such questions as:

> You mean that is true for all . . . ?
> What in your investigations indicated that this was true for all . . .?
> Where and under what conditions would this be true?

Summarizing

Asking students to summarize is particularly necessary when the concepts involved are abstract, vague, or the student reply has been lengthy. The teacher might ask:

> Briefly, please summarize what you have just said.
> What were the main ideas discussed today?
> What is the main point of what you are saying?

Amplifying and Pursuing the Thought

An instructor needs to act as a stimulus to keep the discussion going. This can be done by having students refocus, summarize, consider alternatives and other forces and factors that might move the discussion to a higher cognitive level. This may be done in the following ways:

> I see you have come up with an answer. How did you obtain it?
> What evidence do you have that it is correct?
> You said that this character behaved in an unjust manner. Why do you think that?
> Why do you think the author presented him in that manner?
> What effect do you think this will have?

Considering the Emotional Overtone of the Material

Because of the backgrounds of the students many topics may have emotional content. In discussions where this is the case, the teacher must be particularly careful in phrasing questions so as not to inhibit the rational responses of the students. For example in discussing *The Godfather* in an English class in which there are students of Italian descent, the teacher would not ask: "Why do you think these Italians banded together to form this kind of alliance?" It would be better for the instructor to say: "What forces caused these immigrants to form such an alliance? Why did some of these immigrants behave this way while the majority didn't?"

Paraphrasing

Paraphrase what the student has said when you are not sure that you understand his point, for example, "I hear you say that . . . Am I correct?"

Various Types of Questions

Listed below are examples of questions to solicit student reactions for various purposes.

General Questions to Involve Students in Investigations

1. What do you notice about . . . e.g. this picture, equipment, the environment?
2. What will happen if . . . ?
3. If this is so, then . . . ?
4. This is so if and only if what?

Questions to Stimulate Creative Responses

1. How would you do it better?
2. What would you do to improve the situation?
3. What if you changed the size, shape, color, of . . . ?
4. What if you added or took something away from the . . . ?
5. How would you design an investigation to find out?
6. What hypotheses would you make about . . . ?

Questioning and Listening as Aids to Excellent Teaching 73

7. How would you go about improving the experiment, play, story, crossword puzzle, etc.?
8. What would be a better way to organize . . . ?
9. How would motion affect the . . . ?
10. What other uses can you think of for this object?
11. If you were going to design a better . . . what would you do?
12. If you were going to collect better data, how would you do it?
13. If different materials were used, e.g., in the statue, experiment, homes, etc., what would happen?

Questions to Review a Biography

1. What stimulated the person to do the work he did?
2. Where did he get the ideas for the problems he studied?
3. What procedures did he devise?
4. What effect did society have on his work?
5. What effect did his work have on society?
6. Why do you think he was psychologically "turned on" to do the work he did?
7. What did he achieve?
8. What kind of "self-concept" do you think he had and how did he build it?
9. How did his work contribute to devising better insights or procedures for resolving problems?
10. In what ways did he follow or deviate from what was thought as being the proper way to resolve problems or to create?
11. How did this book affect your feelings about people in this profession?
12. . . . is a human enterprise. How does the book illustrate this?
13. What did reading this book do to you as a person?

Questions to Have Students Analyze Problems, Experiments, and Mathematical Procedures

1. What was the nature of the problem?
2. What was known?
3. What procedures were used in solving the problem?
4. How could these procedures have been improved?

5. What were the hypotheses?
6. What factors or variables were involved in the problem or experiment?
7. What other factors might have been involved in the problem or experiment?
8. How did this problem or experiment contribute to your understanding of . . . ?
9. What assumptions were involved?
10. How were the terms defined?
11. What data were collected?
12. What was the control?
13. How were the data interpreted?
14. What statistical weaknesses were involved?
15. What possibilities are there for further investigation?

Questions Inviting Students to Publicly Affirm Their Values

During the time students are in school they develop values for life. Teachers, therefore, need to help them evolve values but not impose nor moralize about them. More will be said about this later in the text. Listed below are some questions to help students focus and clarify their values:

1. What valuable things have you learned today?
2. In what ways have you been successful today, this week, this year?
3. What makes you feel great?
4. What makes you feel poorly?
5. What do you think about . . . e.g. war, racial conflict, what science and technology do to society, pollution, love, aggression, etc.?
6. What kinds of things hurt your feelings?
7. What would make you jealous?
8. How do you feel about this part of your work?
9. How did you come to this opinion?
10. What other conclusions could you have reached?
11. How do you think your antagonist perceives the problem?
12. How do most people feel about that?

13. What is your personal preference?
14. What have you done about it?

Good Questioning Pays Off

Research indicates teachers specifically trained to ask questions stressing the higher cognitive levels such as those for the upper levels of Bloom's taxonomy do significantly better in constructing questions than do those not having this experience.[3] It must also be remembered that Bloom's taxonomy is used by national testing organizations as a guide in formulating their questions. It is obvious that students having manifold experiences in answering questions on all cognitive levels will be better prepared to encounter achievement and college board tests. With this knowledge in mind, your task is to modify your questioning behavior so as to facilitate better learning and human development by your students. This is a great challenge particularly since there is no end to the degree of sophistication your questioning skill may attain.

Sensitive Listening

It has been said by Krisnamurti, the Indian philosopher, that Americans do not truly listen. They are always judging, composing their thoughts, or preparing salvos for reacting during the time a speaker is discoursing. A person who truly listens in an open, accepting, non-judgmental way probably is a rarity, particularly among teachers. Demonstrating poor listening skills is probably related to how teachers perceive their roles. If they feel their function is mainly to develop some subject matter concept or principle, it is natural for them to focus on its achievement. However, if an instructor perceives his role as mainly enabling students to "self-actualize" through the subject under study, he tends to focus in first on the student as a person and second on the content. He listens intently to what the individual has to say and then when the speaker has finished, and only then, formulates questions and responses to help the student increase his thought processes and self-

---

[3] Virginia M. Rogers. "Varying the Cognitive Levels of Classroom Questions in Elementary Social Studies: An Analysis of the Use of Questions by Student Teachers," Doctor's Dissertation, The University of Texas, Austin, 1969. See also O.L. Davis, Jr., et al., "Studying the Cognitive Emphases of Teachers' Classroom Questions," The Research and Development Center for Teacher Education, University of Texas, Austin, 1969.

concept. There is no substitute for a teacher who is primarily interested in people and their development into better humans.

We all probably both in our daily lives and in teaching need to perfect our listening skill so as to better convey to our friends and students interest in them as individuals. Students often do not achieve well because they have not developed their listening abilities. You as a model of a good listener can aid in modifying this insufficiency. Listed below are a few suggestions to help you improve in this respect. At first you may have to utilize these consciously, but with time and practice, you will find that they become more a pattern of your normal conversational behavior.

Sensitive Listening Techniques

1. *Focus on the person* and what he is saying. Maintain eye contact with the speaker. Endeavor not to evaluate what he is saying until he has completed his statements.
2. *Don't take the discussion away from students.* They are the ones who need to develop their minds.
3. *Give non-verbal signals* to show you are concerned and listening by:
   a. Eye contact.
   b. Concerned posture, e.g., body turned toward the speaker.
   c. Appropriately smiling because student is expressing himself.
   d. Nodding, showing you understand the speaker's statement.
   e. Other gestures, e.g., stroking your chin or brow.
4. *Develop silent-time.* This is similar to wait-time except this is time taken after a student apparently has finished before you reply. Silent-time prevents you from cutting off his statements and allows for others to interject their ideas without your interference. Calm silence also helps to indicate to the student and class trust in their abilities to think and make significant statements.
5. *Look for indicators* that students may wish to say something such as:
   a. Moving in their seats.
   b. Eye contact with the speaker.
   c. Glancing at you or the speaker with a meaningful expression.
   d. Pressing their lips.
   When these occur invite participation, e.g., "John, is there something you would like to say?"
6. *Don't interrupt,* not even to clarify, until you are certain the individual has completed his message.

Questioning and Listening as Aids to Excellent Teaching 77

What indications are there that the students and teacher are practicing good questioning and listening skills?

Consider other things you need to work on to increase your listening ability. The other suggestions in this chapter should give you some help.

Summary

Basic to student-centered instruction is the ability of the teacher to ask stimulating questions facilitating creative, critical thinking and the manifestation of multiple talents. Inquiry oriented questions may be involved in all areas of teaching such as discussion, laboratory demonstrations, student worksheets, visual aids, and evaluations. An instructor may write some questions before class but remain flexible and adapt his teaching as dictated by student interaction. Before outlining questions, a teacher should decide what talents, critical thinking processes and subject matter objectives he hopes to develop and the answers he thinks appropriate.

Questions may be classified as convergent or divergent, according to Bloom's taxonomy, critical thinking processes and/or by the multiple talents the questions are trying to develop. Divergent types of questions and those requiring more cognitive sophistication should be stressed. Multiple, emotionally overloaded questions, and those answered by yes or no responses should be avoided.

The time a teacher waits for a response, or "wait-time," is very important. Most teachers wait less than one second on an average. Five seconds average wait-time results in more responses by slow learners, creative answers, complete sentence answers, questions, and suggestions for experiments.

The developing of good listening skills and environment by focusing on what the person is saying, not interrupting, reacting positively to his efforts, but not over-reacting, encouraging others to respond before the teacher, paraphrasing, clarifying and drawing out ideas enhances the feelings of students toward the instructor and the class.

Research indicates that teachers trained in questioning techniques do change their questioning behavior in the classroom by asking questions requiring greater cognitive ability. Teachers emphasizing higher level types of questions are more likely to have their students do better on national tests which tend to evaluate for all cognitive levels.

Further Investigation and Study

1. Observe a normal conversation and classify the questions asked according to the classificational system suggested in this chapter.
2. Write some discussion questions and classify them according to Bloom's taxonomy, multiple talents, and thinking processes.
3. List as many words as possible which when used as the first word of a sentence would require only yes or no answers.
4. Return to the list of questions asked in the chapter and your answers and review them to see if you would like to alter any of your answers.
5. Read the booklet *Developing Questioning Techniques—A Self-Concept Approach*, Arthur Carin and Robert B. Sund, Charles E. Merrill Publishing Co., 1971.
6. Lead a small discussion and have someone check your wait-time and how well you get students to talk to students instead of students-to-teacher-to-student.
7. Practice your listening and questioning ability using the points listed in this chapter several times in conversation. Rate yourself each time on a 1 to 5 point bases, 1 being poor and 5 excellent.

Answers to Convergent-Divergent Questions (p. 64)

1. Relatively divergent
2. Relatively divergent
3. Very convergent—only yes or no answer possible
4. Very convergent—only yes or no answer possible
5. Very convergent—only yes or no answer possible
6. Relatively convergent—only three answers possible
7. Divergent
8. Very convergent—only yes or no answer possible
9. Divergent
10. Divergent

    Try to rewrite all of the convergent questions to make them more divergent

Answers to Teleological/Anthropomorphic Questions (p. 65)
1. Anthropomorphic
2. Teleological
3. Anthropomorphic
4. Anthropomorphic
5. Teleological

5 Establishing What Is Important in Teaching

Behavioral Objectives—Cognitive, Affective, and Psychomotor

You are about to become a teacher. You have spent several years preparing for entrance into the exciting profession of teaching. You look forward with anticipation to meeting your first classes and taking responsibility for their learning. Why should you have goals?

Suppose an older teacher says to you, "Forget all that stuff about teaching you learned in college. All that theory just doesn't fit the real world of teaching." Do you still need goals? For what purpose are you meeting your classes? Why are students coming to you to be taught? What is your obligation toward them?

Goals provide guidance and direction, and effective teaching requires clarification and understanding of your goals. Every good teacher prepares objectives, because plans for effective teaching have their roots in well-thought-out goals and objectives, without which it is almost impossible to achieve systematic and measurable results. Many teachers experience frustration and disappointment because of the lack of direction resulting from poor or nonexistent goals.

Often the words "goal" and "objective" are used synonymously. We prefer to make a distinction. Goals are broad general statements, sometimes vague in meaning, usually shaping the character of an educational program.[1] Examples are:

---

[1] Robert B. Sund, Anthony J. Picard, *Behavioral Objectives and Evaluational Measures* (Columbus, Ohio: Charles E. Merrill Publishing Company, 1972), p. 1.

> 1. To promote interest and appreciation for the contributions of scholars of the past, or
> 2. To develop the ability to solve problems systematically.

While these goals are laudable, they fall short of providing the teacher with specific teaching objectives. For this reason, recent efforts in education have emphasized objectives, which are stated in performance or behavioral terms.

Behavioral objectives are objectives written in behavioral terms. They must state how a person is to act, think, or feel.[2] Examples are:

> The student should be able:
> 1. When provided with numerical data concerning the daily growth of plants, to graph the data showing the relationship between height and period of growth, or
> 2. When presented with several relevant and irrelevant bits of information concerning a problem, to select the information needed for its solution and outline a method of attack.

Some of the advantages of behavioral objectives are (1) they help the teacher become more precise in his teaching, (2) they clarify exactly what is expected, (3) the teacher plans more carefully because he knows what performance his students should display after finishing a lesson, unit, or course of study, and (4) the teacher knows what materials are needed and is able to give more specific help to students in directing them to outside sources of information. Furthermore, the teacher who prepares behavioral objectives finds them very helpful in evaluation. When preparing paper and pencil tests, the questions can be matched to the objectives and by deciding on certain criteria of performance, questions can be phrased in such a way that the teacher has precise knowledge of the ability of the student to perform certain tasks.

It is customary to think of behavioral objectives in three different areas: cognitive, affective, and psychomotor. These terms come from the work of Bloom and others who developed taxonomies of educational objectives.[3] Cognitive objectives are those that deal with cognition—of knowledge, concepts, and understandings. Traditionally, objectives in this area have received far more attention over the years

---
[2]Sund, p. 2.
[3]Benjamin Bloom et al., *A Taxonomy of Educational Objectives: Handbook I*, The Cognitive Domain (New York: Longmans, Green Co., 1956).

Establishing What Is Important in Teaching

than affective or psychomotor objectives. With increased attention to behavioral or performance competencies, the cognitive area becomes fertile ground for the writing of objectives that stress performance in knowledge and conceptual understandings.

Affective objectives are those that deal with feelings, interests, and attitudes. Teachers are becoming increasingly concerned with this area in our schools today. It seems that neglect or lack of attention to the domain of attitudes has resulted in some unexpected outcomes. Students frequently lose interest in school because of the lack of attention to their needs in the affective domain. Writing affective objectives is usually more difficult than writing those in the cognitive area. It requires more care to formulate behavioral criteria for feelings, interests, and attitudes. It is impossible to peer inside the student's head and determine what attitudes lie there. However, certain overt behaviors are indicative of one's attitudes or interests.

From these observable behaviors, certain objectives in the affective domain can be constructed. When it is possible to identify sufficient groups of behaviors that characterize individuals holding certain attitudes, the use of affective objectives will become more widespread. The value of considering these possibilities lies in the growing awareness by teachers of the need for including affective objectives in the planning for teaching.

Psychomotor objectives concern behaviors involving physical manipulation of apparatus, skill development, and proficiency in using tools, such as instruments and devices. Many of these desired behaviors are not ends in themselves but serve as means for self-learning. Since one of the goals of education is to produce individuals who are self-reliant and capable of pursuing learning on their own throughout their lives, the psychomotor objectives occupy an important place in the overall educational endeavor. Although psychomotor objectives play a major role in physical activities, their importance in other classes should not be overlooked. Examples of psychomotor objectives are:

> For hand-eye coordination,
> When provided with a standard mechanical slide rule, the student will be able to find the product of two numbers and express the result in three significant figures,
>
> or
>
> The student will be able to fill a standard buret and release a prescribed amount of liquid.

How does this activity illustrate cognitive, affective, and psychomotor learning?

Steps in Writing Cognitive Objectives

The task of writing cognitive objectives can be simplified by following certain steps:

1. *Have your overall goals in mind.* What are your general aims for the lesson or unit you are going to teach? Is it improvement of a skill? Developing the understanding of a concept? Stimulating interest in a new area? A combination of these goals?
2. *Select the content desired to achieve the goals of the unit.* In a traditional teaching situation, this may be dependent on the sequence of topics found in a textbook or curriculum guide. But do not let the mere presence of a topical outline dictate your teaching aims. After all, you are attempting to achieve certain goals for a group of

Establishing What Is Important in Teaching

students. The topics chosen should be vehicles to achieve these goals. Usually a number of subject matter topics can be used to accomplish the task. Select those that are appropriate in terms of student interests and needs, teacher interest, suitability to the background of the students, and other factors.

3. *Write tentative statements describing how the student should perform.* Refine these into statements of cognitive objectives that are expressed in terms of performance criteria. Each objective should include a description of the behavior expected of the student, the conditions under which the student must exhibit the given behavior, and the criteria for successful performance.

   "The student should be able:
   When given a list of possible choices concerning environmental practices, to select the one that has the strongest impact on slowing population growth in a given area, giving the justification for his choice."

4. A final step in writing cognitive objectives is to *analyze and evaluate them in terms of their overall contribution to the goals of the unit or course.* Without this analysis, one might easily obtain an imbalance between various levels and areas. Helpful guides are publications by Bloom[4] and Krathwohl[5]. In the cognitive area, Bloom has identified six levels in the hierarchy of educational objectives: Knowledge, Comprehension, Application, Analysis, Synthesis, and Evaluation. The latter ones are higher levels of learning and usually require competence at the lower levels for satisfactory performance.

Tentative Statements of Cognitive Objectives

The following form is suggested to use initially in starting to write cognitive objectives:

The student should be able to:
1. *Hypothesize* what will happen to a slug when placed in salt water (hypertonic solution).
2. *Design* an experiment to determine whether coffee or tea retains heat better.

---

[4]Benjamin S. Bloom, *Taxonomy of Educational Objectives Handbook I: Cognitive Domain* (New York: David McKay Company, Inc., 1956).

[5]David R. Krathwohl, Benjamin S. Bloom, and Bertram B. Masia, *Taxonomy of Educational Objectives Handbook II: Affective Domain* (New York: David McKay Company, 1964).

3. *Infer* that slight environmental changes may cause the death of certain organisms, for example, the slug.

The objectives below are written in a poorer style:
1. The student should circle the numeral representing the number of triangles in a given diagram.
2. The student should join two sets by drawing a single loop around them.
3. The student should indicate the number of objects in each of two sets.

Compare these two sets of objectives. Why is the second set less effective than the first? Note that the phrase "the student should be able to" is written once and only once in the first set. The second set uses the statement over and over again, forcing the reader to read the same expression several times. The reader is mature enough to hold this phrase in his mind after the initial reading, and using the statement once economizes his time.

Note also that the action verbs, *hypothesize, design,* and *infer,* are italicized or underlined in the first set. It is our experience that placing the action verb first and underlining or italicizing it defines the behaviors more accurately. Teachers, as a result, are usually able to determine more easily if a statement is in behavioral terms. Compare the following objectives:

1. *Defines* acceleration operationally.
2. *Understands* the law of conservation of energy.
3. *Knows* how to use it.
4. *Identifies* symbols used in the first year calculus, e.g. $\frac{dy}{dx}$, $F(x)$.

Which of these are written behaviorally? How does the italicizing help you identify the behavior?

Write the Conditions. Detailed objectives should stipulate the conditions under which the student must exhibit the desired behavior. The conditions indicate the clues or stimuli presented to the student, as well as placing restrictions on the student at the time the terminal behavior is sampled. The teacher may identify necessary conditions for stating objectives by asking:
1. What aids will the student be permitted to use?
2. What aids will the student be denied?
3. In what context or situation will the behavior occur?
4. What skills or behaviors should be specifically avoided? Are these excluded by the objective?

Establishing What Is Important in Teaching

Examples of conditions used in objectives are as follows:
1. When given a protractor
2. Given a seed and some water
3. Without the use of a multiplication table
4. Given a chemistry-physics handbook
5. When presented with distillation apparatus

Write the Extent of the Achievement. A criterion of success must be given to determine if the student has achieved the objective. The teacher can indicate the extent of performance by including the response to the following questions in the objective:

1. How often must the learner exhibit the terminal behavior?
2. Is the student with ten correct responses more successful than the one with five correct responses?
3. Has the student who lists three out of five possible responses achieved the objective?
4. Is student X more successful because he responds more quickly than student Y?

Some writers of objectives establish minimum acceptable performance in one or more of the following ways:

1. *Time limit.* The writer specifies that the student must respond or complete the task within a given amount of time. An example would be the statement, "The student must be able to correctly solve at least seven linear equations within a period of thirty minutes." Another would be, "The student must weigh a given sample on a balance to within 1/100th of a milligram within one minute." This practice is questionable from an educational viewpoint, since time limits should vary with ability. Slow learners should be given ample time to meet the minimum acceptable performance levels.

2. *Number of correct responses.* Acceptable performance may also be defined by specifying the number of correct responses. An example of this method is programmed material in which the learner paces himself or is paced by a computer. The learner is permitted to proceed from one unit to the next after he answers correctly all the items in the end-of-unit test or after he correctly responds to 90 percent of the frames in the unit. The percentage of correct responses necessary for success is arbitrary and varies with the difficulty of content and the size of the steps in the program.

3. *Standardized test comparison.* Another means of establishing minimum performance levels is to compare the child with a nationwide sample of children. This occurs when a child is

ranked according to norms on standardized tests. Minimum performance for a child is determined by the norm for children his age or at his grade level. This practice is also being disputed as theories of learning raise questions concerning readiness and rate of development of knowledge.

The extent may not be specifically stated in some objectives, in which case it should be assumed the student will exhibit the behavior whenever he encounters the appropriate situation.

Techniques for Analyzing and Evaluating Objectives

A behavior-content grid is a device for visualizing relationships between content and behavior. It may be used in the selection, formulation, and

BEHAVIORS

CONTENT	Knowledge of Definitions and Terms	Skills and Techniques in Manipulation and Computation	Translation and Interpretation	Analysis-Select Relevant and Irrelevant Data	Follow and Construct Proofs	Verify and Criticize
Non-metric Plane Geometry	X					
Measurement of Length and Angle	X	X				
Simple Closed Curves	X					
Circles	X			X	X	
Constructions	X	X				
Congruent Sets of Points	X					
Area of Plane Regions	X	X	X			
Similar Figures	X					
Graphing Points in a Plane	X	X				

Establishing What Is Important in Teaching

evaluation of behavioral objectives. The example on p. 88 has been constructed for a course in geometry. It may be refined by including subcategories of content and behavior.

To construct a behavior-content grid, make a list of the topics to be covered, list the behaviors you think are important, then arrange the content along one side of a rectangular grid and the behaviors along the other. The intersection of a row and a column is called a cell. A mark in one of these cells represents an objective involving a particular behavior with a specific piece of content. Every piece of content will not necessarily interact with every behavior. Factual content, for example, usually requires only low level cognitive behaviors, such as recall or comprehension.

A set of objectives may be analyzed by locating each objective in one of the cells of the grid. Look at the distribution of the marks on the grid. Are they evenly distributed or clustered? Are there many in one column and few in the others? Does any behavior have no objectives associated with it? Does any content area have no objectives?

In the chart on page 88, notice the heavy emphasis on knowledge of definitions and terms and the lack of objectives requiring higher cognitive behaviors. This is common in initial attempts at writing objectives because low level ones are easier to write. This situation is also common in programs using older curriculum materials.

Notice also that the writer has included several objectives on circles and none on similar figures. Analysis of a test in this way reveals a preference for certain topics. It establishes the content considered important and unimportant by the writer.

If you haven't already done so, try writing a set of objectives, or obtain a previously written set. Now analyze the set with a behavior-content grid. Have you neglected any topics or behaviors? Have you placed too much emphasis on memory and recall? Are additional objectives required? What does this analysis reveal to you about your teaching?

Skill Development[6]

Perhaps you have noticed one characteristic of cognitive objectives that should be discussed further. That is the use of "action verbs" in every statement. These words signify the emphasis on performance that is ex-

---

[6]The Problem Solving Skill is elaborated in "An Analysis and Checklist on the Problem Solving Objective" in Appendix I.

pected of the student. Quite frequently these action verbs appear in the cognitive objectives as infinitive phrases such as "to graph," "to classify," or "to describe." Among the important ones are:

listen	measure	select
search	demonstrate	predict
record	experiment	estimate
compare	describe	group
contrast	repair	operate
classify	construct	dissect
organize	calibrate	apply
outline	discuss	infer
design	explain	name
invent	report	identify
analyze	write	translate
synthesize	draw	state
evaluate	criticize	graph
question		

Notice the absence in the above list of vague terms such as:

know	enjoy	assimilate
understand	believe	conceptualize
appreciate		

The use of these terms makes it difficult, if not impossible, to provide performance criteria by which the student's work can be assessed. What does it mean "to know"? This word in itself does not give clues as to what kind of performance or behavior the student will exhibit as a result of "knowing." Therefore, it is ambiguous and not very useful in an objective statement.

The complaint has frequently been lodged against teaching that students and teachers alike have difficulty expressing exactly what the goals of teaching should be. In taking up this challenge, an attempt has been made to identify the types of skills which students ought to "be able to do better" after having taken the courses in the junior high school and senior high school. We have listed five categories of skills, including the following: acquisitive, organizational, creative, manipulative, and communicative. No attempt is made to rank these categories in order of importance, or even to imply that any one category may be more important than any other. Within each of the categories, however, an effort has been made to list specific skills in order of increasing difficulty. In general, it was felt that those skills which required only the use of one's own unaided senses were simpler than those which re-

Establishing What Is Important in Teaching

quire use of instruments or higher orders of manual and mental dexterity. The categories and the specific skills within them, with some elaboration, are as follows:

A. Acquisitive Skills
   1. Listening—being attentive, alert, questioning
   2. Observing—being accurate, alert, systematic
   3. Searching—locating sources, using several sources, being self-reliant, acquiring library skills
   4. Inquiring—asking, interviewing, corresponding
   5. Investigating—reading background information, formulating problems
   6. Gathering data—tabulating, organizing, classifying, recording
   7. Researching—locating a problem, learning background, setting up experiments, analyzing data, drawing conclusions

B. Organizational Skills
   1. Recording—tabulating, charting, working systematically, working regularly, recording completely
   2. Comparing—noticing how things are alike, looking for similarities, noticing identical features
   3. Contrasting—noticing how things differ, looking for dissimilarities, noticing unlike features
   4. Classifying—putting things into groups and subgroups, identifying categories, deciding between alternatives
   5. Organizing—putting items in order, establishing a system, filing, labeling, arranging
   6. Outlining—employing major headings and subheadings, using sequential logical organization
   7. Reviewing—picking out important items, memorizing, associating
   8. Evaluating—recognizing good and poor features, knowing how to improve grade
   9. Analyzing—seeing implications and relationships, picking out causes and effects, locating new problems

C. Creative Skills
   1. Planning ahead—seeing possible results and probable mode of attack, setting up hypotheses
   2. Designing a new problem, a new approach, a new device or system
   3. Inventing—creating a method, device, or technique
   4. Synthesizing—putting familiar things together in a new arrangement, hybridizing, drawing together

D. Manipulative Skills
  1. Using an instrument—knowing instrument's parts, how it works, how to adjust it, its proper use for task, its limitations
  2. Caring for an instrument—knowing how to store it, using proper settings, keeping it clean, handling it properly, knowing rate capacity, transporting instrument safely
  3. Demonstrating—setting up apparatus, making it work, describing parts and function, illustrating principles
  4. Experimenting—recognizing a problem, planning a procedure, collecting data, recording data, analyzing data, drawing conclusions
  5. Repairing—repairing and maintaining equipment, instruments, etc.
  6. Constructing—building needed items of simple equipment for demonstration and experimentation
  7. Calibrating—learning the basic information about calibration, calibrating a thermometer, balance, timer, or other instrument

E. Communicative Skills
  1. Asking questions—learning to formulate good questions, to be selective in asking, to resort to own devices for finding answers whenever possible
  2. Discussing—learning to contribute own ideas, listening to ideas of others, keeping on the topic, sharing available time equitably, arriving at conclusions
  3. Explaining—describing to someone else clearly, clarifying major points, exhibiting patience, being willing to repeat
  4. Reporting—orally reporting to a class or teacher in capsule form the significant material on a topic
  5. Writing—writing a report describing a problem, the method of attack, any data collected, the methods of analysis, the conclusions drawn, and the implications for further work
  6. Criticizing—constructively criticizing or evaluating a piece of work, a procedure or conclusion
  7. Graphing—putting in graphical form the results of a study or experiment, being able to interpret the graph to someone else
  8. Teaching—after becoming familiar with a topic or semi-expert in it, teaching the material to one's classmates in such a manner that it will not have to be retaught by the teacher

Some questions might be asked concerning the rationale for emphasis on skill development.

Establishing What Is Important in Teaching

1. *Is there a need for skill development?* New courses in elementary and secondary schools emphasize processes as much as the concepts and generalizations. Understanding a process involves skill competencies. Learning "how to learn" requires adequate learning tools. In addition, students need confidence in their ability to perform the tasks needed in self-learning. Skill competency strengthens self-reliance.

2. *Can skill development be guided through a graded sequence of dificulty from simple to complex?* This appears possible because of certain characteristics of skills themselves such as level of difficulty and complexity. For example, skills requiring the use of unaided senses are simpler than skills requiring the use of instruments. It is easier for a student to use his unaided eyes to compare the colors of minerals than to operate a microscope to do the same thing at a higher level of sophistication. Also, groups of simple skills may be included in more difficult complex skills. Graphing, for example, requires competency in the simpler skills of counting, measuring, and using a ruler. In the same way, higher levels of learning, such as analysis, synthesis, and evaluation, require higher levels of skill proficiency.

3. *Does skill development enhance or preclude concept development?* It seems that growth in conceptual understandings would be enhanced by expertise in skill usage. In teaching skills, concepts form the vehicle by which the skills are learned. One cannot learn a skill in a void—there must be substantive information on which to operate. The skill of comparing, for example, is useless there are things to compare. In the same vein, a hierarchy of skills forms a framework on which concepts can be attached. As one moves toward more sophisticated skill learnings, the subject matter (concepts) can be adapted and changed as needs require.

4. *Can achievement of skill competencies be tested?* There is ample evidence that skill achievements can be structured in behavioral terms. Performance can be observed and evaluated. Various performance levels of individual skills can be graded on a continuum from minimum to maximum success. Not only is it possible for teachers to create testing situations using performance objectives but it is equally possible to provide self-evaluation opportunities for students to gain knowledge of their own progress and levels of performance.

5. *What are the implications of the skill development approach in the classroom?* Conditions necessary for success when emphasizing the skill or process goals are as follows:

a. Time must be provided for practice and experience in the skills being developed. One does not become proficient without practice and drill.
b. Teachers must have clear understandings of the skill objectives being sought. Planning must revolve around these objectives rather than traditional content goals alone.
c. Ample materials must be at hand. There must be a "responsive environment" permitting students to operate with the "things of the world."
d. A variety of conceptual materials may be selected to facilitate skill development. Most conceptual themes or topics provide ample opportunities for the teaching of varied skills. In planning for teaching, however, it is important to concentrate on a limited number of skills in any particular lesson.
e. Evaluation emphasis must be placed on performance or behavioral terms, not mere factual memorization or recitation. The superficial coverage of content must be de-emphasized while performance and depth of understanding must be brought to the foreground.

Mere identification of skills to be taught is of course only a first step in the realization of an objective. In order to bring about skill develop-

What skills and attitudes are being developed here?

ment and ultimate mastery of the desired skills, the teacher must devise suitable teaching plans and student activities. It goes without saying that, in this type of learning at least, "learning by doing" is an important maxim. Pupils must be given opportunities to carry out activities which give repeated practice in the skills to be taught. The laboratory becomes an important facility at this point because most of the skills involve procedures which, to a greater or lesser extent, require materials and apparatus.

The Hierarchy of Affective Objectives

In addition to a taxonomy of cognitive objectives, there is also one for the affective domain written by Krathwohl, Bloom, and Masia.[7] The word *affective* comes from the Latin word *affectus*, meaning capable of feeling or emotion. The affective objectives are those in which the instructor endeavors to have his students develop emotions for what they are learning. These include:
1. Appreciations
2. Feelings
3. Values
4. Attitudes

Whenever an instructor teaches anything, he teaches a feeling about it. For example, if he comes into class and says, "We have to study mathematics now. I know you don't like it, and to tell you the truth, I don't either," he is teaching that mathematics is no fun and is boring. As a result, his students develop negative feelings toward the subject. The most important thing an educator can do is develop positive emotions toward what is being learned. If a student learns to enjoy learning he will continue to grow intellectually long after his formal education is finished.

Krathwohl, Bloom, and Masia have classified the affective domain into five main groups as follows:

1. Receiving (attending). The student is at least willing to hear or study the information.
2. Responding. The student will respond about the material being studied.
3. Valuing. The student has a commitment to what is being learned and believes it has worth.
4. Organization. The student has a hierarchy of value—a value system.

---

[7] Krathwohl et al.

5. Characterization by value or value complex. The student has an internalized value complex directing his total behavior. He has integrated his beliefs, ideas, and attitudes into a philosophy of life.

This classification system can be shortened to include three general categories:
1. Awareness
2. Acceptance of values
3. Preference for values

It is more functional to use these three general levels and this hierarchy when beginning to write affective objectives than it is to use the more detailed one. All you have to do is ask yourself, "Do I want to determine whether or not my students are aware of a topic, if they value it, or if their total value complex has changed because of the instruction they have had?"

Overt and Covert Affective Achievement

Some affective behavior can be observed (overt) while some is internalized (covert) and cannot be seen. The latter type can be assessed by indirectly asking the student his values, satisfactions, appreciations, or attitudes about what is being learned. Shown below is a chart outlining these two types of behavior and some methods of determining their attainment:

Types of Behavior	*Measured By*
1. Overt	
a. Verbal	a. General observation
b. Nonverbal	b. Observational rating scales scored by the teacher
2. Covert	
a. Attitudes	a. Self-evaluation inventories; support scales
b. Feelings	b. Semantic differential scales; conversations
c. Values	c. Same as b.

Remember, the covert types of affective attainment are more difficult to determine. Usually the instructor will have to ask a student how he feels, values, appreciates, or he will have to construct instruments to measure these feelings. Self-evaluational inventories are especially useful for this purpose. Brief examples are listed below to help you see their use.

SELF-EVALUATION INVENTORY

1. I like mathematics better than science.
   Strongly agree   Agree   Disagree
2. Mathematics will probably not be very valuable to me in my life.
   Strongly agree   Agree   Disagree

Use of Scale For Science

Place an X in the space of your choice
1. Good ___ ___ ___ ___ ___ Bad
2. Fun ___ ___ ___ ___ ___ Dull
3. Sometimes pleasurable ___ ___ ___ ___ ___
4. Successful ___ ___ ___ ___ Unsuccessful
5. Like ___ ___ ___ ___ ___ Dislike

Sample Objectives

The following are general examples of affective objectives. They have been categorized as being "observable" or "unobservable" and subdivided into problem solving, general, and specific subject area objectives.

Observable Objectives

Problem Solving Objectives:
  The student should:
  1. Volunteer to do additional experiments in areas related to the subjects studied in class.
  2. Volunteer to do additional work in the form of a written paper or oral presentation in areas related to subjects studied in class.
  3. Participate eagerly in laboratory exercises.

General Objectives:
  The student should:
  1. Join (voluntarily) the foreign language club.
  2. Volunteer to attend book fairs when he has the opportunity.
  3. Volunteer to attend optional field trips to museums, universities, etc.
  4. Participate eagerly in classroom activities.
  5. Offer constructive criticism on the improvement of classroom activities.

6. Complete and hand in assignments on time.

Specific Objectives:

The student should:
1. Initiate group action dealing with pollution problems in our community, such as organizing a working committee to determine and publicize sources of pollution.
2. Promote or take part in group and individual activities in preserving natural and living resources in the community.

Unobservable Objectives

Problem Solving:

The student should rate positively, on a self-evaluation inventory, on each of the following:
1. Desire to do additional work on historical topics or related topics not specifically studied in class.
2. Consider problems encountered in an objective manner (example: form conclusions based on logical thought processes, rather than on bias or emotions).
3. Apply good "techniques" in laboratory work.
4. Exhibit self-confidence in terms of solving problems encountered in the classroom.

General Objectives:

The student should rate positively, on a self-evaluation inventory, on each of the following:
1. Want to take another history course.
2. Like history as much at the end of the year as the beginning of the year.
3. Recognize the importance of, and support, research.
4. Voluntarily read outside material related to history.
5. Enjoy participating in group activities in class.
6. Form and change opinions on the basis of new evidence which is discovered.
7. Respond to suggestions and attitudes of classmates.
8. Freely express own opinion concerning topics or problems encountered in class.
9. Be receptive to new or different learning activities in class.

Specific Objectives:

The student should rate positively, on a self-evaluation inventory, on each of the following:
1. Desire to obtain additional information concerning the problem of world over-population.

Establishing What Is Important in Teaching

2. Make decisions concerning the individual's responsibility for conserving natural and living resources.
4. Make decisions concerning the utilization of insecticides, herbicides, and other potentially dangerous substances as each relates to food production, disease control, etc.
5. Utilize good hygenic habits in everyday life (example—maintain a proper diet, exercise regularly, etc.).
6. Decide not to begin smoking.
7. Decide to quit smoking if he has started.
8. Make decisions concerning the harmful effects of drugs and drug abuse.
9. Become convinced of the harmful effects of excessive amounts of alcohol and decide not to use alcohol in excess.

Continuums of Affective Behaviors

Krathwohl points out, in comparing the cognitive and affective domains, " . . . there is a tendency for the counterpart of a low level objective to come from the lower levels of the affective continuum and for objectives at the upper level of the affective continuum to have upper level cognitive counterparts."[8] Not only is there a correlation between emotion and cognition, but there seems to be a positive correlation between the intensity of these behaviors. The more a student "knows" about history and social studies, the higher he values them. Conversely, a student who values science and mathematics will attempt to become more cognizant in these areas.

The implication of the preceding comments is that affective behaviors cannot be ignored. It cannot be assumed they will be achieved as a natural by-product of cognition. Specific objectives relating to affective behavior in any subject must be formulated as carefully as those relating to cognitive behavior. There is admittedly more difficulty in stating observable affective behaviors than cognitive ones as well as less precision in measuring the achievement of affective behaviors. Neither of these difficulties, however, is insurmountable. Kapfer suggests: [9]

1. Stating the affective domain objective as an unobservable behavior (e.g., receiving, responding, valuing, organizing, characterizing) and then stating the related observable area of behavior.
2. Stating finite linear steps in a continuum of behaviors begin-

---

[8] Krathwohl et al.
[9] Kapfer, P., "Behavioral Objectives in the Cognitive and Affective Domain," *Educational Technology* (June 15, 1968): 12.

ning at the "negative" or "neutral" end and progressing to the "positive" end of the continuum.

For example:

Objective: The student increasingly values independent learning as observed in his self-initiating and self-directing behaviors.

Continuum of Behaviors

1. Given a teacher-assigned delimited topic with assigned specific resources, the student follows directions.
2. Given a teacher-assigned delimited topic and assigned alternative resources, the student selects from alternative resources.
3. Given a teacher-assigned delimited topic, the student seeks his own resources.
4. Given a teacher-assigned broad topic, the student delimits the topic and seeks his own resources.
5. Given a student-initiated broad or delimited topic (in or out of of school), the student delimits the topic as necessary and seeks his own resources.

How to Start to Write Affective Objectives

1. Determine your goals.
2. Initially concentrate on writing value-laden objectives. A beginning writer of affective objectives should ignore the first and second levels of the taxonomy, those of receiving and responding, which are involved in many ways with describing the cognitive domain. Concern about writing objectives for the lowest levels of the hierarchy, as well as for the fourth and fifth levels, tends to confuse the beginner as to the function of the affective domain. However, writing value objectives has the opposite effect. Furthermore, writing for valuing or higher objectives is more rewarding and has a greater effect upon the writer than stating them for the first two levels.
3. Write the following phrase at the top of the page once and only once: "The student should be able to:"
4. Select an action verb—refer to the examples of verbs used in the chapter—and write your statement.

    The student should be able to:
    1. Participate in class discussion.
    2. Like mathematics as indicated on a self-evaluational inventory.
    3. Enjoy the class.

Establishing What Is Important in Teaching

Notice that in one of the objectives above, the method for evaluating it is also included. It is probably better to write your objectives and then rewrite them including the method of evaluation and, if necessary, a hierarchy of the behaviors you expect.

Some Criticisms of Behavioral Objectives

While many educators have recognized advantages in specifying instructional objectives in behavioral terms, others have objected strenuously to the present movement. Some of their arguments, with counter arguments by proponents of behavioral objectives, are presented for consideration by the reader.

1. *There may be a tendency to over-emphasize trivial behaviors, because it is easier to state objectives for specific behaviors than for overall general objectives.* Proponents of behavioral objectives view this as an advantage. Recognition of *specific* objectives will assist teachers in preparing general objectives in operational terms because they will be able to scrutinize all objectives carefully and weed out the trivial ones.
2. *Teachers may be inhibited in capitalizing on spur-of-the-moment teaching opportunities if they have many specific behavioral objectives prepared.* Should not *all* classroom activities contribute toward realization of teaching objectives? Having clear behavioral objectives will permit the teacher to judge quickly the relevance of the unexpected activity.
3. *It is impossible to measure precisely certain educational objectives.* This is certainly true. However, evaluation goes on regardless. Should teachers not have at their disposal the best possible *objective* measures based upon performance standards to assist them in the enormously complicated task of evaluating pupil achievement and growth?
4. *Teachers customarily express their objectives, if at all, in vague general statements.* While it is true teachers are generally quite vague about their objectives, there is no reason why such vagueness should occur. To provide quality education, it is reasonable to expect teachers to adopt improved methods of planning and teaching, which include better knowledge of one's objectives.
5. *Behavioral objectives, being specific, imply that the teacher may be accountable for success in achieving them in his classes.*

This is a frequently used argument which expresses a feeling of being threatened in one's teaching role. However, the use of precise objectives can work to the teacher's advantage here. It is no longer necessary to hide behind vague, general objectives with many interpretations. Instead performance criteria and substantiated results can provide parents and school administrators with evidence rather than mere speculation as to the outcomes of class work.

Summary

It is important to have goals and objectives for teaching. Without objectives, teaching becomes a confused and directionless experience, frustrating to the teacher, and ineffective for the students.

Recent years have seen increased attention to objectives stated in behavioral or performance terms. Good behavioral objectives include the expected performance of the student, the conditions under which the performance can be expected, and the level of attainment needed to satisfy the objective.

Behavioral objectives are often divided into cognitive, affective, and psychomotor types. The first pertains to conceptual understandings or knowledge objectives. The second refers to attitudes, feelings, interests, and appreciations. These objectives are difficult to write and evidence of their achievement depends on observations of overt behaviors that are indicative of the affective trait or quality. Psychomotor objectives refer to skills and competencies that involve manipulation, muscular coordination, or sensory achievements.

A characteristic of good behavioral objectives is a statement using "action verbs" signifying performance in observable or measurable terms. Vague terms such as "know" or "understand" should be avoided in writing behavioral objectives.

Many groups have prepared lists of behavioral objectives for their classes or curricula. Such lists should be used as guides for constructing similar objectives for oneself. Occasionally the lists may be used in the original form but care must be exercised in choosing objectives suitable to the overall goals of one's course.

The affective domain deals with appreciation, feelings, values, and attitudes involved in instruction. Affective behavior may be overt or covert.

Overt behavior is evaluated by general observation or by the teacher using a scale as a guide to rate the student. Covert behavior is more difficult to determine since it is not immediately observable. Its achievement may be evaluated by asking the student how he feels about what he is learning, by using self-evaluational inventories, or by applying Likert or semantical differential scales. The steps and the form to follow in writing affective objectives are similar to those of the cognitive domain. The action verbs, however, vary, and it should be remembered that it is possible to describe a continuum of affective behaviors from negative to positive.

The movement toward use of behavioral objectives is significant. While critics have cited certain pitfalls to be avoided, the overall effect appears beneficial. Teachers are more conscious of the performance they wish to expect from their students. Evaluation becomes more precise. Progress toward the attainment of goals is more easily measurable. Teaching assumes a quality that is more satisfying and defensible.

Further Investigation and Study

1. Write five behavioral objectives in the cognitive domain for the subject area you are interested in teaching. After writing them exchange with a colleague for critical analysis. What do you find to be the most difficult part of writing good behavioral objectives?
2. Write five behavioral objectives in the affective domain. Are these objectives dependent on the subject being taught? Good behavioral objectives contain a method of evaluating performance. What method are you using to assess performance in the affective domain?
3. Look at the lists of skills in the respective categories of acquisitive, organizational, creative, manipulative, and communicative. Scrutinize the order of skills listed and attempt to reorder them, ranking them from simple to complex within each category. Do you agree with the order given? Add other skills within the various categories.

6 The Affective Domain

Teachers are becoming more aware of the need to deal with areas of the intellect other than the purely cognitive. Traditionally, schools were mainly concerned with teaching facts, principles, and concepts—what normally would be called knowledge or information. This cognitive domain of the intellect has been given more than adequate attention. Evaluations have been based upon cognition, and progress throughout his school career has depended on the student's cognitive success. Those individuals who were not able to perform certain set standards of intellectual or cognitive ability were dropped by the wayside.

It has become apparent that a very large waste exists when attention is given purely to cognitive goals. Unhappiness abounds and classrooms become unpleasant places in which to spend one's time. The American system of compulsory education to age 16 has produced in some areas of the country, particularly in large urban centers, a type of school which is totally depressing. This has been emphasized in recent books, foremost among which is one by Charles Silberman entitled *Crisis in the Classroom*. Silberman makes the point that in some schools what goes on is reminiscent of penal institutions. Children are under authoritative rule, unmotivated and subject to the autocratic procedures of teachers and administrators. It is a joyless existence and learning is minimal. It is likely that we have succeeded in turning children away from further education and those who manage to survive and go on to successful careers in all likelihood have done so in spite of the system, rather than because of it.

For these reasons it is becoming apparent that we must pay attention to the affective area of concern. This includes feelings, attitudes, appreciations, interests, values, and other more subjective areas of the intellect. We must become concerned with the way children feel about school and about the subjects which they are studying. We cannot continue to force-feed in a dogmatic fashion information with questionable relevancy to children.

It has long been thought that the affective goals and objectives, if important at all, could be achieved vicariously and that they would be fulfilled simply by giving major attention to cognitive goals and allowing the affective goals to materialize concomitantly. Sometimes this has worked, but more frequently it has failed.

One of the important maxims of effective teaching consists of recognition that there appear to be three steps in the learning process, which may be thought of as three corners of a triangle permitting learners to progress satisfactorily. These are interest, progress, and satisfaction. The teacher's goal is to first develop interest. If a spark of transitory interest can be captured, it is then the teacher's responsibility to encourage progress. Progress can only be achieved by providing some form of success on the part of the student, since the normal reaction of humans is to reinforce and perpetuate the areas in which they are successful, and to turn away from the areas of failure and frustration. So this second step consists of providing successful experiences, small though they may be. The third step in the cycle is the natural satisfactions that result from successful experiences, providing satisfying self-concepts and permitting the student to maintain his interest. This brings us back to the original corner of the triangle—that of interest. Interest is furthered by success, and by satisfaction, which has resulted from success. So the cycle is complete and as long as these three links in the chain are not broken, the child will spiral upward to ever-increasing achievements. If at some point, however, the chain is broken, progress ceases. The student is deprived of successful experiences and therefore gains no satisfaction, the triangle is broken, and as far as he is concerned, his learning is terminated in that particular area.

Harry Wong, teacher of a junior high school in California, has recognized this cycle and has had considerable success in working with previously unmotivated, uninterested students. The secret of his success has been love and caring, exemplified in the form of individual attention and the granting of small successes which builds confidence in students who have been previously turned off by traditional teaching methods.

Multiple-Talent Approach

Calvin Taylor, professor of psychology, University of Utah, has recognized the importance of considering areas in human development other than purely academic or cognitive. He has identified six talent areas: creative, planning, communicative, forecasting, decision making, and academic. A junior high school teacher in attempting to facilitate Calvin Taylor's talent approach in his classes has written the following letter to parents of these children in an effort to clarify the aims and goals of the class:

Dear Parent:

Your child has above average talents; however, in the classroom many of these talents are often overlooked and neglected.

Schools usually evaluate a student's work and build the study program around academic activities. It has long been known that success in life and success in the academic school do not necessarily correlate. We can all think of examples where the "A" student in college couldn't hold a job and the student who dropped out of high school owned a business. This being the case we have been in the process of uncovering other talents that ultimately lead to success in later life. These talents have been identified in studies: Academic Talent, Creative Talent, Planning Talent, Decision-Making Talent, Communicating Talent, and Forecasting Talent.

The class activities are selected so that each of the talents must be used. The student then has an opportunity to evaluate how well he has done while using each talent. Through self-evaluations by the student, and evaluations by the teacher, we hope to find the student's strong talents and his weak talents.

This evaluation helps each student. The traditional academic student finds he has definite weaknesses he can strive to overcome. The below average academic student finds he has above average talents that he can use successfully. With each student meeting success at various times, the learning experience is greatly increased and is more realistic in relation to real life. After all, in school we are after the development of the complete individual. We believe this program will better meet that end.

Sincerely yours,
8th Grade Teacher

Thomas Wolfe has provided a quotation which has relevance at this point.

If a man has a talent and cannot use it, he has failed. If he has talent and uses only half of it, he has partly failed. If he has talent and learns somehow to use the whole of it, he has gloriously succeeded, and won a satisfaction and triumph few men will ever know.

Taylor believes that nearly all students are talented. If this seems dificult to believe, one merely is invited to think about the breadth of talents recognizable in society today. There are talents of art, music, mechanics, oratory, organization, creativity, mathematics, and many others. If teachers and school systems are willing to recognize that students who have exceptional talents in one of these areas are worthy of high praise and acclaim, even though their general academic talent may be low, a great step forward will have been made.

The conclusion from Taylor's research is that nearly all students are above average in one or more talents. It is possible using this reasoning to recognize that there is a great deal of high ability in all students. It is only when we severely restrict the talents we are willing to count that we run into the difficulty that we presently find ourselves in —by failing to reward or provide successful experiences for a large number of students, we end up with frustration, failure, school dropouts and a dismal existence.

Multiple talent teaching capitalizes on both subject matter mastery and achievement across the spectrum of each student's ability, which allows an increase in transfer of learning to later schooling or other situations. The multiple talent approach is student-centered and holds hope for reaching nearly every student, as well as helping to increase each student's individuality. Taylor says that students seem to grow more in knowledge when it is the means for developing talents rather than the end or central focus.

A breakdown of the six talent areas identified by Taylor follows:

TAYLOR'S TALENT AREAS

I. *Creative Talent*
   A. Creative—ability to go beyond, putting together seemingly unrelated things or information to derive "new" solutions
      1. Fluency—internal production of ideas is encouraged and sharing these ideas increases fluency and confidence
      2. Flexibility—considering problems from as many points of view as possible
      3. Originality—looking at things in unusual ways
   Creativity production is best developed through steps which stimulate fluency, flexibility, and originality. A basic talent teaching process might be:
      a. presentation of a problem for consideration

The Affective Domain

        b. time to think, list and enumerate
        c. sharing of ideas and refinement of them; all responses are accepted
        d. incubation period
        e. sharing of additional ideas
        f. selecting the best solution
        g. selecting the most original solution
        h. acting in terms of solution and decision

II. *Planning Talent*
    A. Elaboration—ability to tell what to do, what you want to do and what you wish to create or construct
    B. Sensitivity to problems—telling how, why, and when to do something. Deciding what is needed, what cannot be changed, what the effects and consequences of what you do will be
    C. Organizing abilities—being able to organize the materials, time, and necessary resources

III. *Communication Talent*
    A. Expressional fluency—saying what you mean, concisely expressing thoughts, ideas, and needs, including understanding of nonverbal forms of communication
    B. Associational fluency—understanding the interrelatedness of things, seeing interrelations, analogies, similarities
    C. Word fluency—using words to give concise meaning; word usage which adds color, depth, and emotion to expression

IV. *Forecasting Talent*
    A. Conceptual foresight—what are your goals?
    B. Penetration—what are the details, what do you need to know before acting?
    C. Social awareness—how will people around you feel or act? Will changes force unacceptable conditions on others?

V. *Decision-Making Talent*
    A. Experimental evaluations—how many alternatives are there and what are they? What are the limiting conditions?
    B. Logical evaluations—what are the best possible alternatives? What are your goals? What is the best sequence?
    C. Judgment—deciding in terms of alternatives and consequences, conditions and preferences
    A decision is a statement (or act) of preference. Making decisions is basic to living and interacting. Good decision makers are often leaders.

VI. *Academic Talent*
The general school curriculum which is measurable through achievement tests

J. P. Guilford says that the I.Q. index gives a fairly good idea of how the student will do academically, but as for overall intellectual assessment, it is severely limited.[1] Guilford estimates that man has at least 120 high level intellectual talents, but that most intelligence tests measure eight or less of these talents. Ninety-eight kinds of talents are now known, but so far we are able to measure less than 10 percent of these talents. The longer talents remain unused or dormant, the more likely they will never be used to their potential.

How does having fun cause attitudes about school life to change?

Evaluation of Affective Objectives

The long delay in giving proper attention to the affective domain of educational objectives has been due in part to difficulties in evaluation. Whereas the cognitive area is relatively amenable to assessment procedures it is much more difficult to usefully evaluate in the affective area. Recently a few individuals have given attention to the evaluation of affective objectives. Among these are Jay Hackett, in a study entitled, "An Investigation of the Correlation Between Teacher-Observed and Student Self-Reported Affective Behaviors Toward Science," completed

---

[1] J.P. Guilford, *Personality* (New York: McGraw-Hill, 1959).

The Affective Domain

in 1972.[2] In this study, Hackett attempted to answer the question of what correlation exists between affective behavior as self-reported by the student and as observed by teachers. The general affective behavior toward science was described as containing parameters of interests, appreciations, attitudes, and values. Behavioral objectives for these parameters were constructed for eighth-grade students. Two instruments were designed from the behavioral objectives; the first, the Observed Affective Behavior Checklist, contained samples of general affective behaviors commonly displayed by students. This instrument was designed for teacher use in classroom observation of student behavior. The second instrument, the Affective Self-Report Instrument, was a Likert Scale containing the same behaviors as those on the observer's checklist. Six hundred and forty-seven eighth-grade students participated in the study. Teachers observed and recorded the frequency of their student's interests, appreciation, attitudes, and values held toward science. The students then self-reported their feelings about the same parameters. Hackett's conclusions were that teachers demonstrate a certain proficiency in detecting covert affective attitudes held toward science by their students. Students overtly displayed a number of their covert attitudes toward science and honestly self-evaluated their affective achievement. Hackett concluded that valid and reliable affective evaluation instruments can be developed from behavioral objectives in the affective domain.

Gary Downs compared the affective behavior of students enrolled in various high school science courses as measured by an instrument developed using the affective domain continuum.[3] He found that the affective behavior of most science students changed in an unfavorable direction during their secondary school years. High school science students enrolled in physics and chemistry had a more favorable affective behavior toward science than did biology and introductory physical science students, and males had a more favorable affective behavior toward science than did females.

Other efforts at evaluating affective behavior are beginning to appear. In a relative sense, schools now are at about the same stage of sophistication in recognition, use, and evaluation of affective objectives that they were thirty years ago in the cognitive domain. Thus the field

---

[2]Jay Hackett, "An Investigation of the Correlation Between Teacher-Observed and Student Self-Reported Affective Behaviors Toward Science," unpublished dissertation, University of Northern Colorado, 1972.

[3]Gary Downs, "A Comparison of the Affective Behavior of Students Enrolled in Various High School Science Courses As Measured By an Instrument Developed Using the Affective Domain Continuum," unpublished thesis, University of Northern Colorado, 1972.

is wide open and presents endless challenge to alert, professional teachers who wish to become more humane and caring in their conduct of classes under their direction.

How do successful experiences contribute to building self-concepts?

Values and Value Clarification

A holistic approach to education is devoted to aiding the individual develop his total potential toward self-actualization. A person as he evolves develops attitudes and values that in turn affect what he learns. For the school to ignore this aspect of an individual's development is to lessen educational effectiveness.

John Dewey pointed out the futility of failing to attend to values since students during school years are simultaneously developing them and are influenced by the learning environment in their attainment. Piaget's research has substantiated Dewey's thesis in that it has revealed the developmental character of value achievement in the maturation process, particularly during school years.

Piaget found that children's views of the world and ethics passed through various stages as indicated on the following page.

1. Egocentric —Egocentricity characterizes the view of the child up to about four years. A child during this period believes the way he sees things is the way they are for everybody. He is unable to play a game since his rules are the rules. He can't perceive how another person could have different rules.
2. Authoritarian —Age four to approximately eleven. Rules and ethics come from authority figures. They are given from on high.
3. Consensus Derived —Ages approximately eleven on. Rules or ethics may be arrived at by consensus as to what is good, etc. This is the beginning of self-evaluation of values which may continue into full adulthood.

Although the above outline of Piaget's research is somewhat simplified, it conveys sufficient information to understand the essence of this developmental aspect of the individual.

Lawrence Kohlberg, impressed by Piaget's research over the last 14 years, has further investigated value development.[4] He has carried out a longitudinal study of 75 boys starting at ages 10 and 16 and followed their value evolvement past the ages of 24 and 30. As a result of his investigations, he has concluded that value attainment is hierarchical in character consisting of three levels each containing stages (six in all) having a total of 25 different aspects.

The three levels are:

    I. Preconventional or Premoral

   II. Conventional or Conforming

  III. Post-Conventional or Self-Accepting Moral Principles

A brief summary of these as stated by Kohlberg and his colleagues is outlined below:

PRECONVENTIONAL LEVEL

    At this level the child is responsive to such rules and labels as good or bad and right or wrong. He interprets these labels in purely

---

[4]Lawrence Kohlberg and Phillip Whitten, "Understanding the Hidden Curriculum," *Learning* (December, 1972): 11-12.

physical or hedonistic terms: If he is bad, he is punished; if he is good, he is rewarded. He also interprets the labels in terms of the physical power of those who enunciate them—parents, teachers, and other adults. The level comprises the following two stages:

Stage 1: punishment and obedience orientation: the physical goodness or badness regardless of the human meaning or value of these consequences. Avoidance of punishment and unquestioning deference to power are valued in their own right, not in terms of respect for an underlying moral order supported by punishment and authority, the latter being stage 4.

Stage 2: instrumental relativist orientation. Right action consists of that which instrumentally satisfies one's own needs and occasionally the needs of others. Human relations are viewed in terms similar to those of the marketplace. Elements of fairness, of reciprocity and equal sharing are present, but they are always interpreted in a pragmatic way. Reciprocity is a matter of "you scratch my back and I'll scratch yours," not of loyalty, gratitude or justice.

CONVENTIONAL LEVEL

At this level maintaining the expectations of the individual's family, group or nation is perceived as valuable in its own right, regardless of immediate and obvious consequences. The attitude is one not only of conformity to the social order but of loyalty to it, of activity maintaining, supporting and justifying the order, and of identifying with the persons or group involved in it. This level comprises the following two stages:

Stage 3: interpersonal concordance of "good boy-nice girl" orientation. Good behavior is that which pleases or helps others and is approved by them. There is much conformity to sterotypical images of what is majority or "natural" behavior. Behavior is frequently judged by intention: "He means well" becomes important, and one earns approval by "being nice."

Stage 4: "law and order" orientation. Authority, fixed rules and the maintenance of the social order are valued. Right behavior consists of doing one's duty, showing respect for authority and maintaining the social order for its own sake.

POSTCONVENTIONAL LEVEL

At this level there is a clear effort to reach a personal definition of moral values—to define principles that have validity and application apart from the authority of groups or persons and apart from the individual's own identification with these groups. This level again has two stages:

Stage 5: social-contract legalistic orientation: Generally, this stage has utilitarian overtones. Right action tends to be defined in terms of general individual rights and in terms of standards that have been crit-

The Affective Domain

ically examined and agreed upon by the whole society. There is a clear awareness of the importance of personal values and opinions and a corresponding emphasis on procedural rules and reaching consensus. Other than that which is constitutionally and democratically agreed upon, right is a matter of personal values and opinion. The result is an emphasis both upon the "legal point of view" and upon the possibility of making rational and socially desirable changes in the law, rather than freezing it as in the "law and order" stage 4. Outside the legal realm, free agreement is the binding element of obligation. This is an "official" morality of the U.S. government and the Constitution.

Stage 6: universal ethical-principle orientation. Right is defined by the conscience in accord with self-chosen ethical principles, which in turn are based on logical comprehensiveness, universality and consistency. These principles are abstract and ethical (the golden rule, the categorical imperative); they are not concrete moral rules like the Ten Commandments. At heart, these are universal principles of justice, of the reciprocity and equality of human rights, and of respect for the dignity of human beings as individual persons.

Kohlberg's model follows Piaget's in that the individual in his development passes progressively from a rather egocentric view to one of maturity and universal ideals.

In order for value clarification to be effective, Kohlberg recommends that a teacher evaluate the developmental level of each of his students and adjust instruction so that they are confronted with moral problems one stage above their developmental attainment. In the process of doing this the instructor facilitates the student's involvement and tries to present him with his own illogic for consideration. For example, in Kohlberg's level three, the teacher might ask a student whether he dislikes something because of some universal ideal. Generally, the teacher asks questions requiring students to search out and identify certain concepts and principles they hold and their reasons for having them. In doing this, the teacher may vary the activities providing structure or lack of structure depending on the needs of the students and the type of investigation.

For value attainment to occur there must be what Kohlberg calls a "just school" and a "just environment," because he believes that much of what is learned morally comes more from the social milieu than from books and other materials. It is this environment that Kohlberg refers to as the "Hidden Curriculum." He, like Piaget, believes that morality cannot be taught directly but the student through active involvement and the use of his mind must cull out moral principles.

Another leader in American Value education is Dr. Sidney Simon at the Center for Humanistic Education, University Graduate School of Education, University of Massachusetts. Sidney Simon says of students exposed to value clarification processes in the school that they are: "less apathetic, have become less flighty, less conforming as well as less dissenting. They are more zestful, energetic, more critical in their thinking and are more likely to follow through on decisions. In the case of under-achievers, value clarification has led to better success in school."[5]

Dr. Simon, unlike Dr. Kohlberg, has been less interested in research but more concerned with developing techniques of "value clarification" for students and teachers. He not only considers the cognitive processes of moral attainment but feelings and emotions of the person as well. In fact, many of his 79 strategies in his book *Values Clarification* are concerned with techniques involving feelings and emotions.

The purpose of value clarification is to aid students in developing processes to use in determining their own values. It is not to indoctrinate. An instructor must be open and accepting of a student's views while helping him to clarify his values. The teacher, furthermore, must insure that this attitude also prevails among the students about classmates' views. He must also have a clear understanding of what a value is and how it differs from value indicators.

Raths, Harmin, and Simon, in their book *Values and Teaching*, have defined values as having the following characteristics:[6]

Definition of Value
It must be:
1. Cherished
2. Publicly affirmed
3. Freely chosen
4. Chosen from alternatives
5. Chosen knowing the consequences
6. Linked consistently with other values
7. Acted upon

These authors consider beliefs, attitudes, opinions, feelings and morals as "value indicators" which differ from values in that they are guides that have not as yet met all the criteria listed above.

An instructor can identify individuals with values as well as those who are confused by the following characteristics:

---

[5]Reprinted by permission of Hart Publishing Co., Inc., from its copyrighted volume *VALUES CLARIFICATION: A Handbook of Practical Strategies for Teachers and Students* by Sidney B. Simon, Leland W. Howe and Howard Kirschenbaum.

[6]Louis Raths, Merrill Harmin, Sidney Simon, *Values and Teaching* (Columbus, Ohio: Charles E. Merrill Publishing Co., 1966).

The Affective Domain

People Having Values	People Lacking Clear Values
1. Proud	1. Apathetic
2. Enthusiastic	2. Inconsistent
3. Positive in their perceptions and reactions	3. Overconforming
	4. Overly dissenting
4. Purposeful—have goals	5. Confused
	6. Flighty—emotional personality. Tend not to give the impression that they are inwardly at ease.

Fundamental to the clarification of values is a positive self-concept. The individual must feel that "I can," e.g., be creative, do mathematics, write; that "I am somebody," or, in other words, views himself as a capable, lovable human being.

The typical value clarification strategy starts with some area of conflict where students are confused or have not as yet acquired all the characteristics of a person having values. These areas might include such topics as listed below:

Areas of Possible Conflict

1. Sex
2. Politics
3. Contribution of technology
4. Pollution
5. Religion
6. Family relations
7. Individual tastes
8. Culture—what is pleasing in the arts, music, etc.
9. Style—clothing, hair, etc.
10. War and peace
11. Race and other biases
12. Death
13. Authority—how much is needed
14. Rules—which are necessary and why
15. Society and what it does to the aging. What would be a good society?
16. Personality—what is a desirable one?
17. Money—what does it do?
18. Success—what is a successful person?

Typically the instructor in using value clarification strategies may involve students in activities where they do something in response to a problem or he may lead a discussion applying excellent questioning procedures. The teacher may devise procedures to have students perform the following:

1. Make choices.
2. Look at alternatives.
3. Consider thoughtfully their alternatives and the consequences of each of them.
4. Consider what they cherish most relative to the problem area.
5. Publicly affirm their choices.
6. Behave and live their choices.
7. Repeatedly examine patterns and behaviors in their lives.

Such procedures might be used, for example, by a teacher asking the class to decide whether they think "busing for racial integration is likely to achieve its objectives." The students would then be asked to make choices about the desirability of integration. It should be noted that students always have the right "to pass" in giving a response. The teacher may go on to present three or four integration plans and have each individual rank them in order from least to most desirable. The class then would vote on these to determine how they view the situation. This allows students to express their beliefs on the issues and to consider alternatives. They may then be asked to study the consequences of their decisions, a discussion which might initially end by the instructor asking what the students are going to do personally to help solve the problem in their community. Later, the teacher might return to the problem after the students have learned more about the topic and have had chances to behave relative to their decisions and to be-

How does cooperation foster good attitudes in school work?

The Affective Domain

come involved further in the value clarification processes. By so doing, the instructor helps the individual student build his own value system.

An example of one value clarification strategy is called "Are you someone who . . . ?" In this strategy each of the following questions is answered with a yes, no, or maybe.

Are you someone who:
1. likes to break the curve on an exam?
2. likes to stay up all night when friends visit?
3. will stop the car to look at a sunset?
4. puts things off?
5. will publicly show affection for another person?
6. will do it yourself when you feel something needs done?
7. will order a new dish in a restaurant?
8. could accept your own sexual impotence?
9. could be satisfied without a college degree?
10. could be part of a mercy killing?
11. is afraid alone in the dark in a strange place?
12. is willing to participate in a T-group?
13. eats when they are worried?
14. can receive a gift easily?
15. would steal apples from an orchard?
16. is apt to judge someone by their appearance?
17. would let your child drink or smoke pot?
18. watches television soap operas?
19. could kill in self-defense?

(The instructor, as in all value clarification strategies, also does the task and may share his list after the students have ennumerated theirs.)

This strategy allows a person to consider more thoughtfully what he values, what he wants of life, and what type person he is. This exercise can be followed by "I am someone who . . ." sentences.

I am someone who:
1. blushes at a compliment.
2. talks loudly when nervous.
3. has faced death.
4. enjoys intimacy with another person.

The search for self, the who am I of life as a conscious act is a continual on-going process. As a person works and plays, this self adventure becomes a touchstone for living. From knowing one's self, behaviors, patterns, etc. a new confidence, an internal security, a sense of potency emerges which is life giving. Too often in our lives we search outside ourselves for meaning and become preoccupied with assigning blame and trying to change others. A life of meaning lies within each of us by discovering and cultivating what we are right now. Know what you prize and cherish and act on it as you live fully each day of your life.[7]

Teachers are encouraged to use teaching techniques that help students understand and clarify their values. Some strategies for this purpose have been identified by Raths.[8] In these strategies, students are:

a. encouraged to make choices and make them freely.
b. requested to examine available alternatives when faced with choices.
c. asked to weigh alternatives thoughtfully, reflecting on the consequences of each.
d. encouraged to consider what it is they prize and cherish.
e. given opportunities to make public affirmations of their choices.
f. asked to examine reported behaviors or patterns in their lives.

Value clarification can be introduced as part of the instruction in any secondary subject area or it may be instituted as a special course.

Some educators believe that students' attitudes toward a subject can be influenced by illustrating the relevance of the subject to their lives. Teachers need a way to incorporate classroom activities into the daily experiences of their students. For example, they might integrate into their instruction current interests and issues that will affect the student now and in the future. Through the use of value clarifying techniques, teachers could provide a means for students to relate the subject to their lives. Value clarification places emphasis on students clarifying their beliefs and weighing the consequences of their commitments and actions.

---

[7]Unpublished paper by Sidney Simon and Sara Massey, University of Massachusetts, 1972.

[8]Louis E. Raths et al., *Values and Teaching* (Columbus, Ohio: Charles E. Merrill Publishing Co., 1966), pp. 38-39.

Further Investigation and Study

1. Calvin Taylor identified six talent areas for possible use in the classroom. Can you add others? What system could you use to keep a record of pupil progress in each of the talent areas? Do you think all areas are equally important?
2. Write a paragraph or two explaining your philosophy of the multitalent approach to teaching. Assume you were speaking to a parent group in your school. What important points would you emphasize?
3. Initiate a debate in your class on the question "Resolved that value clarification techniques used in classrooms will have an adverse effect on the learning progress of children."
4. Outline the main points of a talk you would give to a group of teacher colleagues in an inservice session devoted to "Values and Value Clarification."

7 Teaching and Learning Methods

Excellent instructors usually use several approaches in their teaching. The choice of the various methods is dependent upon the goals and objectives the teacher wishes to obtain. For example, an instructor may tell the student or class a procedure on how to use a piece of equipment, for example, a table saw, typewriter, slide rule, etc. He is not interested in having students develop their cognitive thought processes in discovering how these operate. He is more interested in having them learn certain skills. He, therefore, decides to lecture and then have students practice performing these skills. For his purposes lecturing has its place. But, it should be remembered that in a lecture many students "tune the teacher out," become bored and listless, eventually causing discipline problems. The attention span of junior high school and high school students for a lecture is, at best, short. Furthermore, if the instructor is concerned about students learning how to think in solving problems, he must alter his teaching to insure that this happens.

Educators concerned with developing cognitive ability have devised various methods and procedures to better insure its realization. Many of the modern curricula and texts are written to help achieve this end. Even though this is so, there is still a need for the teacher to supplement these materials and adjust instruction to the abilities and needs of his students. Texts, for example, are written for an idealized national average student in order for the books to sell well from Hawaii to Maine. An instructor undoubtedly has many students in his class not approximating this ideal. If this is the case, the teacher must modify his teaching so that he helps students manifest their potential and achieve objectives in other ways than just by using the text.

Teaching and Learning Methods

Different teaching approaches are enumerated in this chapter in order that you may become more aware of instructional alternatives. Many of these use class, small group (four or five in number), or student to student discussion techniques. Leading a discussion is an art not easily learned. It is exciting to see a master teacher involved in a dynamic discussion; excellent class discussions do not just happen. The inexperienced instructor may think he will walk into a class and talk about a subject "off the top of his head." After all, doesn't he know more about the subject than the students? It's true you may know about the material, but you are still faced with the problem of getting students to discover and retain this knowledge. To do this takes preparation and creative teaching.

Many of the following teaching methods are discussion oriented. Their format and instructional design should help you considerably in improving your discussion skills. It is suggested that you try several of these, adapting them to the units and subjects you will be teaching. A word of caution, however: many of these teaching styles require considerable sophistication and experience on the part of the instructor in order for them to work well. Don't make a judgment as to their value on the basis of one trial with one class. Classes vary in their receptiveness to new approaches and your ability to use these will change considerably with experience. Remember further, while trying these various approaches you should also continually strive to improve your questioning and listening skills. These are fundamental to all of the following methods.

No attempt is made in this chapter to include all the new teaching approaches. To do so would be beyond the scope of this text. We have, however, carefully evaluated and included those we think useful for developing cognitive processes for several subject disciplines. Those methods and activities particularly appropriate for individualized, creative, and value clarification instruction are discussed later in chapters under these topics.

Inquiry Strategies for Developing Problem-Solving Abilities

John Dewey in his book *How We Think* (Boston: Heath and Company, 1910) pointed out the importance of the school developing critical and reflective thinking in preparing children for democracy. He believed that children should be trained in the schools for a democratic society. This meant to him that they should be involved in problem-solving activities—identifying, defining, organizing, and resolving problems. In order to accomplish this end, the school needed to be organized into small democracies where students would have opportunities of experiencing the frustrations and joys of the democratic processes. Dewey's philosophy had a profound effect on American education in that it slowly found its way into the schools' curriculum and extracurricular activities. Curricula were designed specifically for the purpose of developing problem solving behavior. In extracurriculur activities Dewey's democratic processes were kindled by the organization of student governments, clubs, committees throughout America's educational institutions.

Dewey's philosophy became identified with the Progressive Education Movement in the 1930's toward which there eventually was directed a conservative negative reaction of educators who believed that the fundamental role of the school was to teach the three R's. In spite of this reaction, Dewey's influence continued especially in the development of democratic processes in the social studies and the growth and maintenance of student government.

An outgrowth of Dewey's problem-solving emphasis has been the development of curricula in the 40's, 50's, and 60's specifically attempting to kindle discovery and inquiry oriented abilities. Because Dewey talked of developing democratic problem-solving processes, the first curricula to do this were those in the social studies. Later curricula in mathematics, science, and English adapted this problem-solving processes emphasis to their particular disciplines. The curriculum designers in these subjects, however, became more interested in developing critical thinking processes related to the structure of these subjects; for example, social scientists, when they think and act as members of their profession, perform certain mental processes, such as hypothesizing, designing experiments, etc. It is reasoned that the way for students to understand and learn these processes is to have opportunities to develop and behave in a manner similar to social scientists. Social science curricula producers, therefore, design learning activities involving students in performing these mental operations.

Although the various modern inquiry oriented curricula differ in several respects because of the nature of their particular subjects modes of investigation, they overlap in the sense that they all endeavor to develop problem-solving skills. Thus, Dewey's philosophical tentacles continue to permeate and influence the instructional operations of America's schools.

The Democratic Methods

To understand and operate effectively in a democratic setting requires considerable knowledge and sophistication in behavior, for there are certain ways of behaving in a democracy that differ considerably from those in other forms of government. Since the schools of any society have as their primary function the preparation of individuals to operate within that society, the American schools have the fundamental obligation of providing democratic training. A number of educators such as Charles H. Judd and William H. Kilpatrick in the 1920's and 1930's became concerned with this mandate, and they endeavored to insure the development of democratic processes in the schools' curricula and environments. Their efforts have been further complemented more recently by such men as Herbert Thelen, John U. Michaelis, Donald W. Oliver, James P. Shaver, Byron Massialas, Benjamin Cox, and others. Essentially, all of these educators believe that students should be involved in investigating their social environment. Although they may vary slightly in how they translate this into action, they generally agree that students should perform the following:

Democratic Process Involvement

1. Inquire and reflect about their social and political environment, how to improve it, including interpersonal problems, etc.
2. Develop and model democratic procedures of thought and action.
3. Be actively involved and gain experience in performing democratic processes, e.g., discussing controversial issues, coming to consensus, participating in governmental processes, clarifying values, etc.
4. Be involved in democratic problem solving including: identifying problems, investigating social cause and effect relationships, inferring from data, reflecting on social issues, hypothesizing and using other scientific processes in resolving problems.

In performing the activities outlined above, students must be involved in inquiring about social and interpersonal issues. In so doing, they are encouraged to reflect upon the quality of their environment, and how to improve it. They are thereby participating in activities helping them to better develop their social perceptions, consider alternatives, and negotiate competencies. Several educational approaches have been designed to achieve these ends. One of them has been briefly outlined below.

Herbert Thelen's Investigative Group Approach

Herbert Thelen has designed an inquiry approach for the social studies. It has relevance, however, for other academic areas where students are confronted with problems, such as pollution control in science or determining how to increase interest and awareness by students and parents in the fine arts.

Thelen's procedure includes essentially the following steps:

1. Students are confronted with some information, topic, or a puzzling situation. This may come from the members of a class or the instructor, e.g., a situation may arise where a student is told to leave a place of business because the owner didn't like his appearance, long hair, dirty clothes, etc.
2. Students discuss and explore the ramifications or possibilities of this puzzling situation: Why was the store owner upset? What were his prejudices?
3. The class decides on some problem, such as: What are the roots of prejudice?
4. Class members decide on a course of action, define their roles, organize into groups. For example, one group decides to study the origins of black prejudice, another Chicano, and a third Jewish. One of these groups decides to invite members of the Hari Krishna sect to speak to their class and note the students' prejudice before and after this visit.
5. Students carry on independent and group investigations.
6. Periodic reports are made to the class indicating group progress, procedures, and accomplishments.
7. Information from other groups is considered, feedback given them, or the class may decide to establish a new relevant problem. For example, they may now consider how to reduce prejudice and investigate this problem in the manner and sequence indicated above.
8. Class considers the procedures, social behavior while investigating the problem, and accomplishments, indicating how they might have acted differently to be more effective in using the democratic processes. For example, in operating within their groups, how could they have better shown respect and value for the contributions of their group members?

**Deriving Democratic Awareness Through
the Conflict of Public Issues**

Donald W. Oliver and James P. Shaver have developed a method for making students aware of social issues. Their approach is in many ways similar to those suggested by Dewey, Thelens, Raths and Simon since the students are confronted with social problems and are invited to discuss their resolutions. Their format resembles the Biological Sciences

Teaching and Learning Methods

Curriculum Studies Invitation to Inquiry method referred to later in this chapter in that basic information is given to the students and they are asked to react to it. The information provided as a basis for social conflict in this method usually is in the form of documents and other material involving ethical and legal concepts. The students are asked to respond to these and in the process to develop a clarification of their values, critical thinking, and democratic ways of behaving. The instructor's function is not to impose ethical ideals but to provide an environment where various views are respected and clarified.

Oliver and Shaver outline and encourage the discussion of social conflict issues so that students can better perceive how' individuals in a democratic society may have a multiplicity of purposes. Often individuals have *general values*, such as the desire to contribute to the dignity of our fellow man, which may be in conflict with *specific values*, such as "an individual should be rewarded and gain from his work." A person may hold this to be true yet argue: "Why should the government take away some of my wealth in the form of income taxes?" He apparently does not understand that this wealth is, in part, used to support people needing welfare. What he is really doing is indicating that he would rather keep his private gain and not pay taxes. However, taxes are used to contribute to the welfare and dignity of some people. Therefore, his values are in conflict. These authors present problems likely to engender such conflicts so that students may better determine and realize that in reality the application of values requires considerable flexibility and establishment of a hierarchy. Often specified personal ideals or group ideals may be in conflict with higher more general ones. A democratic society, furthermore, doesn't require that all individuals have the same ideals. Shaver and Oliver argue that on the contrary a democracy should be a pluralistic society. It needs, however, to be characterized by one over-riding ideal, that is, that everything should be done to enhance the dignity of its citizens. In translating this ideal into reality, conflicts of interests, values, etc. are bound to arise, and it is the nature of a democratic society that these must be negotiated, compromised, and worked out by its citizens. Essential to this process must be the realization by society's members that in reality the ideals of the society have dimension. They are not black or white entities and the translation of them into action must be resolved through negotiation and experimentation. Generally conflict among members of the society arise because of a need to clarify:

a. Values that are in conflict

b. Facts related to a problem

c. Semantics—the meanings of the words involved in the controversy.

Depending on the nature of the problem and its conflicts the Oliver and Shaver approach involves all or some of the following steps, as outlined in the excellent summary by Bruce Joyce and Marsha Weil:

1. *Abstracting general values from concrete situations.* The student should be aware of and understand ethical and legal concepts; and he should be able to translate concrete problem situations into ethical and legal terms. To use Oliver and Shaver's example, "If the problem is whether or not Congress should pass an anti-trust act . . . the student must be able to see that the decision can be construed in terms of such general values as property and contract rights, protection of equal rights for large and small businessmen alike, and protection of the interests of the community at large." In other words, the student needs to take concrete problem situations, and attempt to put them into a general ethical legal framework.

2. *Using general value concepts as dimensional constructs.* The student needs to characterize each value on a dimensional basis so that he is able to distinguish degrees of violation or dilution. In other words, students should learn not to use values as all-or-none categories, but to see the possibility of the partial achievement of a value in a concrete situation. For example, in the situation above it simply may not be possible to provide small businesses with equal power to that of large ones, using legal means. To do so might be to violate some of the rights of property of large businesses and others. The values of equality of opportunity and the right to hold property each have to be compromised, probably, in order to arrive at a situation that is not totally unfair to one interest or the other.

3. *Identifying conflicts between value constructs.* In dealing with a concrete situation, the student needs to determine whether more than one value can be abstracted from the situation, and if it can, whether the values abstracted conflict with one another. Returning to one of the examples presented above, the desire to provide equality of opportunity in certain respects can conflict with the desire to protect property rights equally, when it happens that the acquisition of property by one group gives it advantages over the other.

4. *Identifying classes of value-conflict situations.* In other words, the student learns to identify concrete problems in terms of their similarities and differences, and to develop a conception of the types of value-conflict situations that occur during controversial situations.

5. *Developing analogies to the problem which is under consideration.* Analogies enable us to see our consistencies and inconsistencies. If, for example, we identify five situations relating to the

same value, we can tell whether our position on that value is consistent by making analogies which enable us to compare our value position in each situation.

6. *Working toward a general qualified position.* The student is pressed to work toward general policies by which he can make decisions when two values are in conflict, and to apply those policies to fresh situations. For example, the value of free speech in many situations comes into conflict with the need to protect the community. In time of war, should one permit the enemy to send over individuals who will advocate the overthrow of the government? After examining a number of situations in which the value of free speech in communication conflicts with the safety of the community, the student can gradually arrive at a policy statement which will say something like, "Under such and such circumstances, I will sacrifice such and such amounts of free speech, in terms of such kinds of community safety." And the other way around, "In the interests of free speech, I will sacrifice such and such amounts of public safety, and risk the security of the community in order to protect the free communication."

7. *Testing the factual assumptions behind a qualified value position.* When one makes a policy statement, or a qualified value position, he assumes that behaving in a certain way will have an effect of a certain kind. This assumption needs to be tested. For example, "Will permitting free speech of any kind during a war actually affect the public safety in any way?" If the fact is that it will endanger the public safety, then one might say that there is factual merit in the position that one will abrogate the right of free speech in order to protect the community. If, on the other hand, it does not decrease the public safety, that is another matter.

A good contemporary example of this is the controversy over capital punishment. Those who wish to see capital punishment abolished feel that it violates the right to life, and makes the state a legal murderer. Those who are in favor of capital punishment may agree with the preceding position, but feel that the punishment is worth it to protect the community from those who would commit murder. One of the factual controversies, involving both value positions, is whether capital punishment actually does or does not decrease the probability of a murderer committing a murder. If it turns out that capital punishment does not act as a deterrent, then one position obtains an advantage. If it does act as a deterrent, the other position gains an advantage.

8. *Testing the relevance of statements.* Once one develops policy positions, they must pass the test of relevance to any particular situation. For example, welfare payments to avoid destitution of children are sometimes attacked on the grounds that they contribute to the idleness of the parents. The question is, even if that were

the case, whether the idleness of the parents has any relevance to the problem of protecting the children against hunger, lack of medical care, and so on

These eight general operations are the intellectual framework which is to be applied to the analysis of public issues in order to teach students how to sort out the value problems, the definitional problems, and the factual problems, and to come to policy positions that reflect the balancing of values and an appreciation of the dimensionality of values as they apply to particular situations.

The essence of the teaching strategy is to engage the students in a dialogue in such a way that these eight intellectual operations are continuously performed. Roughly, it can be said that there is a good possibility that they could be performed sequentially in relation to a given problem. As stated earlier, this is by no means always true, and it is not important to press for the sequence of operations. What is important is to see that they are performed in relation to the particular issue, so that the student becomes increasingly skillful in performing each of them.[1]

The Seven Inductive Approaches of Hilda Taba

Teaching methods for stimulating cognitive and affective abilities have been devised by Dr. Hilda Taba, now deceased, and her associates Mary C. Durkin, Jack R. Fraenkel, and Anthony H. McNaughton.[2] Although this system was originally designed for an elementary social studies curriculum, the strategies may be easily adapted for use in most subjects on the secondary level.

Several years ago, Dr. Taba became concerned with the development of critical thinking by children. As a result, she constructed techniques and carried out research, striving to perfect a system to stimulate this thinking. She was specifically interested in how students improve their inductive thinking in the process of developing concepts, categorizing, inferring, generalizing, analyzing, and applying generalizations. Essentially, the system that evolved from this work consists of seven major strategies as follows:

---

[1]Bruce Joyce and Marsha Weil, *Models of Teaching* (Englewood Cliffs, N.J.: Prentice-Hall, Inc., 1972), pp. 52-54. Reprinted by permission of Prentice-Hall, Inc. For a very enlightening and detailed description of several different types of teaching strategies we strongly suggest you consult this book.

[2]*A Teacher's Handbook to Elementary Social Studies: An Inductive Approach*, 2d ed., by Hilda Taba, Mary C. Durkin, Jack R. Fraenkel, and Anthony H. McNaughton. Copyright C 1971 by Addison-Wesley Publishing Co., Inc. All rights reserved.

Teaching and Learning Methods

1. Developing concepts
2. Attaining Concepts
3. Developing Generalizations
4. Exploring Feelings
5. Resolving Interpersonal Problems
6. Analyzing Values
7. Applying Generalizations

Taba and her co-workers used these strategies to construct a social studies curriculum. It should be evident, however, that an instructor, in planning lessons for other subject areas, may also use some or all the strategies depending on his objectives. He may, furthermore, choose some of them and combine them with other inquiry approaches outlined in this text. For example: He might start a lesson by having students brainstorm in small groups and place their results on the board and then follow the "Developing Concept Strategy" as outlined by Taba.

The teacher's role in using these strategies is to involve students through questioning. The students, in order to answer the questions, become involved in performing certain mental operations thereby enhancing their mental growth. In the sections that follow, the procedure for using each of the strategies is briefly outlined. These closely follow those suggested by Taba et al. but have been modified slightly to better adapt them to secondary school instruction. You are encouraged to try to use at least three of these in constructing a lesson for your particular subject area.

Developing Concepts

In this first strategy, the purpose is to have students identify and label certain concepts relative to a topic or problem. This may be done in several ways. One approach is to ask a class what they know about a topic, e.g., evolution, integration, algebra, repairing a carburetor, creative writing, etc., and then proceed following the steps in the strategy. Another technique is to involve students in something, e.g., seeing or reading a play, observing parts or all of a film, taking a field trip, watching a demonstration. They are then asked: "What did you find out about . . . ?" Their answers are listed on the chalkboard according to similarities and are labeled as follows:

Developing Concepts Strategy

Teacher	Student	Process
1. "What do you know about, did you see, or need...?"	Gives ideas that are listed on the chalkboard.	Identifying
2. "How would you group these items?" May help in grouping by underlining or arranging cards for the groups.	Groups items based on similarities and gives reasons for these.	Grouping
3. "What would you name these groups?"	Labels the groups.	Labeling
"What members of each could be placed in another group?"	Indicates additional relationships.	Relating
"What could you write or tell the class in one sentence about all the groups?"	Writes or gives a summary sentence.	Summarizing

Attaining Concepts

The concept attainment strategy differs from the previous one mainly in that the teacher gives the class the name of a concept and controls to a higher degree the progress of the lesson. The concept is named, and then the teacher gives several examples of it. Next, a number of related non-examples are listed. This is followed by writing on the chalkboard a mixture of examples and non-examples. The students are then asked to separate these into their respective groups.

The concept attainment strategy is usually used when the meaning of some concept requires clarification prior to the involvement in other lessons, e.g., concepts such as osmosis, diffusion, momentum, mammal, culture, radical, assimilation, etc., may be introduced in this manner and then related to other parts of a unit.

The pattern for this type of lesson is outlined on the following page:

Developing Generalizations

This strategy differs from the previous ones in that the students are involved in higher levels of thinking in relating several concepts. The product of this approach is a sentence, e.g., some scientific principle,

Teaching and Learning Methods

Attaining Concepts Strategy

Teacher	Student	Process
1. "These are examples of, e.g., competition, etc."	Observes and listens.	Observing and Listening
2. "These are or this is not an example of: . . . ."	Observes and listens further.	Observing and Listening.
3. Presents a mixture including several examples and some non-examples. "Which of these things are examples?"	Identifies those that belong to the group from those that don't.	Comparing and Selecting
4. "What do you think an . . . is?"	Shows or States what an . . . is.	Stating
5. "How would you define an . . . ?"	May give a summary or an operational definition.	Defining

"Disease may be caused by micro-organisms," rather than a word concept, e.g., democracy. The strategy generally operates as follows:

Developing Generalizations Strategy

Teacher	Student	Process
1. "What did you notice or find out about?"	Differentiates. States what is relevant.	Selecting and Evaluating
2. "What happened when . . . ?" "Why did it happen?"	Gives explanations.	Inferring
3. "What does this indicate about . . . ?" Followed by, "Why do you think so?"	Makes conclusions.	Inferring
4. "What is the significance of the data?" or "What can you say about, e.g., micro-organisms?"	Indicates implications. Makes generalizations.	Generalizing

Exploring Feelings

(Affective Strategy)

With this strategy, students are involved in exploring their own and others' feelings. By so doing, they better learn how others perceive a situation, understand their own emotions, and generalize when appropriate about a person's affectivity. The strategy is designed so that a student does not feel threatened as might be the case if he were asked directly what his values were about a topic, e.g., mercy killing. Rather, a situation is provided, and the students encouraged to explore and react to it.

The strategy follows the following format:

Exploring Feelings Strategy

Teacher	Student	Process
1. Presents some situation and asks, "What happened in this situation?"	States significant points.	Summarizing
2. "How do you think the people involved felt?"	Infers feelings about each individual or group situation.	Inferring
3. "What experiences have you had that are similar?"	Tells similar situations.	Describing
4. "How did you feel?"	Describes feeling.	Describing and emoting
5. "Why did you feel that way?"	Relates feelings.	Explaining

Interpersonal Problem Solving

(Affective Strategy)

This strategy involves confronting students with conflict problem situations between individuals or groups. The students are asked to relate similar experiences, propose and defend solutions, consider and evaluate alternatives relative to the problem.

Taba et al. points out that a danger in using this approach is that students, because of their own egocentricity, may not proceed to the higher levels of exploring criteria and alternatives in making judgments. This possibility can be overcome by the instructor's moving the group along the other steps in the strategy when he sees this occurring.

The format for this approach is as follows:

Interpersonal Problem Solving Strategy

Teacher	Student	Process
1. A situation is presented involving interpersonal conflict.	Listens.	Listening
2. "What happened?"	Describes events.	Describing
3. "What did each of the people (groups) do?"	Summarizing.	Summarizing
4. "What should each do?" "Why?"	Evaluates and judges.	Evaluating
5. "When has something like this happened to you?" "What did you do?"	Relates past experiences.	Summarizing
6. "As you look back on what happened to you, how would you respond now?"	Recalls and judges.	Evaluating
7. "Why?"	Gives reasons.	Explaining
8. "What things might you have done differently?"	Presents alternatives. Gives reasons.	Evaluating

Analyzing Values

This strategy requires the students to assess the values of individuals or groups. Its purpose is to help students perceive that people may have different values. It differs from other value clarification strategies in that it isn't necessarily trying to have students develop higher values themselves. The approach involves presenting a class with a situation. The students are asked to make inferences relative to the values the individuals or groups have that dictated their responses, ways of living, etc. Students are also asked to analyze their own values relative to the topic presented.

The strategy progresses as follows:

Analyzing Value Strategy

Teacher	Student	Process
1. A situation is presented depicting some value orientation.	Student listens.	Listening
2. "What did they do, e.g., to improve their community?"	Infers and summarizes.	Inferring
3. "Why do you think individuals (groups) do that?"	Infers values.	Inferring
4. "What does this indicate about their values or what they think is important?"	Infers.	Inferring
5. "If you were confronted with a similar situation, what would you do and why?"	Formulates hypotheses and explains.	Hypothesizing
6. "What does this indicate about what you value?"	Infers.	Inferring
7. "How do these people differ in their values compared to you? What differences do you see in what you and other people value?"	Infers and compares.	Inferring

Applying Generalizations

This approach invites students to use generalizations obtained from previous learning and applying them to similar new situations.

The steps of this approach are shown on the following page.

Teaching and Learning Methods

Applying Generalizations Strategies

Teacher	Student	Process
1. "Given these conditions... what do you think would happen if...?"	Students apply what they know to the situation.	Applying
2. "Why do you think that would happen?"	Infers and explains.	Inferring
3. "What is needed for your statement to happen?"	Selects the facts. Outlines the casual associations leading to hypotheses.	Supporting hypotheses
4. "What other explanations can be given for what has happened?"	Gives other reasons.	Inferring
5. "If as you said,... happened, what would happen after that...?"	Formulates hypotheses and applies to new situations.	Hypothesizing

It should be apparent that the teacher may use various parts of this model in class discussion and then break for individual or small group investigation so that students gain more information before continuing to use various parts of the system.

The teacher, when carrying on the discussions, must maintain as much as possible an unrushed open inquiry atmosphere. He often will have to ask for clarification and verification of ideas, e.g., when a student makes a statement that is vague or too lengthy, the instructor might state: "How would you say that another way?" or "How would you say that in a few words?" In the case where a student seems to overgeneralize, the teacher might ask: "What evidence do you have that is true for all?" Teachers must constantly encourage students to focus on the ideas that seem more relevant.

The Suchman Theory Building Approach

J. Richard Suchman has devised an inquiry approach for the purpose of involving students in the processes of constructing and building theories. For this to occur in the classroom, Suchman believes certain conditions are paramount. These are:

1. Students should be presented problems for which they have no immediate solution. In Piagetian terms this means that they need to encounter situations causing disequilibria.
2. Students should be trusted and given freedom to resolve problems without the constraint that they guess what is in the instructor's head.
3. There must be a classroom environment that facilitates students obtaining information and actively working out themselves the construction of a theory.

Suchman found when these conditions were met, students progressed rapidly in their ability to become inquirers and were actually better motivated because of the investigative process itself.

Suchman's approach generally starts with the students being presented a *"discrepant event."* This is a situation that appears strange, unusual, and for which the student has no easy explanation. After the "discrepant event" has been introduced, a discussion session commences. While participating in it, the students are instructed to follow certain rules as indicated below.

1. Students are to ask the instructor questions that can be answered only by yes or no.
2. The student called upon may ask as many questions as he chooses.
3. The instructor does not answer questions when the students are trying to obtain his approval of a theory.
4. Students may confer with each other when they choose or break to obtain further information and perform investigations and experiments as the situation requires.

Note the method has components similar to those used by Thelen, Taba, Shaver, and Oliver. It differs, however, in how students initially are required to phrase their questions so that the teacher can answer only "yes" or "no". After students have investigated the problem and collected information, the teacher brings the class together and acts as a discussion leader in a manner similar to other inquiry discussion methods.

Generally the class procedure goes through the following phases:

Teaching and Learning Methods

SUCHMAN'S APPROACH

1. Presentation of a Discrepant Event
2. Discussion—in which students phrase questions to the teacher that may be answered only by "yes" or "no."
3. Students may investigate to gather further information relative to their theory.
4. Class reconvenes—teacher leads a discussion helping students to develop a theory. Teacher may clarify, focus students' attention on certain aspects of the problem, and summarize their ideas.

A portion of a class interaction, after being presented with a discrepant event and discussing it for some time, is outlined below. Note how the teacher aids the students in understanding and constructing a theory:

Students are shown a photograph of a riot and are asked to respond to what they think is happening. The class participation occurred somewhat as follows:

T. What questions could you ask about this photograph?
S. Are the people reacting to something that scares them such as a fire or an earthquake?
T. No.
S. Are they reacting because they are upset?
T. Yes.
S. Are they upset because they couldn't get in some place—such as a rock concert?
T. Yes.
S. Are they upset because the police are after them?
T. Yes.
S. Are they upset because the police are being brutal?
T. Yes—to some degree.
S. Are the police being brutal because they think these people have broken the law?
T. No.
S. Are they upset because one of the members did something to antagonize the police and the police over-reacted?

T. Yes.

S. Is this a riot?

T. Yes, but what are the causes of a riot?

The class then proceeded to ask several questions related to how riots evolve, the forces that kindle them, how they could be prevented, etc. During the discussion the instructor suggested at one point that the students break up and study individually or in small groups about what causes riots. Later on the class reconvened and continued the discussion. By using this process the students slowly evolved a theoretical model for the causes of riots and their prevention.

Suchman's approach was originally designed to teach elementary students about theories in science. However, with some minor adaptations it can be used in other subjects and with secondary students as well. All that needs to be done is to confront students with some interesting problem situation and then have them theorize about it.

The Pictorial Riddle Approach

Another technique for developing motivation and interest in large or small group discussion is pictorial riddles. These are pictures or drawings made by the teacher to elicit critical and creative thinking responses from students and may be true riddles or just present puzzling situations. A riddle is usually drawn on the chalkboard, poster board, or is projected from a transparency, and the teacher asks a question about it.

Pictorial riddles are relatively easy to prepare. They can be as simple or complex as an instructor desires. In devising a riddle, a teacher should go through the following steps:

1. Select some concept or principle to be taught or discussed.
2. Draw a picture, show an illustration from a magazine, or use a photograph that shows the concept, process, or situation. An alternate procedure is to present something that is atypical or unusual and ask students to find out what is wrong with it. An example might be a picture of a big man being held up on a seesaw by a small man. Ask, "How is this possible?" Or show a farming community in which all of the ecological principles are misapplied and ask what is wrong with what has been done in the community.

Teaching and Learning Methods 141

3. Devise a series of divergent process oriented questions, related to the picture, which will help students gain insights into what principles are involved.

There are two general types of riddles:

1. Riddles showing an actual situation. The instructor asks why it occurred. Figure 1 is of this type.
2. Riddles where the teacher manipulates something in a drawing or a series of drawings and then asks what is wrong with the diagram. Figure 2 is an example of this type.

Shown below are several examples of riddles and some questions that might be asked about them.

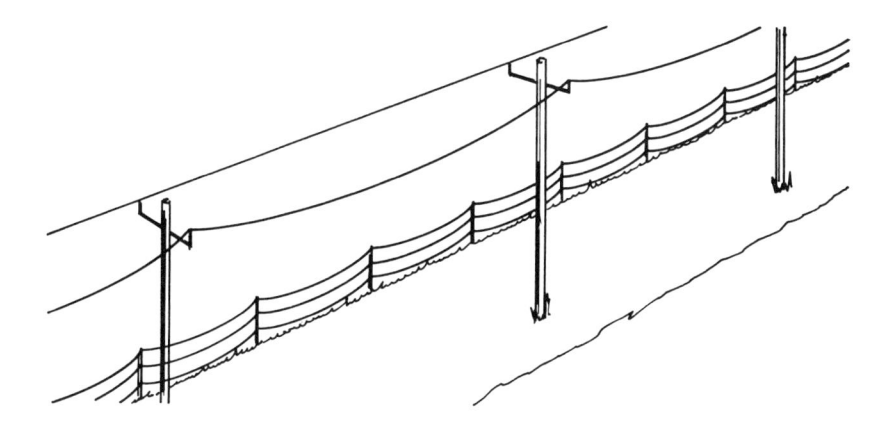

FIGURE 1. Pictorial Riddle (Physical Science)

What do you notice about the things in this picture?

What is similar in the picture?

Why does the fence and the telephone line appear similar?

Why wouldn't you expect to find the two telephone lines so different?

What do you suspect the season of the year would have to be for each line and why?

What does temperature have to do with the appearance of the telephone line and why?

What time of year would you expect to see the sagging telephone line and why?

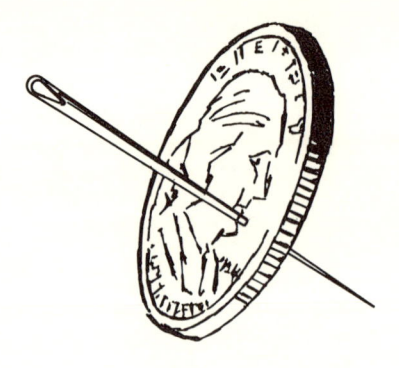

142 Student-Centered Teaching in the Secondary School

FIGURE 2. Pictorial Riddle (Physical Science)

What factors would affect how the needle goes through the coin?

What would temperature have to do with it?

How would the motion of the needle affect its penetration of the quarter?

What type of quarter would be the easiest to send a steel needle through?

What kind of needle would be the best to go through a quarter?

What other questions can you think of related to this riddle?

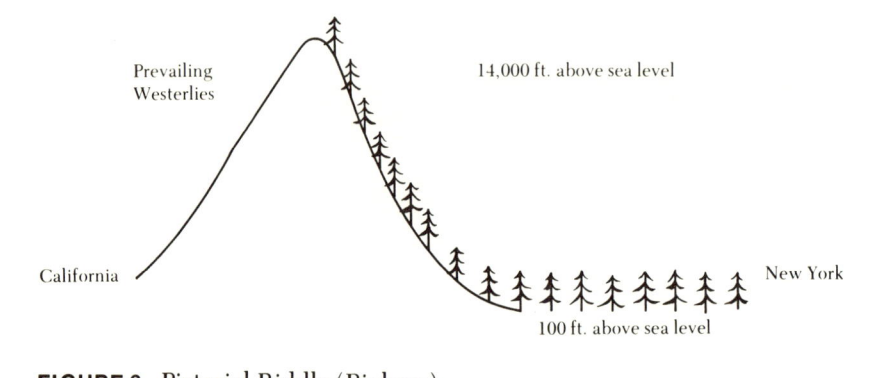

FIGURE 3. Pictorial Riddle (Biology)

Teaching and Learning Methods

What questions can you ask about this riddle?

What is wrong with this diagram?

Where do pine trees grow?

Why do they grow where they do?

If you were going to change the riddle to make it more accurate, what would you do and why?

What does the wind have to do with the ecology of the area?

Where would you expect to find the most and the least amount of vegetation on the mountain? Why?

How could you change this riddle to teach some additional science concepts?

FIGURE 4. Pictorial Riddle (Art and Industrial Art)

What do you notice about this chair?

How would you change the chair to improve it?

How would you modify it to make it more pleasing in design?

How would you change it to make it last longer?

Where would you strengthen it the most?

How many different types of materials can you think of to use in making chairs?

Of those you mentioned, what would be their positive and negative qualities?

144   **Student-Centered Teaching in the Secondary School**

Of those materials mentioned, how would you combine them to construct an entirely different type of chair?

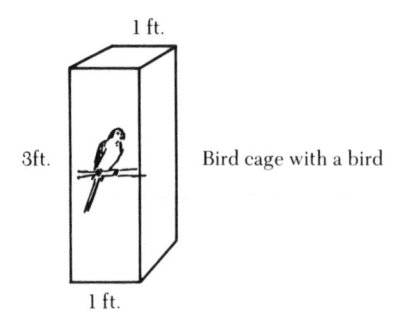

                 1 ft.

3ft.   Bird cage with a bird

                   1 ft.

FIGURE 5. Pictorial Riddle (Mathematics)

What do you notice about this diagram?

If you were going to double the size of the cage what are the ways you would do it and why?

Using the same amount of materials as indicated in Figure 5, how would you maximize the cage volume while reducing the sides that have to be cleaned?

What mathematical riddle type problems can you think of related to building bird cages?

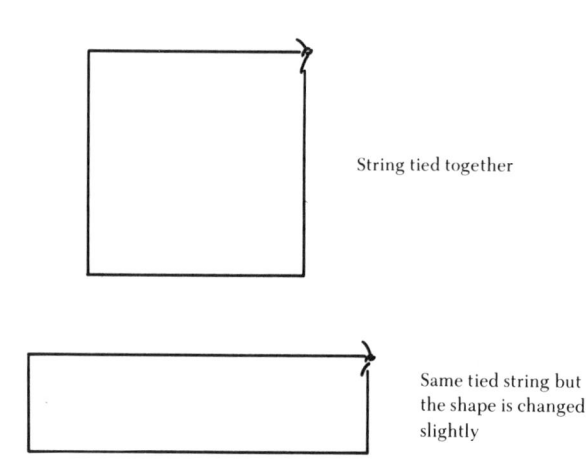

                     String tied together

                     Same tied string but the shape is changed slightly

FIGURE 6. Pictorial Riddle (Mathematics)

Teaching and Learning Methods

What do you notice about how the form of the tied strings has changed?

What has happened to its perimeter?

What has happened to the area enclosed by the string?

What shape would you form the string into to maximize the enclosed area?

What shape would you form the string into so that there were no enclosed area?

How is the enclosed area related to the perimeter of the string as it changes form from a square to a long flat rectangle?

How would you use graph or coordinate paper to verify your idea?

FIGURE 7. Pictorial Riddle (English)

How does this drawing make you feel?

How would you change the drawing to better express your feelings?

How would you change the drawing to indicate that the individuals inside the house believe they are valuable individuals?

What do we communicate about ourselves by the way we keep and fix up our rooms?

If you were going to make a story up about this house what would you say or write?

If you were going to write a story based upon something you have done to your room, home, or yard indicating something about you, what would it be?

FIGURE 8. Pictorial Riddle (English, Languages, and Social Studies)

What do you notice about these figures?

What do you think is happening between them?

If one of these individuals is a member of a minority group and has just encountered a stranger not a member of his group, how is he likely to perceive that person?

What are all the ways the individual from the non-minority group might perceive the other person?

Why do people vary in the way they perceive strangers?

How would you behave if you were one of these people and why?

If you wanted to reduce tension at first meeting between you and a stranger, what would you do?

Teaching and Learning Methods 147

If these two people both speak different languages, what are are all the ways they could communicate?

How can you lessen the likelihood of a stranger feeling insecure toward you if the person comes from a different country and doesn't speak your language?

What are all the ways we communicate?

FIGURE 9. Pictorial Riddle (Social Studies and Anthropology)

What do you observe about these individuals?

Why do you think the one person has his head down while the other has his up?

Which person do you think feels the most secure?

What contributes to a person feeling secure?

What ways do people behave to indicate they are insecure?

What do you need to do to help you feel more secure?

How can we contribute to the feelings of security for *all* the members of this class, school, community?

What happens in society when most people feel insecure?

How can you find out whether or not there is evidence to support your idea?

EXAMPLES OF BEFORE AND AFTER RIDDLES
SCIENCE

Before	?	After
Cell / Cell	?	Cell / Cell
(plant upright)	?	(plant wilted)
Animal Tracks	?	No Tracks
NaOh	?	Precipitate Formed

ENGLISH, SOCIAL STUDIES, ANTHROPOLOGY, HOMEMAKING

Before	What caused change?	After
(two stick figures standing)	?	Running Chasing

148

Indian Pueblo

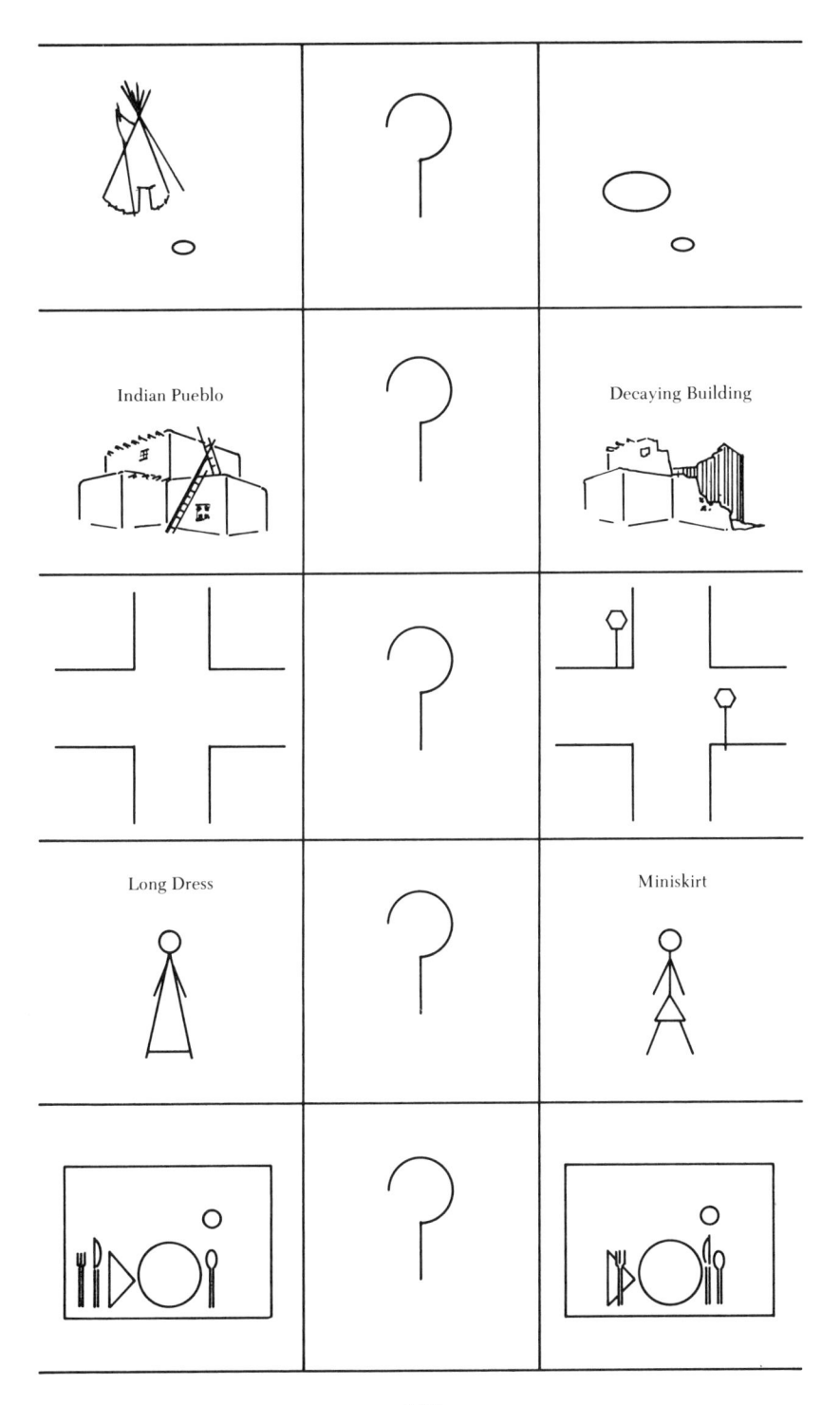

Decaying Building

Long Dress

Miniskirt

149

Before and After Types of Riddles

A format for a riddle lending itself particularly well to overhead projection is the before and after type. Students are presented with a diagram or picture before some factor has been altered and then they are shown another picture illustrating a situation after modification. The student is to hypothesize what happened in the before situation to reach the modification shown in the after diagram as shown in the figure on pages 148-49.

Riddles to Show Relationships

The riddle below is constructed in a manner similar to the face of a clock. Each arm is turned to a different organism and the class asked to state the ecological relationships between them and what would happen if pollution were to eliminate certain of the organisms.

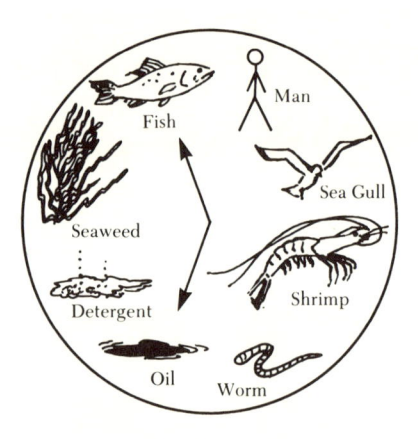

Types of Three-Dimensional Riddles

1. Mobiles
2. Spheres, cubes, hexagons, etc., with a series of related pictures pasted on each surface
3. Collages
4. Objects—i.e. rocks, organisms that are new to the student, a piece of machinery, unique science apparatus, etc.

Teaching and Learning Methods

Some examples of the questions you might ask with three-dimensional riddles are:

    What do you think this three-dimensional riddle is about and why?
    What particularly strikes you about this riddle?
    If you were going to change it, what would you do and why?
    What could be taken away from this riddle without changing its message?
    What would you add to change its message and why?
    What does this riddle suggest that you might construct to give the class an impression of you as a person?
    How would you construct a riddle to attract attention to something you feel strongly about? (Prepare one if you like)
    Of the things you have learned in this course, which would you select to prepare a riddle for and why?

Sources for Preparing Riddles

Riddles may be prepared from many different types of materials as indicated below:

1. Photographs—Polaroid, 35 mm slides, etc.
2. Magazine Pictures
3. Diagrams
4. Cartoons
5. Greeting cards
6. Objects

Other Inquiry Methods

Invitations to Inquiry

The Biological Science Curriculum Study has produced an interesting discussion strategy entitled "Invitation to Inquiry." Although the BSCS has produced forty-four class discussion lessons specifically for biology teaching, the approach, with slight modification, may be utilized in other academic disciplines as well.[3]

---

    [3] For more information see Evelyn Klinckmann, *Biology Teachers Handbook*, 2d ed. (New York: John Wiley and Sons, Inc., 1970).

The main purpose of giving invitations is to involve students in activities in which they learn the structure of the discipline under study. For example, BSCS tries to have students, through these lessons, develop their competence in learning the strategies in solving scientific problems, in the process of which students are involved in activities requiring the following:
1. Using controls
2. Determining cause and effect relationships
3. Using and interpreting quantitative data
4. Graphing
5. Understanding the role of argument and inference in designing investigations
6. Determining how to reduce experimental error, etc.

The Inquiry Role Approach

Following the original work of BSCS and in cooperation with them, the Mid-Continent Regional Educational Laboratory (McREL) published a book entitled *Inquiry Objectives in the Teaching of Biology*. Based upon this effort, staff members of the Mid-Continent Regional Educational Laboratory went on to construct several invitational booklets entitled *Explorations in Biology*, involving students in what they call the *Inquiry Role Approach*. The explorations were given this name because the lessons initially were to be used by students in teams of four, each member of the team being assigned a different role such as team coordinator, technical advisor, data recorder, or process advisor. The members of the team play these roles while working together to resolve problems related to the topic under study such as: Bird Aggression, Bird Population, Food Preferences of Newly-Hatched Snakes, Courtship of Moths, Rat Behavior, Subnormal Children and Venereal Disease, etc. The behaviors for each of the roles and further information about how the teams operate are outlined below:

> *Team Coordinator*—This student heads the team and is responsible for keeping it moving ahead to accomplish its goals. He is the moderator to allow everyone an opportunity to make their point. Each member's data inputs must be coordinated and interpreted. When the group has its evidence and agrees that an answer is correct, the team coordinator works with the data recorder to formulate this consensus of opinion into written form for presentation to the entire class. He also seeks the process evaluator's advice on the team's problem-solving effectiveness.

Teaching and Learning Methods

Technical Advisor—This individual is the analytical task specialist in reading and interpreting the statements so the goal is understood by the group. He aids the team coordinator by listening carefully to what others say and ensures that the team is working on the basic ideas. He should challenge assumptions and be resourceful and creative in problem solving. By evaluating the strengths and weaknesses of the evidence, he serves as the group guide on inquiring deeper into the problem.

Data Recorder—Getting the facts and statements of the group as well as challenging evidence is the data recorder's job. He utilizes a number of resources to gather evidence for any answer that is being debated. He records the group's answers and supporting evidence. He may serve as the group's spokesman and present its position in later intergroup discussions.

Process Evaluator—As guardian of team morale and effective group participation, the process evaluator works closely with the coordinator to develop the quality of the group's inquiry skills. He is concerned with maintaining interpersonal relations and effective sharing in the team activity. This individual is responsible for evaluating the amount and quality of individual participation. The process evaluator will take notes on the group's teamwork for evaluation reports. These reports will be based on the effectiveness of the study quide developed by the teacher in creating a group inquiry experience.

A good team not only develops different jobs and skills, but recognizes which individual is best qualified for each task. Many times an individual does not realize his own potential until other members respond to him and ask him to help them. It is useful to rotate team members on activities to discover where they function best and to let them develop their own experience in various team functions. While it is sometimes hard to discover a member's interest and ability, when found, his motivation is much improved.

A team is really four different individuals functioning together through complementary roles that help them achieve the team goal. Each strives to fullfill the responsibilities of his role at his best capacity so other members can rely on him to do his job as needed. The competitive abilities of the team depend on the pace and pride in high standards of productivity each member sets with his teammates.

Teams should be allowed to compete against each other and select a team name of their own choosing. The teams might be charted by name on a large poster board so everyone can see just how each team is progressing. It would be the data recorder's job to accurately record the team's exercises and group work. This way teams know where they stand in relation to other classes throughout the day. Teams may be allowed to do extra projects or exercises to raise team scores. This keeps team competition and spirit on a high level.

Effective teamwork comes from sharing a common task and holding mutual expectations of what each member is to do. This reciprocal sharing of the task is the rewarding experience out of which group cohesion, loyalty, and spirit evolve. In order to supplement his activities when needed, each student must know and understand the role of the other members.

Team members should complement one another. Teams whose members are supportive of one another take less time in their operation and have a stronger esprit de corps. The individual has strength and support in the group and the group has the coordination of its individual members. The intellectual aim of group inquiry can be reached more smoothly with this cooperation.

It is extremely difficult for the team method of inquiry to function effectively if its members are stymied by the notion that their first approach was the only way to go. Group members have to know that an insolvable problem is really an unusual or discrepant event that does not respond to old solutions and demands a new perspective on that particular problem. This challenge to develop new approaches and new solutions is the kind of problem that develops team creativity. The new frame of reference may help evaluate similar problems, but, more important, it develops student capacity to accept problems as challenges to create new approaches.[4]

Later research by the staff of McREL using these materials on an individual rather than a group basis confirmed that they may be also used effectively in this way. The critical thinking objectives outlined for these lessons by McREL are listed below. Note that many of them have relevance for several secondary academic areas.

Content validity

The original objectives to which EIB items are referenced are as follows:

1. Identifying a phenomenon to investigate.
2. Identifying the question arising from the identification of this phenomenon.

---

[4] A Study Guide to Accompany the Film, "Learning through Inquiry," I/D/E/A, 240 Fourth Avenue, Indialantie, Florida, 32901, p. 5 and 6.

3. From a list of readings, selecting and evaluating reports that might yield useful information about the event noted.
4. Differentiating likely causes of this event from unlikely causes.
5. Selecting a single hypothesis to investigate.
6. Selecting an array of methods appropriate to the investigation.
7. Identifying the independent variable to be studied.
8. Identifying the conditions required for conducting a laboratory study on this topic.
9. Choosing a plan which would yield data affording a test of the hypothesis.
10. Identifying assumptions necessary for interpretation of data resulting from carrying out the plan.
11. Identifying the data which would result from carrying out this plan.
12. Identifying justifiable conclusions from data associated with a class experiment on this topic.
13. From a heterogeneous list of questions, identifying new questions which might arise as a result of carrying out this investigation.
14. Integrating results of this study with those reported by other investigators in related areas.[5]

The format of these booklets generally follows that of the regular BSCS invitations except that more information may be given relative to the problem and that it is sequenced differently. There may, for example, be several photographs, charts, graphs, etc., for the students to observe while arriving at their various conclusions.

Since the Inquiry Role Approach is concerned with curriculum development and effectively helping teachers become more inquiry oriented, McREL has designed several evaluational measures to give teachers feedback. These include a classroom inquiry interaction analysis instrument, an inquiry preference evaluation to determine how aware students are about inquiry practices and whether they prefer them, several Exploration Into Biology Tests to determine inquiry competency, plus several competency measures of social, attitudinal and cognitive growth.

---

[5]Eugenia M. Koos and James Y. Chan, "Criterion Reference Tests in Biology," Technical Report No. 3. Unpublished paper presented at the American Educational Research Association meeting in Chicago, Illinois, April 1972, McREL, Kansas City, Mo., 1972.

Although the invitations of BSCS and McREL have been designed for biology, the approach lends itself well to other subject areas where students are confronted with problems, asked to suggest plans of action or approaches to solve a problem, given more information about its resolution, and asked to evaluate the data and come to conclusions. Teachers given the list of inquiry objectives outlined above have adapted its design to several other secondary subject areas, and presently McREL is considering the possibility of providing similar inquiry oriented lessons for social studies, English, other sciences, and elementary and junior high levels.

Example of an Invitation

An example of a simple invitation, similar to one produced by BSCS, inviting students to form hypotheses and design experiments is given below. Note that the steps in writing it are provided on the left-hand margin as a guide so that you can easily follow them in preparing an invitation of your own.

Steps in Writing an Invitation	Invitation
Problem is presented. Students are asked to design an investigation.	A farmer had a reasonably high mortality rate among his chicks. He wanted to decrease this rate but was not sure what to do. What would you do to insure that fewer chicks died?
More text is given to the student. Students are asked to hypothesize.	The farmer came to the conclusion that the possible cause of death might be related to the heat source keeping the chicks warm at night. He suspected that some of them got cold, but there was ample room for the chicks to get near the white lamp heat source. He wondered whether the lamp itself might have something to do with the death of the chicks. What would you do to test this idea?
More information given. Students asked to suggest further how to design an investigation.	After a period of time he decided to use different colors of light bulbs in the lamp to see what happened. If you were going to test this hypothesis, how would you go about it?

Teaching and Learning Methods

Steps in Writing an Invitation	Invitation
More data are given. Students asked to make inferences.	Out of a flock of 25 chicks in each of the incubators he obtained the following mortality over a 3 day period. *Red Light Source* *Blue Light Source* 1 chick died 2 chicks died *White Light Source* 3 chicks died What do the above data indicate? What can you definitely conclude from these data? How could you be more certain of your answers? How certain are you from this experiment that light was the cause of the mortality? What are some of the other factors that might have caused chick mortality?
Students suggest and design experiments	What experiments would you do to find out?

The above invitation involves students in the following science processes: understanding a problem, outlining experiments, forming hypotheses, interpreting data, and drawing conclusions. It illustrates the application of the scientific method to a realistic situation.

Invitations to inquiry can be written for various levels of learning. They should stress as much as possible the development of the students' cognitive abilities. Students, in addition to being involved in these processes, should also learn about the necessity for having a control, cause-and-effect relationships, when to use quantitative data, how to interpret quantitative data, the role of argument, inference and value clarification in the design of investigations and experiments. Several related invitations concerning the same topic and involving many strategies for investigating and resolving problems can be organized by teachers into unit packets or folders similar to those produced by McREL in the Inquiry Role Approach. The first invitation you write probably won't be very sophisticated, but in the process of writing it you will gain insight into the construction of them plus a better understanding of how to involve students in cognitive processes.

> HOW TO DESIGN AN INVITATION TO INQUIRY.
>
> Outlined below are the steps you need to follow in order to design your own investigations for any subject.
>
> 1. Decide what your critical and creative thinking processes, skills, and subject matter objectives are.
> 2. State a problem related to your objectives. The idea for problems can come from actual creative work or research in your field.
> 3. Devise questions giving students opportunities to set up investigative procedures, make hypotheses, analyze, synthesize (create), and record data. Stress the understanding and structure of your subject discipline as a process using certain cognitive operations.
> 4. Write the invitation as a series of steps. Insert in different parts of it information to help the student progress in depth into the topic or methods of research.
> 5. Evaluate your invitation comparing it with a list of creative and critical thinking processes and rewrite it to include more of these.

Student Prepared Invitations

Secondary students can be shown how to write their own invitations and prepare them for other students to use. Creative and academically gifted students, when given examples of invitations to use as a model and some explanation as to their purpose, experience little difficulty in constructing them. By so doing, they become more involved and aware of inquiry processes and are further motivated to learn the subject matter of the course.

Dividing the Class Period for Inquiry Oriented Investigations

When teachers study discussion methods, they generally think of using them only with large groups. To do so is to limit their effectiveness in developing students' critical thought. All discussion methods can be modified for more student-centered involvement. For example, a teacher might divide a class period as follows:

Teacher's Role	Students' Involvement
1. Teacher presents a problem: e.g., "Write down all the ways you can think of to make our townspeople more aware of Brotherhood Week."	Students individually write down their creative ideas. They spend time as needed. Time: Estimated, 5 minutes

Teaching and Learning Methods

Teacher's Role	Student's Involvement
2. After students have had time to individually write their ideas, the teacher divides the class into groups of 4 or 5 students and tells them: "Look over all of your ideas. Pick one or two of the ones you think are best and develop them. Appoint a reporter to present the ideas you selected to the class."	Students discuss their ideas and what they need to do to implement them. Time: 10-15 minutes
3. Teacher observes class and when he senses the students have more or less completed the task, he asks them to reconvene for large class discussion.	Students reconvene for large group discussion. A member for each group presents his group's ideas to the class. Time: 10 minutes
4. Teacher asks the class which of the ideas they would most like to implement.	Students discuss the ideas as a class and center on those they would like to implement. Time: 10-15 minutes
5. Teacher asks how they should get organized.	Students organize into groups and define their role and assign individual tasks. The implementation of tasks may continue in class or as outside work. Time: 10 minutes

Note that the general format for the previous class activity is as follows:

1. Teacher presents a problem.
2. Students work individually on it.
3. Students confer in groups and share information on the problem.
4. A member from each group reports information to total class.
5. Class discussion occurs. The activity may end here or continue to the next phase.
6. Students do something with what has been done in class.

The above division of a class hour may be varied in several ways. What is important in using this approach is that some time is devoted for *students to work individually,* in small groups, and then finally in large groups. This approach has the advantage over using only large group instruction in that students become more involved. Every individual has the opportunity during some time of the period to contribute to the class's activity. This method also insures that those students who are less secure or outgoing have a chance of being heard at least within their small groups. By so doing, they are likely to believe they have something worthwhile to contribute and thereby change positively their self-concept.

The dividing of a discussion period into varied activities has the advantage, furthermore, of making a class more exciting. Adolescent students seldom like to sit and be involved in large group discussion for fifty plus minutes unless the topic is on a very controversial subject. Breaking the period up into several blocks of time with varied activity lessens boredom. Some classes are not confronted with this problem, for they have students involved in developing certain skills or in creative production which by its nature requires individual involvement and varied activity. Creating something in art, performing dancing, experimenting in science, cooking in homemaking, or building something in woodshop are good examples of this.

What most beginning teachers fail to realize is that it is a rare lecturer who captures the attention of an audience for a prolonged period of time. This is particularly true if the speaker is lecturing to students who are physically tired, have just eaten a meal, or are in a hot, uncomfortable environment, Furthermore, lecturing, if done well, is ex-

What kinds of teaching methods could be used effectively with a group of this size?

Teaching and Learning Methods

tremely fatiguing. No university professor could long survive if he had to lecture the equivalent hours a secondary instructor teaches; he would soon become exhausted. Yet, many prospective teachers see their role, at least initially, as that of a lecturer. The use of varied types of student involvement and discussion techniques as outlined above can help in replacing the lecturing mode. An alternative to lecturing is to provide a certain amount of information for students to read such as is done in the Inquiry Role Approach. Then follow the discussion format outlined above by having each student select from his reading what he thinks is most significant. The students are next divided into small groups to discuss it and finally convened for class discussion.

Summary

Excellent instructors usually use several methods in their teaching, involving students not only in learning subject matter but in clarifying values and in developing critical and creative thinking and other talents. A number of educators over the years have evolved certain methods to facilitate more sophisticated learning. Although these methods may have been specifically designed for certain subjects such as social studies, mathematics, or science, they can be easily adapted for other areas of instruction. For example, the Hilda Taba Inductive Approach was prepared to be used in the social studies field but is an equally powerful technique for use in other subjects when the instructor is endeavoring to facilitate inductive thinking. The democratic approaches as outlined by Thelen, Oliver, and Shaver involve students in investigative discussion-making strategies that have relevance for any inquiry oriented secondary subject.

Invitations to Inquiry and the Inquiry Role Approach are specific methods involving students in problem solving. The class is confronted with a problem or a series of problems, provided information and then asked for the resolution. The Suchman Theory Building Approach may be adapted to any situation where the instructor is trying to have students develop a theoretical framework, whether it be in art, music, social studies, or science.

Student-centered instruction actively involves students in the learning process. All of the methods outlined in this chapter have been designed for this type of teaching. Several of these assume large class discussion while others operate more effectively with small groups. It is suggested that classes be divided often into small groups so that students can better interact with each other and more actively participate in using their talents. Teachers who have become adept in using student-centered approaches are convinced that they contribute to an enjoyable, exciting, and intellectually stimulating learning environment better helping students become more viable humans.

Further Investigation and Study

1. Prepare and micro-teach to your peers a lesson for each of the methods outlined in this chapter. After teaching the lesson, invite your classmates to suggest how it could be improved. Reread, evaluate, and rewrite the lesson accordingly. Then test this revised lesson with secondary school students.
2. Prepare a file containing headings for each of the methods mentioned in this chapter. Obtain some 3 by 5 cards. Whenever you see or have an idea for a lesson using one of these methods, record it on the card and place it in the file to be developed later.

8 Teaching in the Inner City

Introduction

What are the special problems of teaching in a highly urbanized community? Much has been heard in recent years about the unique problems of teaching in the inner city, which has sometimes been called the ghetto. The inner city of our modern large urban centers frequently is made up of minority groups scattered about in their various communities within the inner city. Children of these groups are attending schools often more than fifty years old; the schools are out of date in terms of their structure, and the congestion surrounding them forms an extremely difficult environment for teaching.

It has been estimated that 70 percent of the population of America lives in only 4 percent of the land area. This means that a very high population density resides in the large cities. Our concept of a pastoral America is largely outmoded. Yet, the children being educated in the cities must develop a sense of the interrelationships between human beings and their environment. If they are to develop this sense, they must do it in the context of their immediate community. These children cannot all be transported to the country to view rural America, and even if they could, it would not be a realistic learning experience to them because it is not their home nor the community in which they live. It is necessary to develop real meaning and understanding about the environmental problems of living in a large city. Most of these conditions are man-made but they are no less important and vital to the growing young person.

For teachers working in these communities it requires special understanding to deal with the students of urban minority groups. The urban student is presently a part of a social revolution. The teacher cannot be dispassionate nor separated from the total group of problems involving urban young people. These problems include matters of health, legal problems, political problems, and social ethics. The teacher must take into consideration race, sex, crime, religion, war, drugs and narcotics, smoking, alcohol, problems of space, unemployment, and many other vital issues confronting young people in the urban centers today.

Many times the urban student is thought of as being underprivileged. At first glance this may seem like an anachronism when one considers the vast resources available in the city for education and development. But in many cases, because of poverty, extreme provincialism, racial prejudices, and many other reasons, students from minority groups in the inner city are in fact underprivileged. The resources for them to do school work in their homes are minimal. The interest and motivation to probe into current problems and issues is lacking.

In addition, many of these students have poor self-concepts. They have been told they are deprived. Attending their schools may be adolescents of more affluent middle-class families having different backgrounds, and the urban student may get the impression he is a second-class citizen. Furthermore, because of national origins, problems of language are also very important. Even middle-class English usage may seem like a foreign tongue. Often tests, which are frequently highly verbal, tend to discriminate against the urban student because of this factor.

Students in the inner city find that interpersonal contacts are more frequent than in rural areas. They see a great variety of national, social, and racial backgrounds living in the large city. The inter-dependency on one another is much greater. All of this affects lives in the form of crowdedness, lack of privacy, problems of pollution, and problems of unemployment.

It is important to remember, however, that there are rich resources for good teaching in the inner city. It has libraries, museums, manufacturing plants, small businesses, and all of the vital concerns that make the city an economic entity. The materials for teaching and learning are relatively easily obtained.

The school experience is one of interrelating. How can a student in a class in an ancient school building interrelate with four walls? How does it feel to be imprisoned in straight rows, to be under the constant disciplinary eye of a teacher, to be shunted from class to class, to be counted and graded, and turned loose at the signal of bells? This is a dehumanizing experience. Too frequently conditions such as described above are found in inner city schools.

A recent project called the "Environmental Studies" conceived and developed in Boulder, Colorado, is attempting to combat some of these problems. There is an effort to place a large degree of humanness back in the classroom. The theme is "The real classroom is outside. Get into it."[1] Some of their recent publications advocate:

> "A teacher doesn't teach—he creates an environment for learning"
>
> and
>
> "Teachers who create open learning environments take the risk of trusting students to choose what they want to learn and to invent the criteria for evaluating their learning"

How can students in the inner city use the resources around them?

---

[1] ES/ESTPP Brochure, Environmental Sciences/Earth Science Teacher Preparation Project, Box 1559, Boulder, Colorado, 80302.

Specifically, what can a teacher in the inner city do to stimulate learning? How can he motivate students to become interested in school subjects? How can he make use of the immediate environment to develop a thread of interest in something that seems prosaic to those who have grown up in this environment?

He must be cognizant of the problem. He must recognize that the situation may be far different from what he was led to expect in his teacher training preparation. He must not become frustrated at the constraints placed upon him by a rigid system. He must look around him for resources.

An important key to success in teaching effectively in the inner city is to devise methods of breaking the cycle of frustration students frequently have. Many have been unsuccessful at coping with school work in a rigid system and have developed negative attitudes. The climate for learning must be improved. Creativity should be encouraged, and students should be recognized for their creative talents. The products of creative effort should be displayed for parents, teachers, and other students to see. Instruction should be activity oriented. Emphasis should be put on giving rewards and success experiences. The student's need for success must be served. His image must be changed from one of low status to one of high status, and this can be accomplished by showing appreciation for his efforts. The teacher should begin with things of interest to pupils and allow divergence to exist.

The New Teacher in the Inner City

How can the new teacher prepare himself to teach better in this kind of environment? First, it must be recognized that new as well as experienced teachers need updating in their methods. The role of dispenser of information must be changed to one of guiding interesting activities. Provision should be made for continuous in-service development and teachers should avail themselves of every possible opportunity to improve their academic and teaching competency.

The new teacher beginning work in the large city must make an effort to understand the special problems of the urban student. If it is your intention to teach in the ghetto area or in the densely populated center of a large city, try to have your student teaching experience in a similar circumstance. This experience will be extremely valuable and will allow you to make the transition from college student to practicing teacher in the most effective manner. The student teacher is usually not faced at the outset with the entire responsibility of handling a class as is the regular classroom teacher. Yet, he can learn the methods of handling students and the circumstances under which the inner-city pupil studies and learns.

The new teacher should make an effort to learn about the work responsibilities his students have. What do they do with their leisure time? What are their activities? To gain some of this information he should talk to the regular teachers in the school system. He may find many of these teachers are cynical, resigned, and callous with respect to children. But, instead of becoming discouraged, the new teacher should seek out the really good regular teachers who are sensitive, conscientious, and humane. There are always some in any school system. Their reputations are well known among students and faculty. These people can be useful sources of information and mature judgement, who can assist the beginning teacher in becoming adjusted to the conditions under which he is teaching.

One should look for ways to have stimulating classes. Remember that the urban ghetto students are no less human than rural, suburban, or any other groups. They have needs and desires and expectations. The teacher should attempt to give them successful experiences. In many cases their experiences have been a succession of failures. They have a backlog of poor experiences to overcome. Don't expect immediate trust or mutual understanding.

The new teacher should try to learn the language of the ghetto. This does not mean necessarily to become proficient in a foreign tongue, but simply to be prepared for the kind of speech students in the inner city have. Be prepared for vulgarisms, profanity, and sometimes shocking language. Do not reply in kind. Your job is to use good English but not a stilted or supercilious variety. In time, the students will emulate your good speech if it is not affected, and if it is simple and direct as good English should be. The teacher should try to understand the reasons for the speech mannerisms he finds. Remember that the students' backgrounds may be different from yours. To them their speech is an acceptable way of communicating, and they will continue to use it as long as their peers and friends have the same speech mannerisms. It is important that the new teacher avoid letting unfamiliar speech mannerisms interfere with communicating and developing good rapport with the students in his classes.

Humanizing Teaching

Success in teaching in the inner city perhaps depends on good teacher-student rapport more than anything else. There must be developed a

Teaching in the Inner City 169

feeling of mutual trust between the teacher and his students. The past experiences of the students may have been that of subservience to a rigid disciplinary teacher who teaches in a very mechanistic way and shows poor human qualities. To overcome this, the new teacher should invent ways to stimulate mutual trust, understanding, and dependability. Find reasons to talk to students about their activities, interests, athletic events, travels, and other matters of personal concern. Display human characteristics of love, sensitivity, honesty, and kindness. Do everything possible to treat all of your students impartially and fairly. Try to deemphasize competition for grades. Attempt to develop an inner motivation which encourages students to carry out the activities in your classes because of the satisfaction they gain in being successful.

Try to enlist the help of parents. Even in the inner city the majority of parents are concerned about the education of their children. It is true there is a small minority not interested in the way their children perform in school. They feel that education for them is a waste of time. But the vast majority feel otherwise. Families of minority groups have struggled to bring themselves up to a higher level than their forebears and recognize the importance of education. This can be a very important resource in improving the classroom situation. Make phone calls

What kinds of human relationships are fostered in inner-city schools?

to parents to commend their children for successful endeavors and ask them for assistance when problems arise. Invite parents to school. Make these invitations specific by setting appointments with the parents at mutually convenient times. Do not use the meeting to berate the child but solicit help and cooperation. Show your concern for the education of their children. Give them suggestions for things to do and places to go for resources. Many inner-city families are not aware of the tremendous resources available to them. Point out the availability of the library, museums, and other opportunities for children to learn during their free time in out-of-school activities.

Try to think of each student as an individual with personal feelings and aspirations. Respect his individuality, credit him for his maturity, try to lead rather than coerce, build on his successful gains, and foster an adult relationship. Secondary school students frequently respond favorably when treated as adults. Show that you expect mature adult behavior. Do not expect miracles but look for rather slow changes in development. If you expect the best from these individuals, most of the time you will get it.

Student Activities

The key to successful teaching in the inner city is student involvement. A teacher cannot expect satisfaction and progress in his classes by dwelling on abstractions, reading, and lecturing to the exclusion of other activities of a more participatory nature. Students generally want to see more immediate results. They want to discover the relevancy of school to their personal lives. School must capture their interest in a personal way.

At least as important as involvement is developing an atmosphere of understanding. No technique or method will be successful if students feel misunderstood or alienated from the teacher and the school. Developing an atmosphere of mutual understanding requires seeking avenues of communication between teachers and students. Opportunities must be created to talk with students on an informal basis, soliciting their ideas for ways to improve the class and to maintain interest. The teacher's reaction to these ideas must be open and receptive in a threat-free atmosphere.

Summary

Problems of teaching in the inner city are unique. Most fundamental is that of achieving communication with young people of the urban environment. To do this successfully, the prospective teacher should do his practice teaching in an urban setting. Thus a time of growth and understanding can be provided before assuming the responsibilities and problems of the full-time teacher. Avenues of communication must be developed and mutual understandings must be nurtured.

For effective teaching, students must become involved. Subjects for them should be a "doing" thing, rather than a "reading" or "lecturing" course. The teacher must become resourceful at providing many interesting, creative experiences. Some current helps are being developed by the Environmental Studies Project in Boulder, Colorado.

The challenge of good teaching in the inner city is tremendous. However, the history of education has shown repeatedly that where challenge exists, there are many young people ready to accept it. Perhaps you will be one who builds a successful career of teaching in the most difficult environment of all, the urban school system.

Further Investigation and Study

1. Write for a complete set of Environmental Studies cards, American Geological Institute, Box 1559, Boulder, Colorado, 80302. Use these cards to produce ideas for inner-city activities for junior high and senior high students. With your classmates, discuss the interdisciplinary opportunities made available by these teaching materials.
2. Make a list of the slang words and phrases used by secondary students. How many of these have relevance to school activities? To out-of-school activities? Write a short dramatic skit for presentation in your methods class illustrating the importance of an understanding of current teen-age language for better rapport and communication.
3. Identify several unique features of inner-city teaching. What kinds of training experiences should prospective teachers engage in to best prepare them for these unique problems?

9 Adjusting Instruction for Individual Variation

The bell rang, and students filed into class. Several went to the study carrels and began organizing the material they were to use for that day. Two boys went over to a corner, selected two film cartridges, and were in the process of getting ready to view them on the small rearview screens. Several other students were busy at their desks setting up materials for a learning game. One student was taking a self-evaluational test.

The initial impression of this class might be one of chaos, but upon closer observation it becomes apparent students are simply working in a way different from that of the traditional class. These activities have been organized so that each student progresses at his own rate.

Today, more and more school systems are endeavoring to modify their instructional program so that greater attention is given to individual variation. Psychological research has long indicated there are human differences having implications for teaching and has found that:

1. Individuals come to the classroom with varied backgrounds and experiences. Because their experiences and genetic differences vary, not all students readily learn in the same way. They are, therefore, as Piaget has pointed out, at different cognitive levels.
2. Individuals vary in the rate at which they learn concepts. Some students must have a relatively prolonged contact with concepts before they grasp them.

Teachers, although mindful of these facts, traditionally have done little to adjust for individual differences other than to give an extra reading assignment to the more advanced students. Teaching to challenge the individual potential of students generally has not been done, for several reasons.

REASONS FOR RESISTANCE TO INDIVIDUALIZED INSTRUCTION

1. Traditional ways of instruction have been barriers to change.
2. Logistics problems. If students progress at their own rates this necessitates the addition of more courses, materials, and equipment. A modular system allowing different number of modules for various courses may have to be adopted. The class period, for example, may have to be lengthened in a laboratory situation. Adopting a scheduling system allowing variations of time spans, depending upon the activity or class assignment of students, presents logistics problems, particularly in the larger schools.
3. Teachers trained for group instruction often feel insecure when confronted with the idea that not all students in a class will be performing the same tasks at the same time.
4. Group instruction is comparatively cheap and easy to direct and control.
5. Facilities for individualized instruction are more costly because they require more space.

In spite of this resistance to change, there are patterns of instruction which have received acceptance because of a belief that they will offer a greater chance for each individual to realize his potential.

Open School, Individualized Study, and Continuous Progress

There is an exciting development in American education changing instruction from a teacher-centered to a student-centered endeavor. This approach strives to let each student progress through course work according to his ability. The anecdote on the first page of this chapter describes a class organized for student-centered instruction. Not all members of a class are doing the same thing at the same time; this is truly the essence of individualized study.

The schools using the individualized approach generally employ one of three plans.

1. *Continuous Progress Plan.* One approach to individualized teaching is called the continuous progress plan. It allows students to progress

from subject to subject with no time restriction. If a student finishes biology in ten weeks and passes an examination, he then may move into units from another course. This approach has been worked out at the Laboratory School at Brigham Young University; at Bryce Valley High School, Tropic, Utah; at Nova Middle and High School, Ft. Lauderdale, Florida, as well as at several other schools.

2. *Term Oriented Individualized Instruction.* A second approach is term oriented individualized instruction. It lets students work at their own rate, but when they finish the normal work required they remain in the same class and progress on to enriched material. For example, if a student finishes a year's course work in 25 weeks, he does not pass on into another class but studies the subject further in depth. This plan is being tried at many schools in the country. It has the advantage of eliminating scheduling and classroom utilization problems found in the other plans when students are allowed to pass from subject to subject throughout the school year.

A brief list of those involved with this approach are: Cape Kennedy High School, the University School, Florida State University in Florida; Meeker High School in Colorado; Middletown High School in Rhode Island; Pampa Senior High School in Texas; Appolo Junior High School in Nashville, Tennessee; Bacon School in Evanston, Illinois; Mineola High School in Garden City Park, New York, plus many more.

3. *The "Open School."* A third approach is the "open school" concept. Its major philosophical emphasis is on providing a more humane educational environment allowing students considerable freedom and self-direction. Although there are several schools trying modifications of this approach, the Wilson School at Mankato State College, Mankato, Minnesota, is probably one of the best examples of how this concept operates.

The Wilson School schedule is changed daily and the students choose from it the topics they want to study. They may pursue an area from 3 to 103 weeks. Although there are students enrolled from lower primary to upper high school age levels, the school is ungraded. When students have completed the necessary units of work they graduate. Students from all age levels may be working in the same room. The learning may be going on in small group activities or individually. Attendance at classes is optional and students may go home if they wish for part of each day. Students progress at their own rate. The teacher acts as a facilitator and guide, providing stimulation and direction.

The British have been using open classroom instruction in many of their schools, particularly on the elementary and junior level, since the Second World War. In these schools the learning arises from the interest of the individual. It is guided and kindled by the teacher but not imposed. In a typical classroom there may be considerable diversity of activities; one student may write a poem, another prepare a newspaper, a third reads, a forth prepares a collage, etc.

The British government found from an extensive evaluation of children coming from these schools that they do academically as well on national examinations as those from more traditional institutions. The students from open classrooms, furthermore, read more, liked school more, dropped out less, and had fewer discipline problems, even in slum area classrooms, than did those from traditional modes of instruction. Their Ministry of Education has been so impressed by these results that it has encouraged further development of these types of schools.

One American educator who observed several of these schools for several weeks was asked to compare them with our typical ones. She said in summary: "In the English open schools, I never saw unhappy children in the classrooms."

The open school concept has become increasingly a concern of educators and parents in this country. Most of them presently operating are private, although some school districts have established open schools on an experimental basis. Undoubtedly, what will happen in this country is the development of several of these schools designed around the open concept, which will probably evolve into a unique American institution. This is exciting to contemplate because these schools will offer an alternative to the traditional instructional system, the outgrowth of which should provide data and direction for improving all of our schools.

Advantages of Individualized Instruction

Although individuals vary physically and cognitively, and have not had the same experiences nor learn at the same rate, the traditional mode of instruction operates as though this were not so. Individualized approaches make no such assumptions and endeavor to respond to the overwhelming evidence about individual variation. They are efforts to respect the "person." Teachers who have gone from group-centered to more open or individualized instruction often state they didn't realize how futile it was in the traditional approach to try to have all students learn particularly difficult material at the same rate. The fact that the slow academic student is not demeaned and frustrated because he doesn't learn rapidly or the gifted student is not held back until his classmates catch up is perhaps the major advantage of this approach.

There is, furthermore, a shift in emphasis from extrinsic to intrinsic rewards. A student doing an assignment at his own rate achieves self-confidence and a sense of competence which may not manifest itself so easily in group instruction. The real joy of learning in this manner comes in the student's completing the task on his own initiative, not because of an "A" given by the teacher.

Other advantages have been outlined by Dr. Sidney Rollins of the Middletown Project in Rhode Island.

ADVANTAGES OF INDIVIDUALIZED INSTRUCTION

1. Pupil progress ranges from a year or more ahead of where pupils would be if they attended a graded school to half a year behind the usual achievement of a given grade level.
2. Dropout rate (less than one percent at Middletown) is drastically lower than the national rate of 30 percent.
3. Pupils recover from extended absences from ungraded schools more quickly and easily than from graded schools.
4. Pupils stimulate themselves to greater effort—even in April, May, or June when they normally begin to ease up on studies.
5. Pupils seem to appreciate the opportunities for avoiding the boredom and frustration that the ungraded structure can offer.[1]

Problems of Implementing an Individualized Approach

Although an individualized approach has ideally many practical advantages, there are also several disadvantages. A teacher considering taking a position in a school or seriously thinking about the implementation of such a system should be aware of these before making pertinent decisions. Generally, the problems involve facilities, scheduling, materials, and cost, as indicated below:

1. *Facilities.* Seldom do schools implementing student-centered instruction completely individualize their courses, for to do so means there must be facilities available for large and small groups as well as individualized learning. In order to design and provide facilities to accommodate these various modes of teaching, architects must know in advance how many of each type is required in order to insure maximum utilization of the plant. No school system can afford to construct rooms that are vacant several hours a day. Unfortunately, most faculties are not sufficiently experienced to be able to predict to a high degree of accuracy their needs nor do they understand that a large lecture

---

[1] S. P. Rollins, "Ungraded High Schools: Why Those Who Like Them Love Them," *Nation's Schools*, LXXIII (April, 1964): 110.

complex cannot be constructed solely for their department's use one or two times a day.

Because individualized instruction usually involves considerable use of multi-media, special facilities providing the use and maintenance of machines and media must be available and these mean considerable cost.

2. *Scheduling.* Because of the diversity of the program and this type of instruction scheduling becomes a complex problem. For example, if there is one large group instructional room, it must be scheduled and used by several departments to insure maximum utilization. Obviously, this use by various departments limits the flexibility for any one program because the instructors will be only able to use the room when they are scheduled to do so.

3. *Staff.* Individualizing a department necessitates the faculty operating as teams. Instructors also have to be well prepared in several subjects because as at Nova High School in Fort Lauderdale, Florida, they may be supervising a large laboratory containing 70-100 students working on units spread over several areas in three different subjects. Because students often are working on different units within each of these subjects, it is impossible for a teacher to read a chapter ahead of the students the night before in order to be prepared. Individualized teachers must know the subjects and curriculum well in order to interact appropriately with each student's needs.

Many teachers, furthermore, find they have difficulty adjusting to individualized approaches because of their psychological orientation and educational philosophy. A teacher who views teaching as a telling-covering activity rather than as a means of facilitating learning is bound to have difficulty with this type of approach.

Acting as a member of a fully functioning team often presents problems because of the disparity of how members view their functions as teachers and what they think are appropriate requirements for the learners. For example, if some teachers believe students should be directed to cover a lot of material and others think they should be given considerable freedom to become autonomous investigators, there are bound to be conflicts among the faculty team members.

Individualized instruction does not mean students are given total freedom and that there is little or no direction and structure. Discipline must be imposed by faculty when necessary. Unfortunately, in schools using this form of instruction some teams haven't defined what constitutes an infraction of acceptable class behavior, and because there are no assertive members on the team, class chaos occurs. The faculty must help students devise appropriate standards for providing a suitable learning environment respecting the rights of all and must insure

Adjusting Instruction for Individual Variation

that these are carried out. Students must realize that they do not have the right to be non-productive nor to hinder the learning of the other members of the class. The faculty must impose the necessary controls to see that students act accordingly.

4. *Materials.* Individualized instruction demands far more reading matter and audio-visual aids then does conventional teaching. This is so because multi-level learning aids must be available so as to adjust the materials to the various academic abilities of the students. For example, the intellectually gifted may read a college level book or listen to a "teacher-prepared taped talk" about the subject topic.

Unfortunately, there are not sufficient commercially prepared materials to provide multi-level resources for all topics in a course. This means that teachers have to prepare these which requires considerable time and competence. It has been found that on a typical faculty team the ability to construct effective learning aids varies considerably caus-

How are individual differences being accommodated in this mode of instruction?

ing some teachers to have to work harder in order to make up for their teammates' insufficiencies. This often leads to disenchantment with the team.

5. *Cost.* Because of the need for multi-level, multi-learning aids for varied student abilities, individualized instruction is more costly than traditional approaches. This is particularly so because students wear out filmstrips, 35 mm slides, and tapes, etc. at a more rapid rate than when they are used solely for group instruction. The problems of maintenance of these and the audio-visual machines requires that a resource center be staffed by technically competent people, causing a further need for increased financial support.

Syllabuses for Individualized Instruction

Science

Shown below is a small part of an individualized syllabus in science to go with the Earth Science Curriculum Project book *Investigating the Earth*. The complete syllabus actually contains an introduction, behavioral objectives, a list of the required and enrichment activities, self-tests, and several guides for enrichment activities for each area. Only the list for the required and enrichment activities is shown below to give you some idea of how a simplified student syllabus might be constructed:

CHAPTER 5
FORCES AND FIELDS
FIELDS, MOTIONS AND FORCES

Sections 5-1 to 5-3

REQUIRED ACTIVITIES

Investigations
5-1 B.____
     C.____
5-2 B.____
     C.____

Complete Section 5-1—"Investigating a Temperature Field."

Complete Section 5-2—"Investigating the Behavior of a Falling Object."

Read Section 5-3—"How is Motion Described?"

Read Section 5-4—"Forces are the Cause of Motion."

Adjusting Instruction for Individual Variation

SUGGESTED ENRICHMENT ACTIVITIES

Activities in
this Syllabus
1
2

Complete Activity page 107.

Complete "Investigating the effect air has on the behavior of falling bodies."

Complete the *Sample Problem* on page 111 with the following data: 160 Kilograms and an acceleration of 7 meters per second.

Using the formula in the above *Sample Problem* determine mass when the force is equal to 600 Newtons and the acceleration is 25 meters per second.

Complete Vocabulary Exercise—"Fields, Motion and Forces."

Answer questions in figure 5-5, page 109.

Answer questions in figure 5-8, page 111.

Answer and give an analysis of the questions and diagrams in figures 5-6 and 5-7, page 110.

Answer the following "Questions and Problems" page 126-127: A) 2, 3, 4, 5, 8.

Complete *Thought and Discussion* questions.

Make a written or oral report on the following article. Elsasser, Walter M. "The Earth as a Dynamo" *Scientific American* May, 1958 (Scientific American Offprint #825).

Determine the acceleration using an elapse time and top speed of a drag racer.

Social Studies

Shown below is an example of a student syllabus for social studies entailing several weeks of work depending on the capability of the student. This is a refinement of several previous unit designs done at Nova High School, Fort Lauderdale, Florida. It was produced mainly by the social studies supervisor, John M. Clark.

THIS IS AN INSTRUCTIONAL LAP.   NOT FOR STUDENT USE.

THE AMERICAN PRESIDENCY:
The Presidents and Their Roles

LEARNING ACTIVITY PACKAGE #42

The Nova Schools
Social Studies Program
John M. Clark

Name _____

Section _____

Date Begun _____

Target Date _____

Date Completed _____

RATIONALE

What are the president's roles?

What makes a president great?

Can there be only one desk in all the land bearing the sign, "The buck stops here!"?

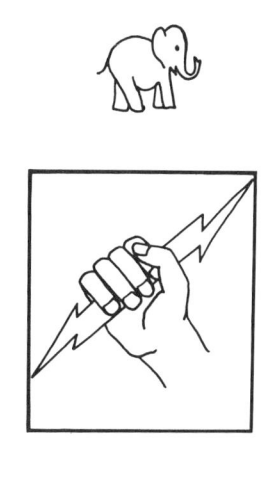

Does the president have too many roles to play?

Is the presidency a killing job?

Who were the great presidents?

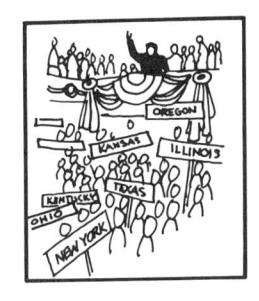

THE PRESIDENTS AND THEIR ROLES

OBJECTIVES:

_____1. After completing your prescribed course of study, you will be able to name or identify six Presidents who are considered to be strong or great Presidents.

_____2. After playing the game *Plus Fiver* several times and when given a random list of the Presidents you will be able to identify those considered to be great, average and poor.

_____3. After completing your program of study you will be able to distinguish between the Constitutional and Developmental Roles of the President by listing five roles of each type.

_____4. Given a list of major current and historical issues from the American scene you will be able to identify the major role the President would use in dealing with each issue.

_____5. Given the book *Quotations From Chairman LBJ* you will be able to choose at least one quotation representative of each of the following Presidential Roles:
   a. Chief of State
   b. Chief of Party
   c. Chief Spokesman of the People
   d. Chief Diplomat
   e. Commander-in-Chief

_____6. After completing your prescribed course of study you will be able to discuss in a small group the relationship of Presidential Greatness to the man and to the events which may or may not have forced greatness upon the man.

UNLESS OTHERWISE NOTED, FULFILLMENT OF OBJECTIVES WILL BE MEASURED ON THE PROGRESS TEST AND/OR ON THE POST TEST.

RESOURCE MATERIALS:

READING: (Teacher prescribes what is to be read.)

_____ *Contemporary Issues*, pp. 214-226.
_____ *Comparative Political Systems*, pp. 136-142.
_____ *The Challenge of American Democracy*, pp. 84-90.
_____ *Politics and Progress*, Unit III.
_____ *Quotations From Chairman LBJ*
_____ *America and Its Presidents*
_____ *Our Presidents and Their Times*
_____ *The American Presidency*

Adjusting Instruction for Individual Variation

AUDIO-VISUAL:

_____ Talking Book: "The Role of Presidential Leadership" (Teacher Prepared)
_____ Filmstrip: The President—Office and Powers
_____ Sound/Filmstrip: The American Presidency—The Powers
_____ Sound/Filmstrip: The American Presidency—The History

ACADEMIC GAMES: (Teacher may assign if student likes games.)

_____ *The Presidential Role Game*
_____ *Plus Fiver: A Game of the Presidency*

SELF-ASSESSMENT

I. In each of the following groups of our Presidents, there are two who are generally considered to be strong or great Presidents, and one generally considered to be weak or poor. In the space provided to the left of each group you are to write the number of the weak or poor President.

( ) 1. Wilson   2. Pierce   3. Washington
( ) 4. Jefferson   5. Theodore Roosevelt 6. Grant
( ) 7. Andrew Johnson 8. Jackson   9. Lincoln
( ) 10. Truman   11. Harding   12. Franklin Roosevelt

II. Following is a list of the Roles of the President. In the parentheses to the left of each role you are to place a "C" if it is a Constitutional Role or a "D" if it is a Developmental Role.

( ) 1. Chief of State
( ) 2. Chief Executive
( ) 3. Chief of Party
( ) 4. Chief Diplomat
( ) 5. Chief Spokesman of the People
( ) 6. Chief Legislator
( ) 7. Chief Executive of Metropolis
( ) 8. Protector of the Peace
( ) 9. Chief of the Alliance of the Free World
( ) 10. Chief Administrator
( ) 11. Commander-in-Chief of the Armed Forces
( ) 12. Chief Financier

III. Listed below are several issues that the President of the U.S. might have to deal with at a moment's notice. Making use of the above list you are to place the number of the role which the President would most likely use in coping with each issue in the parentheses to the left of each issue.

( ) Enactment of a Tax Reduction Law
( ) Summit Meeting with Soviet Premier
( ) National Calamity in the Mississippi Delta

( ) Cuban Artillery Bombards Guantanamo Naval Base
( ) Federal Aid to Education
( ) The Presidential Baseball Toss

DEPTH OPPORTUNITIES (Must talk to teacher first, so academically slow student doesn't pick difficult tasks.)

1. For the embryo artist: Develop and illustrate a series of cartoons depicting the president of the United States as he deals with each of the following issues:
   a. The Berlin Blockade
   b. Preparation and Execution of the Budget
   c. Distribution of Federal Patronage
   d. Rioting in a Major Metropolitan Area

2. For the musically inclined: Prepare an audio tape of the music associated with five or six of the defeated Presidential candidates since 1932. In a narrative section of the tape discuss how the music was used in the campaign.

3. Read pertinent sections of several weekly or monthly magazines such as *Time, Newsweek, Atlantic, New Republic,* or *U.S. News and World Report,* and basic position taken in regard to President Nixon. Are they pro-Nixon, anti-Nixon or neutral?

4. Read the recent best seller *The President's Plane is Missing* by Robert J. Serling and try to establish empathy with Frederick James Madigan, the Vice-President. After formal essay in which you discuss the Office of the Vice-Presidency compare its present organization to an organization that you recommend.

5. This is to remind you that the purpose of this section of the Learning Activity Package is to allow a student to work in-depth in a mode and style that he finds most rewarding. Depth Studies may or may not be required depending upon the given situation.

Adjusting Instruction for Individual Variation

English

Shown below is a student syllabus for English produced at Nova High School, Fort Lauderdale, Florida.

NOVA HIGH SCHOOL
LEARNING ACTIVITY PACKAGE
31

HUMANITIES I

ROMANTICISM

I have reviewed this package for content in
terms of curriculum and appropriateness.

(Supervisor)

Written by: Pat Galbreath

Copyright 1972 - Nova High School

RATIONALE

This unit marks the transition from primitive man's concern with the supernatural to his awareness of nature.

Primitive man, having given a supernatural essence to the unexplained, now views nature and sees within it a spiritual quality and in so doing, idealizes and colors his environment.

During the course of this unit, the student will reexamine in the light of romanticism, the literary terms: microcosm-macrocosm, motif, symbolism, and antithesis. He will also explore those aspects keynoting romanticism: individuality, freedom of emotions, idealism, and pantheism. As in previous units, the concepts will be illuminated by an exposure to the fine arts.

This LAP insures individualization by allowing each student to select his core reading and to proceed at his own pace and level.

PERFORMANCE OBJECTIVES
ROMANTICISM

Using your reading, viewing and listening for reference, be able to discuss orally or in an essay of not less than one page, how nature is given a divine or sacred quality.

From your required reading, viewing, and listening, be able to select at least five passages which keynote individuality.

Using your required reading, viewing, and listening, locate and describe a minimum of three examples of idealism.

Using your required reading, viewing, and listening, locate and discuss a minimum of six passages which are examples of freedom of emotions. Determine what emotion is being expressed in each example.

STUDENT PERFORMANCE REQUIREMENTS

During the course of this study the following will be expected of the student.
a. Read all of the required selections.
b. Perform all the activities under Concepts 1, 2, 3, and 4.
c. Define all of the vocabulary words for use in class discussion and in written work.
d. Choose one activity from the activity selection for your final product.
e. Take all objective evaluations.

CONCEPT #1   *Pantheism*

Pantheism is the belief that all forces in nature are guided by a sacred spirit; the belief that God is everything and everything is God.

OBJECTIVE

Be able to discuss orally or in an essay of not less than one page, how nature is given a divine or sacred quality, using your readings for reference.

VOCABULARY
>   divine -
>   sacred -
>   noble savage -

REQUIRED ACTIVITIES
1. Read: a. Blake, William. *Adventures in English Literature,* "The Tyger," p. 331.
   b. Cummings, E. E. *Adventures in Reading,* "i thank You God," p. 192.
   c. Tennyson, Alfred, Lord. *Adventures in Reading,* "Flower in a Crannied Wall," p. 247.
   Wordsworth, William. *Adventures in Reading,* "My Heart Leaps Up," p. 184.
2. Using your required readings as a basis to formulate your own ideas, choose one of the following topics for a theme of not less than three pages. Consult Warriner's *Complete Course: English Grammar and Composition,* pp.386-397 for your information on how to write an effective theme.

Adjusting Instruction for Individual Variation

    a. A comparison of outdoor life with that of cities
    b. A consideration of the attention given to nature by modern Americans
    c. A description of some place of natural beauty
    d. A modern noble savage
    e. Another topic suggested by the student and approved by the teacher

CONCEPT #2   *Individualism*

The individualist is one who pursues an independent course in thought or action.

OBJECTIVE

From your readings be able to select and discuss at least five passages which keynote individuality.

VOCABULARY

    rebellion -
    reform -

REQUIRED ACTIVITIES

1. Read: a. Burns, Robert. *Adventures in Reading,* "Bannockburn," p. 236.
         b. Priestley, J. B. *Adventures in Reading,* "Walk in a Pine Wood," pp. 257-258.
         c. Walsh, Maurice. *Adventures in Appreciation,* "The Quiet Man," pp. 127-139.
2. Using your required readings, answer the following *essay* questions in a minimum of one paragraph each.
    a. In what different ways do the characters in the readings express individualism?
    b. Which characters are the active rebels? Which ones are passive rebels?
    c. What various methods of reform do the characters attempt?
    d. What relationship does love of nature have to individualism in the lives of the characters in the following readings: "The Quiet Man" and "Walk in a Pine Wood"?

CONCEPT #3   *Idealism*

The dreamer and the utopian are idealists who see man and his world as perfectible.

OBJECTIVE

Using your required readings, locate and describe a minimum of three examples of idealism.

VOCABULARY

    utopian -
    perfectible -

REQUIRED ACTIVITIES
1. Read: a. Brooke, Rupert. *Designs in Poetry*, "The Soldier," p. 104.
          b. Kipling, Rudyard. *Adventures in Reading*, "If," pp. 228-229.
          c. Noyes, Alfred. *Adventures in Reading*, "The Last of the Books," pp. 216-217.
          d. Tennyson, Alfred, Lord. *Adventures in English Literature*, "Ulysses," pp. 481-483.
2. Using your required readings and viewings, write *two* short one page essays. One is to be titled "The Dreamer" and the other "The Utopian." In these essays cite examples from your readings to illustrate the titles.

CONCEPT #4 *Freedom of Emotions*

Running the gamut from ecstasy to despondency, the romantic indulges in freedom of emotion.

OBJECTIVE

Using your required readings, locate and discuss a minimum of six passages which are examples of freedom of emotion. Determine what emotion is being expressed in each example.

VOCABULARY

   melancholy -
   sentimentality -

REQUIRED ACTIVITIES
1. Read: a. Browning, Elizabeth. *Designs in Poetry*, "How Do I Love Thee?" p. 44.
          b. Keats, John. *Designs in Poetry*, "Proem from Endymion," p. 94.
          c. Lowell, Amy. *Designs in Poetry*, "Solitaire," p. 62.
          d. Robinson, Edwin A. *Adventures in Appreciation*, "Aaron Stark," p. 373.
          e. Yeats, William B. *Adventures in Appreciation*, "The Lake Isle of Innisfree," p. 311.
2. Select six passages from the required readings which are examples of freedom of emotions. In a paragraph for each, using quotes to justify your explanation, explain the emotions being expressed.

ACTIVITY SELECTIONS
1. Gather from various magazines color pictures of flora and fauna characteristic of the nature scenery depicted in your romantic core reading. Now search your reading for poetic passages attributing to nature a sacred or spiritual quality. Match these passages to your pictures as a photographic essay with accompanying text. A model example of a photo essay with matching text may be obtained from the teacher.
2. In water colors, pastels, or oils capture the "forest girl," Rima, in the wild paradise of *Green Mansions*. Convey pictorially the pervading pantheistic nature of this "half-way heaven."

Adjusting Instruction for Individual Variation

3. Act out a scene, or present a dramatic reading of a brief passage from Noel Coward's play *Blithe Spirit* to comment on the role of nature in affecting human character.
4. Investigate and write a detailed, analytic paper on nature worship as depicted in *The Golden Bough* by Sir James Frazier.
5. Read Somerset Maugham's *The Moon and Sixpence* for a fictionalized account of Gauguin's search for the transcendental in nature. Write a formal paper commenting on Gauguin's mysticism and pantheism.
6. Working in water colors, pastels, or oils, depict several of the elements of romanticism illustrated in your reading.
7. Construct and choreograph a creative dance interpretation of the elements of romanticism highlighted in the unit: pantheism, idealism, individuality, and freedom of emotions.
8. Choose any romantic composer or romantic piece of music and research background material to analyze and comment on in a critical paper of not less than five pages.
9. From the romantic selection you are reading, draw an episode which you feel you could expand to a short story of your own. Be sure to include in your short story many of the elements of romanticism.
10. Research the career and poetry of any great romantic writer: Wordsworth, Byron, Keats, Shelley, Schilling, Pushkin, etc., analyze and comment on elements of romanticism in their careers and poems.
11. Create, in the art media of your choice, oil, charcoal, ink sketches or pastels your interpretation of romanticism. Write a one-page paper describing the elements of romanticism represented in your art work.
12. Substitute and complete another choice of activity with the approval of the teacher.

SELF-ASSESSMENT TEST

1. Write a brief definition of the term *pantheism*.

2. Explain in your own words why primitive man would have been what we label a pantheist.

3. TRUE—FALSE: Primitive man was directed by reason and therefore concerned only with the world of reality.

4. Artists associated with romanticism are:
   - _____a. Gericault
   - _____b. Corot
   - _____c. Millet
   - _____d. Delacroix
   - _____e. Gauguin
5. Write the title of a representative poem for each of the following elements of romanticism.
   a. Idealism_____
   b. Individualism_____
   c. Fredom of Emotions_____
   d. Pantheism_____
6. Essay: Choose one of your required readings and explain in paragraph form why it is representative of romanticism.

SOURCES AND MATERIALS

Connolly, Francis X. and others, eds. *Adventures in Reading.* Classic Edition, "The Adventures in Literature Program" series. New York: Harcourt Brace Jovanovich, Inc., 1968.

Coward, Noel. *Three Plays.* "Blythe Spirit," New York: Dell Publishing Company, Inc. 1941.

Frazer, Sir James G. *Golden Bough.* New York: The Macmillan Co., 1967.

Hudson, W.H. *Green Mansions.* New York: Dell Publishing Company, Inc., 1967.

Inglis, Rewey Belle, and Spear, Josephine, eds. *Adventure in English Literature.* Olympic Edition, "The Adventures in Literature Program" series. New York: Harcourt Brace Javonovich, Inc., 1952.

Maugham, W.S., ed. by Shefter, H. *Moon and Sixpence.* New York: Washington Square Press, 1969.

Nordhoff, Charles, and Hall, Norman. *Mutiny on the Bounty.* New York: Pocket Books, 1969.

Perrine, Laurence and others eds. *Adventures in Appreciation.* Classic Edition, "The Adventures in Literature Program" series. New York: Harcourt Brace Javonovich, Inc., 1968.

Peterson, R. Stanley. *Designs in Poetry.* Macmillan Literary Heritage, New York: The Macmillan Company, 1968.

Warriner, John E. *English Grammar and Composition: Complete Course.* New York: Harcourt Brace Javonovich, Inc., 1957.

MULTI-MEDIA MATERIALS

Record:

    Beethovan, Ludwig. Symphony No. 6, "Pastorale," Eugene Ormandy Philadelphia Orchestra.

Films:
Mutiny on the Bounty
Green Mansions
Lyric Poets

Partial Individualized Instruction

Another attempt to give greater attention to individualizing instruction is to use some large-group instruction in a team-teaching situation on certain days, with small-group and individualized instruction other days. This is a compromise between having traditional group instruction and individualized instruction. This approach has the advantage of releasing teachers during the time the large-group instruction is taking place to better prepare and organize materials. When this method is used, there is no reason why the students can't be taught on an individualized basis when the group is broken down into smaller ones. One danger in this approach is that the large-group instruction may be overemphasized.

In schools such as Nova in Florida it has been found that total individualized instruction particularly in some subject areas was considered undesirable by the majority of students. When consulted, the students, for example in social studies, indicated that they wished some large-group instruction for the purpose of dicussions, group investiga-

What is the best use of resources in individualized instruction?

tions, films, etc. When the instruction accordingly was altered to approximately 80 percent individualized and 20 percent group instruction, the students did as much work during their individualized time as they had done previously when their total time was devoted to self-pacing instruction.

With some individuals, particularly those with high social talent, potential total individualized instruction may inhibit their development. Then too, if a school or a teacher decides to operate only an individualized system, the opportunity of experimenting with other possibly effective modes of instruction such as the Taba Inductive approach or synectics is eliminated. It seems reasonable, therefore, that most individualized approaches should be partial and remain flexible depending, of course, upon the subject. After all, man is a social animal and what we know about teen-agers indicates that they have strong group peer orientations. To ignore this totally is to fail to meet the needs of the social talents of your students and invites greater discipline hazards.

Gifted Students

Traditional economics held that a country was richly endowed if it was rich in raw materials. This outlook was modified when it was realized that some countries lacking rich resources, such as Japan and Switzerland, have a comparatively high standard of living. These countries are rich because they possess one of the most important resources—creative and gifted manpower. A country's survival and development is dependent upon its caliber of manpower. This is most apparent in modern technology. In order to maintain a high standard of living, more and more raw material must be withdrawn from poorer raw resources. The genius of the scientist and technologist must be brought to bear in order to accomplish such a feat. It is primary, if we are to maintain our standard of living with an increasing population and decreasing raw materials, that we utilize to a greater extent our potential of gifted manpower.

Educators and national leaders aware of the importance of this have for many years endeavored to discover and offer special enrichments for the gifted students. In large schools special classes for the gifted have been devised, or individual attention has been given to gifted individuals in regular classes. Many extracurricular activities have been specially designed for the gifted and have been supported by school districts, business, industry, and state and federal governments.

Gifted students—or, as some psychologists and educators prefer to call them, the academically talented—are generally defined as individuals who are in at least the top 20 percent of their class and have an I.Q. above 120. They are good in reading and abstract reasoning, spatial visualization, memorization, ability to apply knowledge, and persistence in solving problems.

Business, Industry, and Universities Support Gifted Students' Programs

Business and industry, because of the wide concern for improving the quality of the manpower supply and a greater realization of community responsibility, have fostered many programs for the gifted student. Often these have been developed in cooperation with the public schools or with a professional group.

Summer Work Experience

Many school districts offer special programs for the gifted during the summer. Often these students are assigned work experience with some company. The participating industries attempt to match students with specific jobs in their plants that will be highly stimulating.

New York City formed a committee to help gifted students obtain work experience during the summer. The employed gifted students were usually given preliminary lectures about the plant in which they were going to work and then assigned to a member of the professional staff. Each student received a modest salary plus considerable help and guidance from the staff. The general program has met with wide acceptance and has been enlarged since its inauguration.

Surplus Equipment and Sponsors

In addition to the activities mentioned above, business and industry have made surplus equipment available to schools and have provided mathematicians, computer specialists, scientists and engineers to act as consultants for gifted students working on research projects. Many Chambers of Commerce and local branches of the National Association of Manufacturers have now appointed educational representatives from their membership. When contacted these individuals endeavor to meet requests for consultants, speakers, surplus equipment, or other services that the members of their organization can provide.

Extracurricular School Programs

There are many extracurricular programs sponsored through the schools for the academic, artistic, musical, and mechanically talented. Model

United Nation programs, speech contests, debating teams, essay contests, school publications of artistic work and creative writing, musical recitals, and future teacher clubs are only a few of the activities, many of which are particularly appealing to the academically gifted individual.

Science and Mathematics Nights and Days

Some schools may sponsor science fairs or foster science and mathematics nights or days. The types of activities presented at these night or day programs may be similar to those found in science fairs, the only difference being that more students may be involved and that the students may be present to demonstrate or explain their projects or work. Science fairs have been criticized for emphasizing the dramatic or the "showy" part of science rather than experimentation. Visiting school nights (or days) have been an attempt to get away from this by having students present to explain the purpose of their research. Participation in these programs usually has not been limited to talented students and should not be. Students of varying ability and from various classes should be represented so that the public understands the effort of these departments to encourage the learning of science and mathematics regardless of the student's capability. It is, however, natural for faculty to emphasize the accomplishment of their best students and give them some special recognition.

Inner-City Programs

Many schools in the inner city with the help of grants from the federal government, local business, industry, unions, and universities have fostered special programs for those interested in the sciences, medical professions, and other occupations. For example, Manual High School, Denver, Colorado, a school with a black population of over 90 percent, has a special program operating in cooperation with the Colorado University Medical Center. Twenty-five students are bused to the Medical Center each morning where they receive special lecture demonstrations, tours, and work experience. In the afternoon, they return to their high school for regular class instruction. During the summer many of these students are employed by the Center. The purpose of the program is to try to interest and prepare more individuals from minority groups to go into the medical fields. Another popular project has been one in which students in cooperation with and sponsored by the construction unions completely build houses for sale in the community.

Adjusting Instruction for Individual Variation

Advanced Placement Programs for the Academically Talented

School programs for the academically talented usually consist of special classes, the general pattern of which includes more advanced subject courses or seminars. The Advanced Placement Program is specifically designed for this purpose. It consists of college-type courses offered on the high school level.[2] The program is operated by the College Entrance Examination Board, a nonprofit organization founded in 1900. Its purpose is to encourage college level courses for advanced students in high school, make suggestions for these, provide examinations, and urge colleges to grant credit to freshmen who have completed such work. Most colleges recognize these and accept a completed course for college credit.

Small Schools

Small high schools seldom are able to offer special classes for the gifted. They have, however, encouraged students to do course work more or less on their own. The procedure is usually to have one or two students study a film series by television instruction, read texts and do research. The students may not have direct supervision, although an instructor meets with them from time to time to discuss their work and assignments. This plan has the advantage of developing more self-direction and responsibility on the part of the students, and gifted students usually respond well to this type of operation.

Activities of Professional Groups for the Academically Talented

Many professional societies and agricultural associations are actively interested in improving instruction. They may conduct seminars, sponsor special conferences, or provide liaison personnel for school systems to help students. Most states, for example, have academies of science. A part of the program sponsored by these academies is the Junior Academy in which outstanding science and mathematics students in the secondary schools, who are members of the Junior Academy, are invited to the conventions of the state academy where a time is set aside for the junior members to report their research. The agricultural associations sponsor and encourage the development of Future Farmers of America

---

[2]College Entrance Examination Board, *A Guide to the Advanced Placement Program*, 1964-65 (Berkeley, Calif., 1964), p. 4

clubs in the high schools. Provision is made for boys and girls of this and similar groups to display the accomplishments of their projects in state fairs.

Academically Poor and the Culturally Deprived Students

Educators have become increasingly concerned about what the school does for the academically poor student. There are a number of reasons why students do not do well in school: they may come from disadvantaged homes; have low academic potential; or have the potential but, for emotional and other reasons, underachieve. This group does not include the mentally retarded. The slow learners are usually defined as having an I.Q. under 90 and not achieving above the fiftieth percentile on the DAT Verbal Reasoning and Numerical Ability Tests. This group of individuals would fall within the lower 20 percent of student population. However, this is a national figure; in socially and economically deprived district schools over 50 percent of the students may be in this category, whereas in an upper socioeconomic area the proportion of students in this category may be less than 5 percent.

Students in the lower 20 percent of the student population do not achieve well in the traditional courses. These individuals often do not do well in school because they lack verbal fluency making it difficult for them to read and write. However, when instruction is activity-centered and reading is deemphasized, they often achieve many of the objectives of a course through the use of their other talents. It is important that teachers perceive these valuable humans—with mechanical, social, artistic, and athletic talents—as valuable and capable individuals and work through and reward the strengths of their talents. There are volumes of research indicating that when an individual begins to participate in athletics, in by far the majority of cases, his academic achievement increases. When teachers look upon a person as being valuable he usually returns value. Teachers have had an academically slow student help them get their cars to run when they failed. Who was slow then? When you look for the student's talents and strive to kindle them, the student's belief in himself changes. He begins to believe more in himself, that he can control his fate, and it is this that may cause him to try harder to develop better his less gifted talents such as reading and writing.

Adjusting Instruction for Individual Variation

Suggested Teaching Activities for Individual Differences

Listed below are some suggestions on how to give better individual attention in teaching. The list is not exhaustive; a wise and creative teacher unafraid to experiment with new approaches will undoubtedly discover many more.

1. *Individualize* the class instruction as suggested in the first part of the chapter.
2. Encourage students to *make an extra-credit file*. Allow students to include in it reports about all types of activities in which they participate. For each project the student should place in the folder a note about what he learned. Reports about the following might be included: (a) Completion of some "programmed" material. Presently many companies are producing programs and teaching machines for many subject areas. Since a student can progress through these at his own rate, they allow for individual differences. (b) Newspaper articles, journals, and books. (c) Resolution of some problem or experiment. These can be library, community, laboratory and other field problems. (d) Making a collection—classifying and keying the items in it. (e) Special demonstrations presented to the class. (f) Special additional experiments done at home, in the field, or in the laboratory. (g) Trips to museums, planetariums, observatories, parks, or research facilities. (h) A summary of an educational-television program. (i) Participation in fairs and other educationally related programs.
3. *Individualize class assignments* whereby the students progress at their own rates and at the end of the period hand in what they have accomplished. This may be laboratory assignments or written assignments.
4. *Extend special recognition to a student who goes beyond a minimum acceptance level* for doing and formulating investigations for the manifestations of his various talents.
5. *Use multiple resources* including cassette teacher-prepared tapes and texts in class. If a slow student has difficulty reading one text, endeavor to find another or attempt to have him learn the material in ways other than through books, such as by tapes and/or 35mm slides.

6. *Encourage talented students to do research, investigations, creative work, organize activities.* Have talented students from the upper grades go to some of the lower grades and perform some educational activity. This technique is especially appreciated by junior high school students who enjoy watching students from the upper grades with high status present activities. This approach also has the advantage of giving recognition to students and motivating them to greater achievement and the manifestation of their various talents.
7. *Encourage parents* to obtain books, take trips, and discuss educational topics with their children. Parents often welcome a suggestion from the teacher about books and types of trips to help enrich their children's education.

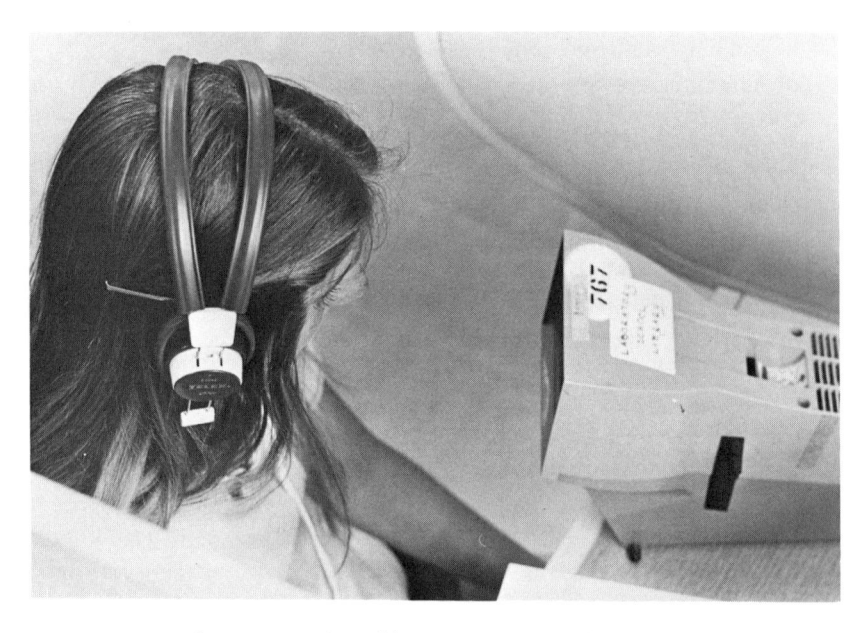

What part is played by equipment and materials in individualized instruction?

Pacs

Many of the schools using individualized approaches have constructed "pacs" for students to use. UNIPACS, for example, are produced under the direction of Teacher UNIPAC Exchange, 1653 Forest Hills Drive, Salt Lake City, Utah, 84106. These pacs are prepared by classroom teachers. Instructors interested in learning to write them can obtain help and direction through correspondence with this center. If an instructor submits a pac to their bank, he then has access to others from it.

Recognition

Secondary school teachers often have given too little consideration to the importance of recognizing achievement and multi-talent. They should learn from their colleagues, the coaches. Coaches award pins, blankets, cups, and ribbons; see that the activities of their teams are publicized; and put on athletic shows. They are masters in the techniques of giving and getting recognition. All students, not only athletes, like to receive some recognition for their work. An instructor should utilize the techniques of public relations and adapt these methods for giving recognition for achievement in his subject. Write-ups in the local newspapers and school paper on what is happening in your subject field are as important to the student involved in it as the sports page is to the athlete. Display cases containing student projects, club pins, letter blocks similar to the athletic letter ones worn on sweaters, plaques, and certificates are all forms of recognition used by schools. Creative, well-trained teachers will find many ways to enhance students' self-concepts by the use of proper recognition. Excellent teachers use varied methods of giving recognition, and the end result of their efforts is a contribution to better learning. How wonderful it must be to a student to be able to progress according to his ability, not devalued but given recognition for contributing as best he can.

Summary

Students come to the classroom with varied backgrounds and experiences. They differ cognitively, affectively, in the development of their multi-talents and in several other ways which makes them uniquely different humans. Schools usually have not given much attention to these differences because of high costs, poor facilities, and poor equipment. In spite of these problems, many schools are endeavoring to change the traditional pattern of instruction. Individualized instruction, continuous-progress, and open classrooms are operating successfully in many schools. In individualized instruction a student works according to his ability at his own rate; he remains in the class throughout the semester or year. In the continuous-progress organization a student stays in a class until he has finished the required number of units. He may finish an entire year's work in a matter of weeks; if so, he takes another subject. In the open school, the student completes several units of work, the selection of many of which may arise out of his interests. After completing and demonstrating competence in various areas he graduates. Some schools have taught for individualized differences by making film courses available. These are often arranged on a seminar basis, or there may be extra laboratory sessions to supplement the film instruction. Students view these film courses several times if they wish to.

The advent of new curriculum developments and a wealth of educational materials, including self-pacing programmed aids and pacs, has made it possible for teachers more easily to adapt classes for individualized instruction. One problem, however, in making the transition to individualized approaches is that the teacher must become mainly an organizer and a facilitator rather than a teller. Many teachers because of their traditional role find this difficult to do.

Educators and government, professional, business, and industrial leaders have become concerned about motivating the gifted student, particularly if he is from a minority group. As a result of this concern, several programs have been specifically sponsored for these students, including special seminars, work experiences, summer institutes, scholarships, congresses, junior academies, advanced placement programs, special materials, science and mathematics days and nights, and fairs. Greater efforts are also being made to help the culturally deprived and academically slow learners. This group constitutes about 20 percent of the student population nationally, numbering several millions.

There are numerous, diverse activities that can be used to teach for individual differences. These may include—in addition to total individualized instruction—programmed instruction; use of pacs; book reports; written reports; collecting; performing special demonstrations or experiments; reports about trips to museums, planetariums, observatories, or research facilities; special studies of live areas; reports of research; production of a newspaper and other creative work; and participation in fairs, school nights or other extracurricular nights.

Recognition should be given for student accomplishment and the manifestation *of all human talents*. By being rewarded, individuals are more likely to gain positive self-concepts, thereby increasing belief in their ability to be successful in areas other than those receiving recognition. There should be, therefore, an active public-relations program in the school and community emphasizing achievement in various subjects, including scholarships and awards of all types for outstanding achievement.

Further Investigation and Study

1. Suppose that you are head of a large, fairly traditional department in a large metropolitan high school. What would you do to get the department to teach more effectively for individual differences?
2. What is the difference between individualized instruction, continuous-progress, open school concept, and grouping? Which of these do you think is the best approach and why?
3. Describe a class designed for individual achievement. Assume that the class has thirty students.
4. Why hasn't there been more attention given to individual differences?
5. How does the traditional role of the teacher change in teaching for individual differences?
6. What are the advantages of individualized instruction in science?
7. How have the modern curriculum developments contributed to the possibility of better individualized instruction?
8. What are some of the ways in which you would try to give the gifted student a better education?
9. What would you do for the academically slow learner?
10. What kind of teachers do slow learners and students from minority groups require?
11. What is done in some of the small high schools to teach more effectively for individual differences?
12. In what ways has the government tried to improve the education of the gifted and the economically and academically deprived?
13. In what ways have businesses tried to improve instruction for the gifted?
14. If you were going to provide a gifted-student course in your subject, what would you do?
15. Suppose you are a supervisor convinced little is being done for the slow learner. You are responsible for instruction in five high schools and eight junior high schools. What would you do to improve instruction for the academically poor student?
16. How would you design a class situation to give recognition to individual variation?
17. How would you maximize the development of all human talents in your classes?

10 Creativity—The Way to "Being" More Human

Abraham H. Maslow in the late 1930's was struck by the realization that modern psychology, to a large degree, was based on the study of sick individuals, which he thought gave a limited perception of man. He, therefore, set about to study the mentally healthiest individuals he could find. At first, he carried out rather extensive interviews observing how these people live and act. Slowly, he realized that mentally healthy individuals have a number of characteristics in common. They are very active people, dedicated to something they believe in and are very much involved in their commitments. Eventually, Maslow characterized them as being "self-actualized." This means that they have the will to and do use to the best of their ability their maximum human potential.

One of Dr. Maslow's students, Richard Craig, became interested in correlating creative human characteristics with those of self-actualized individuals. He found the overlap was very high. Maslow concluded from this and other work that anything that would contribute to improving a person's creativity would also affect positively his mental health.[1] From research of this nature, he argues that all teachers, rather than just a few, and all courses should strive to develop creative ability.

---
[1]Abraham H. Maslow, *The Farther Reaches of Human Nature* (New York: Viking Press, 1971), p. 73.

By so doing, students will move toward greater self-actualization and consequent mental health. He says in this respect:

> And why should not every course help toward creativeness? Certainly this kind of education of the person should help create a better type of person, help a person grow bigger, taller, wiser, more perceptive a person who, incidentally, would be more creative as a matter of course in all departments of life.[2]

Definition of Creativity

A number of other psychologists during the 1960's and early 1970's have become increasingly concerned about creativity. They have endeavored to define, characterize, and develop it, all with various degrees of success. A leader in this endeavor has been Dr. Paul Torrance. He says:

> I have chosen to define creative thinking as the process of sensing gaps or disturbing missing elements; forming ideas or hypotheses; and communicating the results, possibly modifying and retesting the hypotheses.[3]

Creativity is generally thought of in two ways. Some believe it should be restricted to the production of a new entity or idea never before known to man. Others have a more inclusive definition including all productive endeavors unique to the individual. This latter view is the more useful for teachers trying to develop creative ability and helping individuals to self-actualize.

Creative Abilities [4]

Psychological research has revealed that creative abilities may be separated into the following categories:

---

[2]Abraham H. Maslow, "A Holistic Approach to Creativity," in *Climate for Creativity*, Calvin W. Taylor, ed. (New York: Pergamon Press, 1972), p. 289.
[3]Paul Torrance, *Guiding Creative Talent* (Englewood Cliffs, N.J.: Prentice-Hall, Inc., 1962), p. 16.
[4]For greater elaboration of these see: Sidney J. Parnes paper, "Programming Creative Behavior," in *Climate for Creativity*, Calvin W. Taylor, ed. (New York: Pergamon Press, 1972), p. 198.

1. *Fluency*—Proposes many similar ideas for a problem.
2. *Flexibility*—Produces many different classes of ideas for a problem.
3. *Originality*—Gives responses uniquely different from other people.
4. *Elaboration*—States many details related to the creative response indicating how it may be constructed, implemented, etc.
5. *Sensitivity*—Generates many problems in response to a situation.

Review the above list again. What questions would you ask to stimulate the development of each of these abilities for the subject you teach?

Characteristics of Creative Individuals

Creative individuals vary in motivational, intellectual, and personality traits. Individuals with creative potential can be most easily recognized by the following characteristics:

1. Curiosity. This probably is one of the easiest signs by which a teacher can discover creative individuals.
2. Resourcefulness.
3. Desire to discover.
4. Preference for difficult tasks.
5. Enjoyment in solving problems.
6. Drive and dedication to work.
7. Flexible thinking.
8. Responds to questions and has habit of giving more answers to questions than do most students.
9. Ability to synthesize and see new implications.
10. Pronounced spirit of inquiry.
11. Breadth of reading background.

In addition to the above, the creatively talented have a marked ability to form abstractions, analyze, and synthesize information. They demonstrate persistent and sustained concentration and are usually sensitive and individualistic. Given freedom as well as direction, creative students often surprise the instructor with their capabilities and interests.

HAVE FUN BEING CREATIVE:
What Could You Produce from the Above?

Predictions of Creative Ability: I.Q. and Teacher's Grades

Considerable research has been done on the identification of creative individuals. Such research indicates that I.Q. tests generally do not reveal creative ability and are, in fact, not good instruments for this purpose. Traditional measures of intelligence generally evaluate only a few of an individual's abilities. Dr. Paul Torrance states, "If we were to identify the children as gifted on the basis of intelligence tests, we would thereby eliminate approximately 70 percent of the most creative."[5] He says further, "If the intellectual capacities of the individual are to be fully developed, the abilities involved in creative thinking cannot be ignored. The traditional measures of intelligence attempt to assess only a few of man's intellectual talents."[6] Because traditional tests do not reveal creative potential, psychologists have devised a number of tests which attempt to identify creative ability on the junior high and high school level.

Although creativity and intelligence do not necessarily have a high correlation, there is some indication that very creative professional individuals do have high intelligence. Ann Roe found that the minimum intelligence required for creative production in science was higher than the average I.Q.[7]

Attempts to identify creative individuals by the use of school grades generally have been unsuccessful. Grades are usually given in school for mastery of information, and Taylor reports that "sheer mastery of knowledge does not seem to be a sufficient condition for creative performance." He found, in studying creative scientists, a low correlation between academic achievement in school and production in industry.[8] MacKennon, professor at the University of California, in studying adults with outstanding creative ability found that the majority received "C's" and "B's" in school rather than "A's". The fact that creative students did not obtain high grades indicates that schools either have not recognized this ability or have not rewarded it.

Hutchinson, professor at the University of Utah, studied two methods of teaching, using the same group of students. In the first half of the school year, students in some classes were taught by the "receive and reproduce" method while those in the other classes were involved in the "think and reproduce" approach. In the second half of the year, these methods were switched for each of these groups. In evaluating the students under these methods, he found generally those with high achievement under one approach did not do well in the other. Students who memorize and reproduce are not the good thinkers.[9] Mueller in reviewing the problem of whether the schools can foster creativity states that there is:

---

[5]Torrance, *Guiding Creative Talent*, pp. 4-5.
[6]*Ibid*.
[7]"The Psychology of the Scientist," *Science*, Vol. 134 (August 18, 1961): 56-59. Copyright 1961 by the American Association for the Advancement of Science.
[8]Calvin Taylor, *Creativity: Progress and Potential* (New York: McGraw-Hill Book Co., 1964), pp. 110-111.
[9]Discussed in Calvin Taylor, "Creativity and Science Education," *News and Views*, Vol. VII, No. 4 (December, 1963): 1.

Creativity—The Way to "Being" More Human

> A formidable paradox in current research on creativity in the classroom: studies of the creative process stress the view that truly creative minds are invariably free minds—free to make choices and hold convictions in the face of society's restraints. Yet the public schools are a myriad of controls and forces that necessarily restrict the learner to culturally prescribed and approved learning tasks.[10]

Frank Barron, a leader in creative research, says in this respect:

> One of the most provocative findings in recent research on creativity in children is that the school system itself has a dampening effect on spontaneity and originality.[11]

However, Barron stresses that this need not be the case. He goes on to say:

> There is no doubt at all that school can be made a most diverting, happy, and creative experience.[12]

Research in Creativity: Implications for the School

An accumulation of psychological research in the field of creativity has attracted the attention of educators to the problem of improving the possibilities for manifestation of creative ability in the secondary schools. Findings of this research are:

1. *All people of all ages and races are creative* to some extent.
2. *Individuals differ considerably in the degree of their creative ability* and expression.
3. *Freedom to be creative has an effect on mental health.* Torrance emphasizes this point further when he says:

   > Scattered evidence from a variety of sources leaves little question but that the stifling of creative desires and abilities cuts at the very roots of satisfaction in living and ultimately creates overwhelming tension and breakdown. There is little doubt that one's creativity is an in-

---

[10]Richard J. Mueller, "Can the Public School Foster Creativity?" *Saturday Review* (December 19, 1964), p. 48.

[11]Frank Barron, "Travels in Search of New Latitudes for Innovation," in *Climate for Creativity*. Calvin Taylor, ed. (New York: Pergamon Press, Inc., 1972), p. 53.

[12]*Ibid.*

valuable resource in coping with life's daily stresses, thus making breakdown less likely.[13]

4. *Students can learn more effectively in a creative situation.* Taylor says in this respect,

> Recent experiments have suggested that many things can be learned more economically in a creative situation than in an authoritarian one and that some people who learn little by authority can learn much creatively.[14]

5. *Some schools have been particularly successful in developing creative talent.*
6. *Outstanding creative individuals in society often were not high academic achievers* in school.
7. For schools to be effective in developing creative endeavor, they have to *provide an environment conducive* for its manifestation.
8. *Overuse of positive reinforcement* in class discussions may inhibit creative responses by students.
9. *Longer wait-time contributes to creativity.* As was pointed out in Chapter 4, there is a high correlation between the nature of questions asked by an instructor and a student's creative responses. The types of questions a teacher asks, the time he waits for answers, and the role of reward has much to do with creative production in class.

Research in questioning procedures indicates there is a high correlation between intelligence and creativity measures on tests as long as the students are not allowed very much time to respond. This correlation, however, drops to insignificance when students are not time restricted. Mary Budd Rowe, in analyzing the time allowed students to respond to questions, found if teachers waited on an average of five seconds compared to their normal one second of wait-time the students:
   1. did more speculative thinking
   2. made better inferences
   3. changed their judgment of who was a slow student.[15]

---

[13]From *Creativity: Progress and Potential* edited by Calvin Taylor. Copyright 1964 McGraw-Hill Book Co. Used with permission of McGraw-Hill Book Co.

[14]Taylor, p. 53. Used with permission of McGraw-Hill Book Co.

[15]Mary Budd Rowe, "Wait-Time and Rewards as Instructional Variables: Influence on Inquiry and Sense and Fate Control." Prepared for the symposium at Kiel, Germany, September, 1970. Unpublished paper, New Science in the Inner City, Teachers College, Columbia University.

What is the relationship among creativity, interest, and self-concept?

Early Development of Creative Potential

Research indicates that creative potential will not manifest itself well in adult life unless the individual encounters early, stimulating environments. Dr. Hess has experimented with rats to determine how experience affects later behavior.[16] He took two groups of rats and blindfolded one group from infancy. He allowed the other group to develop from infancy to three months without blindfolds. Then he blindfolded them. Both of these groups were then allowed to run free in cages containing a number of objects. At the age of five months the two groups of rats were confronted with maze problems. The group which had not been blindfolded until three months achieved significantly greater success in solving maze problems.

[16]Robert D. Hess, "The Latent Resources of the Child's Mind," *Journal of Research in Science Teaching*, Issue I, Vol. 1 (1963): 21.

Dr. Hess did another experiment in which he took one group of rats home and raised them as pets. They were allowed to run about the house a considerable amount of time. The other group was left at the laboratory in cages. After several weeks, tests were given the rats. The performance of the rats raised as pets was significantly higher than that of the laboratory rats on ability tests. Other research in anatomy and biochemistry on similar groups of animals indicated that those with enriched experiences showed an increase in cortical tissue and in the cholinesterase activity of the brain.[17] Dr. Hess states the implications of his research as follows:

> (1) There is reason to believe that the potentialities of the human mind as genetically determined do not unfold naturally and inevitably, but require active participation of a stimulating environment in order to attain normal development. (2) It is important that this stimulation occur as early as possible in the child's experience. (3) The range and variety of early experience directly affected the possibilities of later learning and set limits to the flexibility and adeptness of the adult mind by limiting or expanding the network of concepts, meanings, and symbols through which the individual experiences his world. (4) The early deprivation of suitable stimulation probably results in some permanent loss of mental ability. (5) One of the primary purposes of elementary school education is the maximizing of mental capabilities by systematic stimulation and exercise of mental faculties.[18]

Although what Dr. Hess has to say pertains directly to the elementary school, it also has relevance to junior high and high school education. The research reported above clearly indicates the role teachers should play. Teachers have the responsibility to insure that students have numerous opportunities to develop their creative faculties in order to unleash dormant creative potentials.

The Stimulating Creative Class Environment

Jack R. Gibb in working with various types of businesses, industries, and governmental agencies has found that creativity within the organization can be enhanced by increasing trust, free communication, and self-de-

---

[17]Edward L. Bennet et al., "Chemical and Anatomical Pascity of the Brain," Science, 146 (October 30, 1964), pp. 610-19.
[18]Hess, p. 21.

termination, and decreasing control.[19] How Gibb's ideas might be adapted for teaching is briefly outlined below.

Enhancing the Release of Creativity

1. Develop high trust and reduce fear.	Indicate that you trust students to be productive, don't censor ideas, show less disapproval.
2. Encourage a free flow of communication.	Encourage creative work from all students. Strive to develop the idea that creativeness is an excellent way of behaving for all the members of your class. Be open and accepting of student suggestions.
3. Allow self-determination of goals and self-assessment.	Consult students on what they are interested in and what it is they would like to do. You may present ideas but students are encouraged to accept or reject these and determine their own if they choose.
	Don't grade creative work. Encourage students to evaluate their work, e.g. how they may alter it in the future if they choose, etc.
	Don't make statements as to what is good or bad. Ask what other ideas arose from producing something creative. Ask how the works of the class differ. Encourage students to assess their work, not from the point of view of its being good or bad but from the viewpoint of what it was they were trying to do, how they did it, and what, if anything, they might wish to change.

---

[19]Jack R. Gibb, "Managing for Creativity in the Organization," in *Climate for Creativity*, Calvin Taylor, ed. (New York: Pergamon Press, Inc., 1972), pp. 23-32.

4. Insure that control is not tight.	Do not require conformity for your own and student behavior, e.g. "Let's all make a pot." Encourage students to experiment with work and various learning procedures. Encourage and accept conflict and disagreement with your ideas. Give high priority to diversity and creativity over conformity.

Gibb has found that creative managers and/or teachers are individuals who believe that people are self-motivated and responsible on their own, likely to be creative if restraints are removed, work best when they set their goals, and manifest fantastic potential when allowed to do so.

Rewarding Creativity in the Classroom

Rewarding creativity by grades may inhibit a class's creative production. Gibb worked with a large governmental agency to determine the effect of giving rewards for creative work. Through systematic interviews over a prolonged period of time he found that workers rewarded for creative endeavor were more likely to hoard ideas and were cautious about sharing them. He further found that supervisors gave ideas to workers under them who then submitted these and split the rewards. This was done because management assumed that the supervisors would, as a normal course of their work, submit procedures for improving the organization without receiving extra financial reward. Gibb states that rewarding creative endeavor actually tends to develop deceit, deception, and reduced communication between individuals so necessary for stimulating creative excitement and zest.

Although rewarding creative enterprise, for example, by good grades, on the surface seems desirable, in fact it may be detrimental to the productivity of the class. Gibb further found that students who were rewarded by grades for creative production tended more to behave for the purpose of getting grades than for learning [20] Grading may further impose a system of extrinsic or external rather than intrinsic or internal rewards. The real and lasting reward for producing something creative comes from the internal self-realization that "I can be crea-

[20] Gibb, p. 27.

Creativity—The Way to "Being" More Human 215

tive." It's very self-satisfying to the individual to discover and know he has this human ability.

Individuals who are grade motivated may cease to be productive once the external rewards are no longer present. On the other hand, the individuals who reap the intrinsic rewards of creative self-discovery are more likely to continue their creative activities and learn throughout their lives.

Methods for Developing Creative Talent

To teach for creativity you will have to be creative in the methods and assignments you devise. Unfortunately, if you are a typical student or teacher you probably have not had many creative instructors to model yourself after. If you do encounter one, analyze what he does and endeavor to develop similar capabilities.

Other than providing the proper environment as suggested by Gibb, there are certain specific teaching techniques instructors may use to stimulate creative enterprise. Creative questioning, as outlined in Chapter 4 on Questioning and Listening, is basic to becoming a more

How do you think the teacher stimulated creative activity in this class?

creative teacher. Most of the following activities hinge on the teacher asking questions requiring creative responses.

Questions That Stimulate Creative Abilities

As has been pointed out earlier in the chapter, there are different types of abilities that have been defined as creative behaviors. Outlined below are examples of questions teachers might ask to encourage the development by students of each of these behaviors.

Creative Questioning

Type of Creative Ability	Example of Questions Teachers Might Ask and Possible Student Responses
1. *Fluency* (Pose many similar ideas for one problem)	Teacher: What ways can you use this barbed wire to convey your feelings? Student Response: Twist and turn it into a shape of hands lifted upward to show a feeling of "reaching out," make a statue showing contentment, etc.
2. *Flexibility* (Generate many different classes of ideas outside the usual category for a problem)	Teacher: What unusual ways can you use a clothes hanger? Student Response: Use it for a skewer, to make a fence, to make a cage for animals, to make picture hangers, guides for plants.
3. *Originality* (Give responses unique or statistically uncommon from those proposed by other individuals)	Teacher: What ways can you use a clothes hanger? Student Response: Place several of them together and mold them to form a model of a heart. Place them on the bottom of shoes to protect the leather.

Creativity—The Way to "Being" More Human

4. *Elaboration*
 (Give many details that spell out an idea)

 Teacher: What ways can you use a clothes hanger?
 Student Response: Make it into a mobile by cutting into three, six, or eight pieces of varying lengths and then stringing these together. Hang small rockets down from parts of the hanger.

5. *Sensitivity*
 (Sense problems from a situation)

 Teacher: From what you have read in this report, book, or seen in this film, etc., what are all the problems that come to your mind?
 Student responds by enumerating several problems.

Another way to insure that you develop your creative questioning ability is to ask questions allowing for divergent response and requiring certain types of creative thought processes as illustrated below:

Creative Mental Processes

	Teacher Question
1. Originate problems	What do you think is the problem? (See others above)
2. Formulate hypotheses	What do you think will happen if . . . ?
3. Design an investigation or experiment	How could you go about finding out?
4. Infer	What do you think is the significance of . . . or what does this data indicate?
5. Evaluate an experiment, research, mathematical problem, artistic production, etc., and tell how to modify and improve it.	What do you like about . . . ? If you were going to do . . . ? what would you do differently?

	If you were going to repeat or redo the problem, experiment, etc., what would you do?
6. Invent new uses for objects	What are all the things you could make out of . . . or what are all the ways you could use . . . ?
7. Develop new approaches	What are all the new ways or approaches you can think of for resolving the problem, situation, etc.?
8. Produce orginal art, literature, dance, musical forms, etc.	How would you convey the feeling, message, view, etc. of . . . ?
9. Communicate uniquely, e.g., in reporting or summarizing	What would be the best way to convey . . . to be sure that individuals understood its message?
10. Produce analogies	What are all the ways you can think of that this is like . . . ?

As you become more proficient as a creative teacher, you will probably discover other general types of questions. These should be added to the above list.

Creative Listening

Students generally are taught in school to listen mainly for the purpose of memorizing or recalling information. They should, however, also be encouraged to listen creatively. This means using listening to spark their imaginations, such as listening to a poem, story, historical presentation, or music and then becoming involved in conveying its meaning in different ways or using it to leap in thought to new ideas. Students also may be asked to attend to the ordinary, for example, sounds of the steet, something falling and hitting the floor, the ocean, noises in the community, sounds in a forest or park, and then be asked to pick out the unusual or a little known aspect of what they hear. They may also be asked to encourage free associations as they listen; for example, students can listen to Paul Horn's recording made in the Taj Mahal and then express the thoughts flowing from their minds.

Creativity-Synectics

William J.J. Gordon and his colleagues have produced an approach for stimulating creative talents called Synectics.[21] Gorden believes creative processes of thought can be described, developed, and generalized to most subject areas including both the arts and sciences. He further thinks that the emotional and irrational components of the creative enterprise are initially more importatnt than the intellectual and rational ones. Many of the early activities of the synectics system include, therefore, non-rational group interplay. These are followed by a pattern of instruction that eventually evolves into rational solutions and problems.

Synectics basically centers around students being invited to form three types of metaphors to gain different perceptions of a problem. These are used to break mental "structural-fixedness" or "psychological set" in looking at a problem thereby contributing to the stimulation of creative thought. The three forms are:

Types of Metaphors

1. Direct analogy—compares two objects.
2. Personal analogy—identifies with object, e.g., how would you feel if you were it?
3. Compressed conflict—two words describing phenomena that contradict each other.

In making direct analogies, students are mainly asked to compare two objects or concepts stating how they are similar. For example, they might be asked to compare the following:
1. A lawn mower with a pencil sharpener
2. Peace with love
3. A bicycle seat with a bird

After originating several metaphoric comparisons, the students are next invited to make personal analogies, in which they are asked to identify, with the object or concept—in other words, to become it. The teacher might ask: "How would you feel if you were a bicycle seat?" The students then list their various feelings. The teacher may use the enumer-

---

[21] Synectics Educational Systems, 121 Brattle Street, Cambridge, Mass. 02138.

ated personal analogies to form part of the next kind of metaphor—compressed conflict. In this type the students take one of their previous statements and give a contradiction or an opposite for it. These may in turn be used by the instructor to return the class to making direct analogies related to the original problem. Because of the nature of the sequence of this metamorphic involvement, the students now should perceive the problem in a far more diverse and creative manner.

These three metamorphic forms are used in the synectics curriculum in two general ways: (1) *for exploring something that is unfamiliar* or (2) for *creating something new*. The teaching procedures for each of these two purposes generally pass through phases as indicated below:

I. EXPLORING THE UNFAMILIAR TEACHING TECHNIQUE

1. Teacher or students provide information relative to the topic, e.g., about minorities.
2. Problem may be stated: What is it like to be a member of a minority group?
3. Students are asked to make *direct analogies* and list these, e.g., Being Black is like being a tornado, etc.
4. Student makes *personal analogies* and is asked to be one of the direct analogies—and "feel" being it, such as, How does it feel to be *like* a tornado?
5. Student selects one of these analogies, identifies with it, and compares it with one of the original direct analogies. Being Black is sometimes like a tornado in that you feel like a swirl of entrapped energy. Being Black is to be entrapped in a swirl of cultural energy.
6. Student explains where the analogy would not fit with other students' analogies. Being a tornado is not like being a martyr because: . . .
7. Students discuss their analogies as a means of investigating the topic further.
8. Students are asked to return to the original starting point of the problem to generate a new series of direct analogies. From these, they might write a short paragraph or essay stipulating their new creative insights into the topic.

Creativity—The Way to "Being" More Human

II. CREATING SOMETHING NEW TEACHING TECHNIQUE

1. Teacher or student presents topic area.
2. Students asked to describe it as they see it—the topic may be related to objects, concepts, personal, and social problems.
3. Problem or task is defined by students and/or teacher.
4. Students make and list *direct analogies*.
5. Students select one of the direct analogies and use it as a basis of a *personal analogy*.
6. Students use personal analogy for compressed conflict, e.g., feeling like a rejected person is like . . . but not . . . .
7. Students take one of these contradictions and use it for making a new *direct analogy*.
8. Students move back to original task using the last analogy or any of the others to better create new solutions or concepts related to the task.

Before using the above teaching strategies Gorden suggests that students should be involved in stretching exercises, which are introduced to the class "to warm them up" for making metaphors. For example, the teacher might ask students to respond in writing to the following:

"How is a sea shell like a holy place?"
"Imagine you are a young tree in a winter storm. Be the tree! How do you look and feel?"
"The Northern Lights are like: _____"

After the students have gained some confidence in doing these exercises the instructor may then begin the general synectics procedures as indicated above.

An example of how the synectics procedures may be used in the classroom is shown on the following page.

FEATURES OF SES MATERIALS

INTERDISCIPLINARY
(Social Studies/Science Example)

Roger Williams disagreed with the elders of the Massachusetts Bay Colony. Therefore, he and his followers moved away to what is now Rhode Island. This was typical of how the American colonies grew.

Below is a picture of how an amoeba looks when it is reproducing. HOW IS THE GROWTH OF THE AMERICAN COLONIES LIKE THE AMOEBA REPRODUCING? _____

| single amoeba | nucleus begins to divide | amoeba with two nuclei | two amoebas |

STUDENT CENTERED
(Builds on the Students' Knowledge & Experiences)

WHAT IN YOUR EXPERIENCE IS LIKE THE COLONIES OR THE AMOEBAS? _____
Explain your idea: _____

ANALYTICAL SKILLS

HOW IS YOUR CHOICE *UNLIKE* THE AMOEBA OR THE COLONIES? _____

CREATIVE ANALYSIS

WHO IS LONELIER? A SOLITARY COLONIST OR AN AMOEBA WITH ONLY ONE NUCLEUS? _____
Why do you feel that way? _____

Creativity—The Way to "Being" More Human

CREATIVE WRITING
(Non-fiction Example)

    Look back over what you have just written. On the lines below put your thoughts and connections into a short description of how you feel about the expansion of the American colonies in terms of the amoeba reproducing.

_____
_____
_____
_____
_____
_____
_____

An adaptation of the Synectics Approach, shown below, has been prepared by Shan Cunningham of the Experimental College at Minot State College:[22]

IDEAVENTURES IN COOPORTUNITY

(Another funfilled adventure with Synectics Man)

---

[22]Shan Cunningham, "Ideaventures in Cooportunity," The *Journal* of the Experimental College at Minot State College, Minot, North Dakota. April, 1973.

Our story opens with a typical E.C. class on a typical first day of a new quarter:

> Let's make plans.
> What should we do?
> How about reading some books?

We did that last time.
What a drag!
Boo!

> Wad-ja-do over quarter break?
> I'm bored.
> What time is it?

Let's get inta something.
Okay, let's decide.

> Wad-i-ya wanna do, man?

Suddenly, from out of the woodwork, a strange creature appears.

> What's that, man?
> A new student?

My long lost dog?
A strange visitor from another planet?

> Wow! Who's that farout dude?

STRANGE CREATURE INDEED! . . . IT'S SYNECTICS° MAN

> (Well, not really, of course.
> Actually it's Chester P. Faralant,
> third son of an itinerant chicken
> sexer from East Jesus, North Dakota,
> who has been magically transformed into
> a creative problem solver by mumbling
> the mystical names of Parnes, Prince,
> and Gordon.)

°Synectics: A new method of directing creative potential to the solution of technical and theoretical problems.

Here I come to save the day—SYNECTICS MAN is on his way!

STEP ONE: I need . . . (fill in the blank with whatever words, like, happen to you.)

Help	to be happy	trust	interaction
adventure	friendship	experience	old hats
to be awake	free	novelty	to look
activity	dumb	responsibility	to see
sunshine	advance notice	fun	continuity
reasons	food	information	sharing

Creativity—The Way to "Being" More Human

ideas	acceptance	education	discussion
direction	fulfillment	security	books
reminders	coffee	productivity	everything
direction	enthuisiasm	new words	people
cooperation	credit	new thoughts	reaction

STEP TWO: Is non-sense. I want you to put together new words by recombining all words from before, like:

lifeportunity	funsability	cotrust
ideaventures	trustability	helpexperience
chancaction	seebooks	cornbook
discussabooks	foodtime	peopleivity
helpways	richstruction	
allways	relaxaction	
cooportunity	credaplace	
trustafriend	flexaventure	
directionshine	enthusability	

STEP THREE: O.K. Let's break it there and go on to the next step. This time make up word phrases from the non-sense words.

enthusability experience	self-wakeability
to see lifeportunity	sharing selfdom
popcorn people	trust-a-friend reaction
to see nude thoughts	self-instruction security
understand cornbooks	self-information cooperation
nude flexipuncture thoughts	new word funshine
sharing funshine	understand Rich-instruction
popjobeducation	hairy production
fulfillability experience	new ways education
nude freedom reaction	cooportunity experience

STEP FOUR: Now make sentences out of the word phrases.

Self-instruction security may mean novel life security and hairy producivity.

Can popcorn people stand the heat of sharing shunshine?

Sharing selfdom through trustafriend reaction.

Create fulfillability experience by rich people interaction.

Trust new ways of self-education.

To see lifeportunity, you must have self-waketivity and self-trustability.

New ways of education allow food time flexibility.

People and feedback sharing sunshine produce cooportunity experience.

Lifefreedom enthusiasm can lead to self-instruction.

STEP FIVE: O.K. Let's leave that alone for awhile. Go back to the non-sense words and select the ones you like.

self-sharing
standication
flexication
funshine
ideaventures
enthusability
cooportunity

STEP SIX: Next, select one of those words that we can work with:
IDEAVENTURE

O.K. Our aim is to answer this question: In what ways can this class be an IDEAVENTURE? Why is it important to you to answer this question?

1. We want to create and share enthusiasm.
   WHY?
   2. We want to lead ourselves to learning.
      WHY?
      3. We want to become independent.
         WHY?
         4. We want to become self-fulfilling.
            WHY?
            5. We want to become more secure with ourselves.

STEP SEVEN: Now decide which of those statements best fits your needs:

"In what ways can I become self-fulfilling?"

Fill in the blank: To become self-fulfilling, I should _____

walk
evaluate continually
go to the park
ask questions
ride bikes
solve a community problem
read a book
look for new things in old things
share perceptions about a book
take a trip and ask questions
do a book with writing and pictures and expose it to feedback

build things
draw pictures
be quiet and hear myself
use a telescope
go out under the dome and share perceptions
let a child lead you
plan a place
spend a day communicating without words
break a habit
study all night
meet for a whole day or week
build or fly a kite
train a dog, or a frog
sleep under the dome
plant trees to sit under
paint a wagon

STEP EIGHT: O.K.   Now decide on some things that you want to do.
Decide how you want to do them.
Write a contract
AND DO IT.

It should be evident that not all of the stages necessarily have to be used as indicated. For example, if a teacher has a few minutes at the end of a period, he might have students just prepare a few direct or personal analogies related to the topic under study. He may also decide to have students continue doing some of the phases as homework.

Teachers from most secondary subject areas have been taught synectics procedures and have used them effectively in the classroom. Gordon and his group have also produced synectics oriented curricula for the sciences, mathematics, social studies, and the language arts.

The Forced Relationship or Morphological Analysis Approach to Solving Problems Creatively

Dr. Fritz Zwicky has devised a system for stimulating creative problem solving by inviting students to identify and relate various independent variables or factors.

Essentially the approach involves the following steps:

1. A problem is stated in as general terms as possible.
2. Students are invited to identify as many different independent variables as possible.

3. Students state these variables-factors in as many ways as possible.
4. Each of these factors becomes an axis on a grid of a two-dimensional or three-dimensional model as indicated below.
5. Students then combine the axes to come up with multiple ways of looking at and resolving the problem.

It is suggested that instructors first start using the two-dimensional system with students and once they have become familiar and proficient with it, they move on to three-dimensional form.

An example of how the two-dimensional approach might be used is outlined below:

Procedure in Using the Morphological Analysis Method

Problem is presented by the teacher or arises from students. e.g., Teacher asks:	What different ways could you make a collage?
Students list several things (Independent Variables) out of which the collage could be made:	Materials a. different color b. shape c. texture d. type of material, etc.
Students, choosing from the above, list two of these if they are going to use a two-dimensional grid or three for a three-dimensional grid	Shape Type of material
Students then list how many ways these two factors may vary and place them on a grid as shown in Figure 10.	Draw Grid
The last step is to consider the combination of factors from each axis of the grid to broaden their thinking in preparing a collage. Note in the example below, nine types of materials and five shapes are listed on the grid. The combination of these gives 45 different ways materials could be used for the collage.	

Creativity—The Way to "Being" More Human

In addition to the ideas given above for stimulating creative enterprise, you as a teacher should endeavor to do as many of the following as possible.

Independent Variables

Types of Materials

Factors	triangle	circles	rectangles	multiple shapes
Plastic				
Sandpaper				
Tissue Paper				
Newspaper				
Various types of cloth				
Rocks				
Wood				
Sticks				
Rusty Wire				
Factors	triangle	circles	rectangles	multiple shapes

Independent Variable—Shape

FIGURE 10.

In using the above, students would combine, e.g., triangles made from several substances: wood, sandpaper, plastic, etc. in making their collage. This approach helps students to broaden their focus relative to the problem and stimulates them to be more diverse in their responses.

A more complex and creative utilization of this method is to use more independent variables placing them on three axes to increase the number of possible relationships. The Harvard Bridge Case below illustrates how this might be done. The problem is: How to Get Something from One Place to Another Via a Powered Vehicle. Arnold describing the resolution of the problem says:

> Certainly, one of our independent variables would be the type of vehicle used and we could subdivide that into (1) some kind of cart, (2) some kind of a chair, (3) a sling, and (4) a bed (we could list many others, but this will be enough for our example). A second independent variable might be the media in which our vehicle operates, and here we might list air, water, oil, hard surface, rollers, rails, and a solid, frictionless surface. A third independent variable would be the power source, and this could be broken down into compressed air, internal combustion engine, electric motor, steam, magnetic fields, moving cables, moving belt, and atomic power.

Let us assume for the moment that these are the three independent variables that will completely describe some device for getting something from one place to some place else. This may be an oversimplification, but it helps make our chartmaking much easier, for a three-dimensional body is easily visualized and sketched on a two-dimensional sheet. Our chart [Figure 11] then becomes a three-dimensional body which can be thought of as a filing cabinet with drawers operating or opening in all three directions. The contents of each of these drawers will be defined by one of the variations of each of the three independent variables. Note the three drawers arbitrarily singled out on the chart. Drawer #1 is characterized by a bed-type vehicle, moving over rails, powered by compressed air. Drawer #2 would be a sling-type vehicle, moving through air and powered by electricity, and Drawer #3 would be a chair-type vehicle, moving through water and powered by a moving cable. With the subdivisions we have chosen for the three independent variables, we have constructed a morphological chart that contains 224 drawers, which is more combinations than the average person could produce by any process of free association or than most groups could assemble by "brainstorming." We could, of course, easily increase the number of variations along each axis and thereby greatly increase the possible number of combinations.[23]

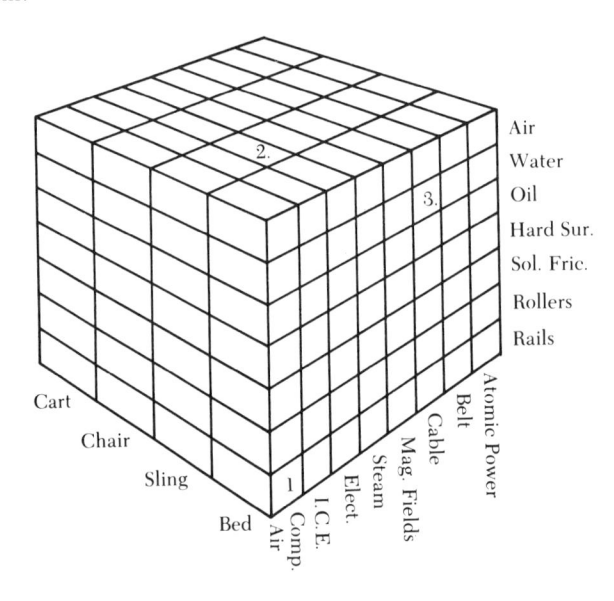

FIGURE 11.

---

[23]Arnold, F. "Useful Creative Techniques" in *A Source Book for Creative Thinking*, edited by Parnes, S. and Harding, H., (New York: Charles Scribner's Sons, 1962), pp. 256-57.

Using Acting and Dance Creatively in Academic Subjects

Mathematics, social studies, English, and home economics teachers usually do not think of using creative acting or dance to accomplish academic goals. However, as suggested earlier, using acting in the Inquiry Role Approach has been found to be an effective way for students to learn. Teachers may use a modification of this approach by placing students into groups and giving them basic roles to play. In social studies, for instance, a group may be formed and given basic descriptions of each of the following roles: a nazi leader, a German Jew, a white American citizen, or an English civil servant. The actors playing these roles are assembled around a large table and told that all of them are in a restaurant in Switzerland prior to World War II. They are then asked to react according to their role assignments.

Another role method would be to have some students act out the meaning of some concept. In science this might include such concepts as osmosis, photosynthesis, ionic bonding, or how an engine works. The students work in small groups to develop how they would act out the assignment.

Dance may be used in a manner similar to acting. A mathematics instructor might ask students to demonstrate through dance what ratios, proportions, and algebraic equations mean. A social studies teacher could similarly involve students in concepts related to population or family security.

Initially there may be some trepidation among students in using dance or drama in an academic subject. This can be lessened by the teacher explaining to the students that he believes in stimulating creative ability and developing their multi-talents, and that being involved in creative activity often results in better learning.

Boys particularly may think of dance as being effeminate. This can be overcome by asking all students to stand and follow the teacher as he goes through the motions of throwing a baseball. The instructor demonstrates by counting up to six as he carries out the motions, each number representing in sequence a different position in throwing the ball. The students then follow the instructor as he counts. After doing this a couple of times, he may slow the count down to get slow-motion or speed it up to get a rapid dance motion. The teacher then explains that by making these motions they are illustrating the movements of a baseball player in the form of dance. He may use this involvement as a basis for asking students in groups to develop a dance to demonstrate some concept that the class has been having difficulty in learning.

The use of creative drama and dance and its effectiveness in stimulating creativity and learning is largely dependent on how secure you are as a person and how open and free you are as a teacher. If you think you will never use it in teaching, you should ask yourself, "why?"

Other Suggestions for Developing Creativity

1. *Encourage new ideas.* Ask students what they think. What would be fun to investigate, do, etc.?
2. *Encourage student presentations, demonstrations, and experiments.*
3. *Give creative homework* assignments.
4. *Encourage project work* or research requiring creative responses.
5. *Do not rush pupils* to cover material.
6. *Study the lives of creative individuals* and the implications of these for the student.
7. *Be creative yourself* in the methods you use.
8. *Don't overemphasize teamwork.* Creative persons often like to work alone.
9. *Show the class creative work* done by other students.
10. *Encourage diverse forms of creative expression,* i.e. experimentation, field work, art, poetry, and writing related to the subject.
11. *Encourage inquiry, discovery, and invention.*
12. *Develop as an instructor longer wait-time* in discussion.
13. Confront the students with opportunities to sense possibilities for producing art work or stories.
14. Encourage students to prepare or become involved in any of the following:
    a. *Attribute Games.* List as many characteristics of an object as possible particularly stressing different and unique descriptions.
    b. *Brainstorming.* Involve students in listing without evaluating all the ways they can resolve some problem or produce some invention.
    c. *Thematic Apperception Tests.* Have the students prepare or look at a picture, preferably one that shows some possible emotion, like a person with a face that may appear sad, and describe or write several different things that might be happening.

Creativity—The Way to "Being" More Human

- d. *Completing* part of a poem, story, piece of art or film they have read or seen.
- e. *Constructing various types of learning puzzles* and games.
- f. *Role Playing.* Act out the role of Voltaire, Beethoven, Oppenheimer, a member of a minority group, etc.
- g. *Recording,* after reading or listening to something, *as many different ideas as possible* that come to them about the topic.
- h. *Making posters* conveying some message, their feelings, etc., which strive to be particularly creative in character.
- i. *Resolving some problem* from a series of clues.
- j. *Rewriting something* that has been written to make it more appealing or modern.
- k. *Listing all the ways they can be creative* in their home, class, during vacations, etc.
- l. *Writing paradoxes.* A situation or a belief that seems contrary to common sense but can be true.
- m. *Writing a discovery or inquiry oriented lesson* for other students to do.
- n. *Producing some work of art or music.*
- o. *Making pictorial riddles.*
- p. *Producing creative and provocative* questions.
- q. *Writing answers for which others will have to guess the question* or problem.
- r. *Imagining how it would be* if . . . or how it must feel to . . . or how to improve some piece of equipment.
- s. *Communicating* something by sound in an unusual manner, e.g., making three lines on a board and asking what geometrical shape it could be.
- t. *Making innovative kites* conveying a message related to what is being studied in a class.
- u. *Using a commercially prepared filmstrip,* film loop or film in some innovative way. e.g. stopping the presentation and asking the other students if they were preparing the audio visual material, what they would do next.
- v. *Making a filmstrip, film loop, film or a series of polaroid or other types of photographs* creatively expressing what is under study.

w. *Making a cassette recording* conveying information, a story, music etc. related to a class' activities. For example, a newspaper reporter's description of the English battle with the Spanish armada, Dunkirk, and interview with Custer, Pasteur, Redi, Picasso, etc.

x. *Devising activities to better develop sensitivity.* For instance, how does it feel . . . e.g. to be successful, creative, skilled, to listen to a person's problems, to be respected.

y. *Construct learning puzzles,* such as crossword puzzles, math puzzles, etc.

z. *Making learning games,* such as a game to show sterotypes, feelings in the ghetto, identification of historical discoveries and events, how it feels when . . . etc.

aa. Rolling out a long piece of Butcher paper and asking each student to place or draw something on it depicting the topic under study or indicating his uniqueness as a person. Students might draw something related to environmental studies, the civil war period, applications of mathematics. Shakespeare's England, etc. One class drew prison bars and then caricatures of themselves plus something that indicated how they differed from other students. This mural was then placed on the hall wall outside of the class for others to see.

bb. *Making collages* about the subject illustrating some concept, principle, theory, feeling, value, etc.

cc. *Making a personal coat of arms, flag, model or representation of a room* representing a person's personality.

dd. *Constructing something to leave in the class* to indicate they have been there.

ee. *Coming to class in some way* indicating they have made some personal change.

ff. *Constructing a light symphony.* Use various transparent color wheels made of cellophane and flash light through them to obtain the impression of changing light.

gg. *Turning numbers different ways to write something* e.g.

hh. *Listening creatively* to music or a poem and letting the sound stimulate a flow from one thought to another. It may help to close the eyes to do this. Listen to most things in

Creativity—The Way to "Being" More Human

ii.
: class to stimulate imagination rather than just to recall and memorize.

ii.
: *Recording on a pad near the bed just before sleeping or awakening, a creative idea that comes into the mind.* Act upon these ideas when you completely awake later.

jj.
: *Compiling a list of problems* or things that would be fun to investigate.

kk.
: *Publishing* a creative class newspaper.

ll.
: *Drawing cartoons* or a comic series related to what is being studied.

mm.
: *Making a booklet* containing drawings, diagrams, photographs etc. arranged in a creative manner.

nn.
: *Constructing* something out of the following to convey feelings, concepts, values about what is being learned, e.g. stick figures showing emotion.
    1. pipe cleaners
    2. straws
    3. beebees
    4. popsicle sticks
    5. barbed wire
    6. string or rope
    7. cardboard
    8. bones
    9. bolts, nuts, screws, wire, parts of machines, etc.
    10. colored paper
    11. waste materials—e.g. tin cans, bottle caps, glass, foil etc. A teacher might ask: What artistic things could you make from garbage?

oo.
: *Using different devices to make a story with shadows.*

pp.
: Making a presentation to the class using your hands, painted with ink to form faces that talk about the subject.

qq.
: Constructing puppets, writing a script, and giving a play related to things being studied. Rewriting part of a novel in play form, historically recreate an event or a conversation between individuals.

rr.
: Constructing a diagram or taking a photograph of something in which there may be possibilities for individuals to perceive several different objects.

236 **Student-Centered Teaching in the Secondary School**

ss. Reading creatively. Using reading as a springboard for new ideas. After reading something coming up with a new idea, concept, or invention related to it. After reading a story improving on it, writing the author's outline or preparing a completely new outline.

tt. Writing a series of analogies, such as Math is like . . . Democracy is like . . .

uu. Writing paradoxes.

BE CREATIVE: Use these forms as creatively as you can to depict something about, for example, your feelings, this class, this course, how your values are developing.

Creativity—The Way to "Being" More Human

Clearly, using this list of activities requires creative investment on the part of the student as do many other activities designed in an inquiry mode. Free inquiry by its nature, however, is likely to elicit more creativity than this type of guided inquiry.

Influence of Modern Curricula on Development of Creativity

Few published materials, except those specifically designed to do so, do a good job of eliciting the creative processes of thought, for seldom do such materials require students to suggest problems for study or to design investigations. However, if students are encouraged and given some guidance early in a course in how to do this, it is surprising how they reveal their talents as the course progresses.

A creative teacher must modify most of the materials he uses and break away from a text at times in order to really stimulate creative activity. The typical secondary text has been written for the average teacher, it has to be in order for it to sell and have a wide market. A teacher who is going to be above average must, therefore, not be limited by the text if he wants to develop more creative processes in his students.

Awareness of creative ability, and a striving by instructors to stimulate its fruition, can do much to make this valuable human resource available to society. A teacher who accomplishes this end separates himself from a mass of instructors to become truly a master teacher. Research in creativity is accelerating, and new insights into the creative process are undoubtedly forthcoming, with implications for educators. As a professional person you should strive to keep abreast of these and translate them into action in your classroom.

Creative Time Rating Form

The following form is presented to assist you in evaluating your progress toward becoming a more creative instructor. The form may be used in conjunction with listening to a cassette tape recording of your class or with you estimating the amount of time spent as indicated below. It is advisable to retain the forms and compare them through the year and from year to year.

Teacher Time

Teacher presents material: explains, lectures, clarifies, talks during discussions.

Time in minutes _____ What should it be? _____ minutes

Routine Time

Teacher performs routine tasks: takes role, gives directions, disciplines, but no real learning of course material is taking place.

Time in minutes _____ What should it be? _____ minutes

Student Involvement Time

Amount of time students are involved in learning activities:

	Actual	What should it be?
Involved in individual activities	_____ minutes	_____ minutes
Involved in small groups	_____ minutes	_____ minutes
Involved in large groups	_____ minutes	_____ minutes

Percentage of time devoted to: (in minutes)

Fluency	Flexibility	Originality	Elaboration	Sensitivity

Percentage of time devoted to:

Non-creative work _____ minutes

Wait-time _____ minutes

Summary

Abraham Maslow in studying outstanding mentally healthy and self-actualized individuals concluded that creative involvement is fundamental to a feeling of psychological well-being and to the development of human potential. Based on his research, Maslow believed a teacher should endeavor to maximize the creative talents of his students so that they better build their self-esteem and confidence in their value as persons.

Although there is some disagreement on a definition, it is suggested that teachers think of creativity as the process of an individual producing something unique for himself. It is important for teachers to realize that individuals of all ages are creative to some degree but differ considerably in this ability. The gifted creative student may be recognized from those less talented because he is more curious, is resourceful, likes to make discoveries, prefers difficult tasks, enjoys solving problems, has drive, is a flexible thinker, responds relatively rapidly to

If you were this student's teacher; how would you use this situation to stimulate creativity?

questions, has a pronounced spirit of inquiry, and reads extensively. The creatively gifted do not necessarily have high I.Q.'s nor do they necessarily achieve well in traditional academic systems. Research indicates that I.Q. and creative ability generally do not correlate highly. To try to identify creative students on the basis of I.Q. and teacher's grades is not likely, therefore, to reveal a number of highly creative students.

Maslow and Torrance believe freedom to be creative affects mental health positively, thereby making it possible for students to learn more effectively. Some students learn well *only* during the times that they have opportunities to be creative. Grading and rewarding creative endeavor, however, may inhibit a class's creative production. An environment stimulating creative enterprise has the opposite effect if it establishes trust, encourages open communication, allows for self-determination of goals and self-assessment, plus reduces control in the sense of conformity.

Research indicates that if creative potential isn't tapped in the school it might never fully manifest itself. Teachers should encourage new ideas, give creative assignments, refrain from overemphasizing teamwork, provide opportunities for students to design and improve equipment, display the creative work of students, and stimulate discovery and invention and the other mental creative processes. It takes time to be creative. A long wait-time in discussions, therefore, should be encouraged since it allows needed time for individuals to develop creative thoughts.

Modern curriculum developments do not necessarily encourage creativity. Most published materials were written for the average instructor to use. A teacher wanting to be above average must modify or supplement these and originate many activities to better stimulate creative enterprise. The approach and methods teachers use in their classes, especially in developing questioning techniques and establishing freedom, may stifle or encourage creative work. When enlisting students to originate problems, hypothesize, design techniques of investigating, make discoveries, speculate, invent, or form metaphors, inquiry oriented and student-centered activities contribute considerably to the development of this most viable human talent.

Creative teaching requires that teachers themselves continue to devise and become proficient in establishing a creative class environment. By so doing, they become more fully functioning individuals and move toward the greater realization of their self-actualization as persons.

Further Investigation and Study

1. Outline some ways you would encourage creative endeavor in your subject.
2. Prepare a synectics type lesson for your subject.
3. Outline the creative types of abilities and write questions for each for the subject you will teach.
4. In what ways does the present classroom organization contribute to the stifling of creative individuals?
5. What did Dr. Hutchinson's report indicate about the method of instruction and creativity?
6. Why might it not be good to reward creative ability with high grades?
7. How would you determine the presence of creative potential in a class?
8. Define creativity in your own words and give reasons why you consider this an acceptable definition.
9. How are creativity and I.Q. related?
10. Mr. Mueller states, "Truly creative minds are invariably free minds" and suggests that this presents a dilemma to the school. What does he mean? How much direction need there be in the school? What is the role of direction in stimulating or restricting creativeness?
11. What implications does Dr. Hess's work have for teaching?
12. Devise a lesson you think will give opportunities for creative responses.
13. It has been said that creativeness is contagious. What would you do as a teacher to insure the contagion?
14. In what ways does knowing the creative questioning techniques help in designing lessons?
15. Outline three types of creative assignments you would like to invite students to do.
16. What relationship does "feeling" have with creativity?
17. What relevance does wait-time have for developing creative ability?
18. How would you modify a curriculum in the subject you will teach to make it more creative?

11 Evaluation

Probably nothing is so well known and so little understood by teachers as evaluation. Evaluation involves the total assessment by the instructor of a student's learning and development, including understanding of cognitive critical thinking processes, subject-matter competence, multiple-talents, values, self-concept, laboratory skills, and ability and willingness to work. Not only the progress of the student toward his self-actualization, but the objectives of the course and school and the effectiveness of the instructor are also considered. Good evaluation indicates the strengths and weaknesses of instruction. Once a teacher has made a thorough assessment, he has an indication of how to improve his teaching, for evaluation acts as the feedback in the experimental process of teaching. A teacher must be experimental if he is to progress and try to become more skilled. He must be willing to try new ways to interact as a person with students, methods and techniques and in so doing move toward teaching excellence. An experimental approach assumes collection of data to verify the success of the teaching strategy. The data in this case must come from the evaluating techniques, and the better the evaluating instruments the greater the information available to the teacher for improving his course and instruction.

Evaluation

Types of Evaluational Instruments

Listed below are general evaluational techniques used by teachers. It must be emphasized that testing is only a small part of evaluation and probably receives too much attention at the expense of other methods.

A. *Commercial Tests*
   1. *Standardized tests.* There are several standardized tests prepared for the various subject areas. Many of the new curriculum studies have produced standardized tests or are in the process of doing so. These include (a) achievement tests in specific subject areas, (b) aptitude tests, (c) understanding of processes, e.g., in science or critical thinking, (d) tests to determine creative ability, interest, personality, intelligence, and self-esteem inventories, (e) readiness tests. The format of these various instruments may involve several of the tests listed below.

B. *Teacher Prepared Tests*
   1. *Essay tests.* These should require a sufficient sample of the subject matter. A teacher should refine his essay questions by studying student performance on past tests and insure that his questions are really reflecting his most important goals.
   2. *Problem tests.* A problem or a situation is presented, and the students are asked to suggest plausible answers. This type usually involves investigative procedure or evaluating information.
   3. *Simple recall tests.* Avoid these.
   4. *Multiple-choice tests.*
   5. *Matching tests.* Avoid these.
   6. *Self-tests.*
   7. *Completion tests.*

C. *Non-test evaluations*
   1. Behavioral records. These are based on class, laboratory or field observations. The teacher prepares a checklist and evaluates how the individual functions in each situation.
   2. Analysis of talents, e.g., creative work. This may involve the production of some project, art work, or activity.
   3. Student self-evaluation of his performance, interest in the course or unit, or self-esteem.
   4. Interpretation of written and oral presentations.

Because of the complexity of evaluation it is strongly urged that teachers obtain some advanced special training in testing and measurement. Some states now require this for certification. In the sections that follow, not all aspects of evaluation are considered because of the need for economy of time and space.

Testing

Look over a segment of the following test. Consider what is good and bad about it.

Select from Column B the answer which best fits Column A.

	Column A		Column B
1.	Roundworms	a.	Mammalia
2.	Flatworms	b.	Echinodermata
3.	Snakes	c.	Aves
4.	Birds	d.	Platyhelminthes
5.	Paramecium	e.	Nemathelminthes
6.	Dogs	f.	Protista
7.	Starfish	g.	Porifera
8.	Sponges	h.	Reptilia
9.	Whales	i.	Protozoa
10.	Fishes	j.	Rotifera
11.	Diseases and pathogens able to pass directly from one host to another within a population	k.	Anopheles Mosquito
		l.	Mosquito (Aedes)
12.	The parasite which is the causative organism of a disease	m.	Contagious
		n.	Aerobic
13.	The insects which, along with man, are alternate hosts for malaria	o.	Anaerobic
		p.	Pathogen
		q.	Slime mold
14.	The vector insect of yellow fever	r.	Louis Pasteur
15.	Oxygen-requiring bacteria	s.	Charles Darwin
16.	A visible living protist which glides along an amoeboid movement	t.	Animalcule
		u.	Pasteur
17.	The scientist who definitely killed the idea that microbes might arise spontaneously from dead materials	v.	Protista
		w.	Euglena
		x.	Rickettseae
18.	Discovered the world of microscopic life in the 1670's	y.	Anticoagulent
		z.	Leeuwenhoek
19.	The name which represents the whole group of subvisible creatures	aa.	Linnaeus
		bb.	Salivary glands

Evaluation

20. Means little animals
21. The man responsible for the great classification system in 1750's

cc. Denitrification
dd. Nitrogen cycle
ee. Vector
ff. Flagellate
gg. Noctituca
hh. Rickettsibe

Refer to the test again. What is wrong with this format? Where will the students place the answers? What of the number of answers to match the questions? How well does it evaluate the objectives of the course: principles, understanding of science as a process, scientific attitudes, science as a human activity?

Tests Should Evaluate Your Objectives

Just as Bloom has pointed out that there is a hierarchy of objectives, so too are there levels and degrees of sophistication in testing.

The above examination, you will probably agree, is a poor one. It tests mainly for memorized information giving the student little chance to apply, create, and evaluate what he has learned. It probably also doesn't really assess the objectives of the course. No gifted instructor would be content with just evaluating regurgitation of information. Education is far more than that. It's worth repeating that students tend to learn the way they are tested. Are the things emphasized in this test really the important goals of the subject? How many of them will be retained one week, a month, a year after the course? Research indicates that irrelevant facts are soon lost to the mind while concepts and principles a student has learned to use and apply in his life attain a high retention level. It is this prolonged retention that we as professional teachers strive to achieve.

If the state or school district insists upon or a teacher decides to use behavioral objectives, then tests should be designed to evaluate them. This is true whether the objectives are student or teacher defined. It is relatively easy to write behavioral objectives, but to evaluate their achievement is often difficult.

Most beginning teachers, at first, tend to want to write only essay types of questions. It is easier to do this than write multiple choice questions for the same objectives. However, essay questions have limitations as indicated on the following page.

Limitation of Essay Questions

1. They limit the sample. Since few questions can be answered in the time allotted, only a small sample of the total learning is made.
2. They require extensive correction time. Remember you shall probably have 100 or more students a day in your classes. If each student writes 4 questions requiring 15 seconds of correction time per question, on an average you will need:

   100 students x 4 questions x 15 seconds per question = 6000 seconds

   $$6000 \text{ seconds} = 100 \text{ minutes} = 1 \text{ hr., } 40 \text{ min.}$$
   $$60 \text{ sec/min} \quad 60 \text{ min/hr}$$

   This is a considerable amount of time.

Although learning to write multiple-choice questions initially requires considerable time, in the long run, an instructor will be ahead because they require far less correction time. Furthermore, they may be corrected by students in class.

Writing Test Questions for All Levels of Bloom's Taxonomy

Recall that Bloom stipulated there were five cognitive levels of objectives. There should, therefore, be test items to evaluate each of these levels. Outlined below are examples of how this might be done. In some of the sections, the behavioral objective is stated followed by the question evaluating it. If you have written excellent behavioral objectives and use them as a guide for constructing your tests, your examinations probably will be better than those prepared by many experienced teachers.

1. Recall. Knowledge Level

The matching test above mainly stresses recall. Simple recall is the lowest level of learning. It requires only memorization of information—and information is not knowledge in the broad sense. Animals can memorize. Teachers have often devoted too much time to this level because recall questions are simple to write. Other levels must become a part of all tests. In most instances probably no more than 20 percent of any test should consist of simple recall questions.

2. Comprehension

To comprehend is to understand. Students may know something, for instance, osmosis, momentum, density, democracy, ratio, poetic li-

cense, but not understand it. Comprehension types of questions ask students to:
   a. Interpret a statement.
   b. Translate—describe a process or idea in their own words.
   c. Extrapolate—go beyond the data.
   d. Interpolate—supply intermediate information.

You are probably already fairly familiar with the knowledge and comprehension levels of Bloom's taxonomy. For this reason greater attention is devoted to its higher levels. On the following pages is a portion of the "Summary Description of Grade Nine Science Objectives and Test Items" (Revised Edition) prepared at the direction of the High School Entrance Examinations Board, Department of Education, Edmonton, Alberta, March 1965. The Board has endeavored to test for all levels of the taxonomy. Their booklet is provided to the Alberta teachers so they see how their junior high school students will be evaluated by the Department of Education and to encourage teachers to prepare similar types of tests. Many school systems and state departments of education have used Bloom's taxonomy for the same purposes. Note in the following sections a brief description of each level is presented first. This is then followed by examples of objectives and essay and multiple-choice test items to evaluate them.

   3. Application
      ... Given a problem new to the student, he will apply the appropriate abstraction without having to be prompted as to which abstraction is correct or without having to be shown how to use it in that situation.
      ... In application the student shows that he *will use* the abstraction correctly given an appropriate situation in which no mode of solution is specified.
      ... In all cases, however, the task should use material the student has not had contact with, or take a new slant on common material or use a fictional situation. If the material is familiar, comprehension or recall is required, not application.
      Some Objectives
         1. Applies scientific concepts and principles used in class to the phenomena discussed in a paper.
         2. Predicts the probable effect of a change in a factor on a chemical solution previously at equilibrium.
         3. Applies scientific principles, postulates and other abstractions to new situations.
         4. Finds solutions to problems in making home repairs employing experimental procedures from science.

Some Items
1. What effect would an increase in pressure in the boiler of a steam engine have upon the performance of the steam engine?
2. A baseball can be made to curve. How can this be explained?
3. Would the air in a closed room be heated or cooled by the operation of an electric refrigerator in the room with the refrigerator door open?
    - °A. heated, because the heat given off by the motor and the compressed gas would exceed the heat absorbed.
    - B. cooled, because the refrigerator is a cooling device.
    - C. cooled, because compressed gases expand in the refrigerator.
    - D. cooled, because liquids absorb heat when they evaporate.
    - E. neither heated nor cooled.

Items 4 and 5 are based upon the following situation.
The boiling and freezing points of water were determined and marked on the glass of a new, and as yet "blank" thermometer. If these two points are 9 inches apart, how far apart would the degree markings be if it were desired to make

4. A Centigrade thermometer?
    - A. 9/180 inch
    - °B. 0.09 inch
    - C. 0.9 inch
    - D. 9/16 inch
    - E. 9/32 inch
5. A Fahrenheit thermometer?
    - °A. 0.05 inch
    - B. 0.5 inch
    - C. 0.90 inch
    - D. 9/100 inch
    - E. 9/32 inch
6. An automobile weighing 3,300 lbs. goes up a hill 160 ft. high in 20 secs. The output of the motor in horsepower must be
    - A. 8
    - °B. 48
    - C. 412.5
    - D. 10,560,000

    Note: Item 6 should be classed as "Comprehension" if it is parallel to, or similar to items taken in class. In Items 4 and 5 the situation is probably novel—it has a new twist. Item 6 might be made novel to most students, for example, by including the length of the hill.

4. Analysis

. . . Analysis emphasizes the breakdown of the material into its constituent parts and detection of the relationships of the parts and of the

Evaluation

way they are organized. . . . evaluation involves more than analysis or even critical analysis in that, when one evaluates, in addition to analyzing a judgment is made in terms of some criteria as to its adequacy.

Some Objectives
1. Recognizes unstated assumptions.
2. Distinguishes facts from hypotheses.
3. Distinguishes conclusions from statements which support it.
4. Checks consistency of hypotheses with given information and assumptions.
5. Distinguishes cause and effect relationships from other sequential relationships.
6. Detects the purpose, point of view, attitude, or general conception of the author.

Some Items
1. "Light is produced indirectly in the fluorescent lamp." What would be another way of expressing the conclusion implied in the above statement?
2. 1 liter = .88 qut. Are there more quarts than liters in a container whose capacity is 1000 cc?

Item 3 contains a pair of statements which are either in agreement with each other or not in agreement, and either of the statements may be true or false. Study the pair of statements and choose
    A. if statements I and II are in agreement and both false.
    B. if statements I and II are in agreement and both true.
    C. if statements I and II are not in agreement; I true, II false.
    D. if statements I and II are not in agreement; I false, II true.
3.   I. At absolute zero the molecules of a substance do not move with respect to each other.
    II. No heat energy is possessed by a substance at absolute zero.
    (Key: (B) Note: This pair of statements is only illustrative as other pairs of statements could be added to make use of the same alternatives.)

The following paragraphs concern the action of a geyser. Read the passage carefully before answering Items 4-8 inclusive.

A geyser is a hot spring that erupts at intervals. It is made up of a more or less crooked or constricted, turbular fissure that extends into the earth and is filled with water. A source of heat near the bottom of the fissure heats the water.

After an eruption the tube fills with water from an underground source. The water throughout most of the length of the tube, and especially in the lower part, becomes heated to a point above the normal boiling temperature (212°F.) of water but does not become quite hot enough to turn to steam. However, sooner or later, some of the water in the lower part of the tube at the source of heat reaches the boiling point and turns to steam. The steam raises the whole column of water above it and causes some water to overflow from the geyser pool at the surface. This overflow acts as a trigger, permitting the whole column of water in the tube to flash into steam which blows from the fissure in an eruption.

For each of Items 4-6 choose
- A. if the statement is true and pertains directly to the action of the geyser.
- B. if the statement is true but is not directly concerned with the action of the geyser.
- C. if the statement is false.

4. If the tube were not crooked and constricted the water throughout the tube would come to nearly the same temperature by unrestricted convectional circulation, the water would boil, and a boiling spring rather than a geyser would result.
5. The boiling point of water in the bottom of the tube is lower than it is at the top.
6. The water in the tube does not turn to steam although it is above the normal boiling point because of the pressure of the overlying water. (Keyed answers are: 4 (A), 5 (C), 6 (A).)
7. Air pressure on a fine day is usually higher than on a stormy day. Thus, the geyser will erupt more often during stormy weather. This statement can best be evaluated as
    - A. a wild guess.
    - °B. true, because it can be predicted from known principles.
    - C. false, because it cannot be predicted from known principles.
    - D. true, because it is based on statements in the above passage.
    - E. false, because it contradicts the statements in the above passage.
8. An investigation of which one of the following hypotheses concerning the boiling point of water is most suggested by the observation of a geyser?
    - A. the boiling point of water decreases with increasing altitudes.
    - B. the boiling point of water is that point when the vapor pressure equals the atmospheric pressure.
    - °C. the boiling point of water in a pressure cooker is above 212°F.
    - D. the boiling point of water in a hot water heating system is above 212°F.

    Note: Item 4 is classified as Analysis, 5 as Knowledge of Specifics, 6 as Comprehension, 7 as Evaluation, and 8 as Synthesis.

5. Synthesis

Synthesis emphasizes the putting together of elements and parts in such a way as to constitute a pattern or structure not clearly there before. Generally this involves a recombination of parts of previous experience with new material reconstructed into a new and more or less well-integrated whole...

Some Objectives
1. Describes an original experiment conducted by a student.
2. Proposes ways of testing a hypothesis.
3. Integrates the results of an investigation into an effective plan or solution to solve a problem.
4. Develops schemes for classifying chemicals.
5. Formulates hypotheses to explain adequately a wide range of seemingly interrelated phenomena and be internally consistent.
6. Makes deductions from basic theories.

Some Items°
1. How could you construct an oil barometer from oil which floats on water?
2. Given: 1. Work = fd.
   2. Power is work per unit of time.
   3. 33,000 ft. lb. per min. = 1 H.P.
   Develop the formula for Horsepower H.P. =
3. You suspect that a certain soluble compound contains hydrogen. Which of the following would be a way of checking your suspicion?
   A. prepare a solution of the compound and subject it to electrolysis, using Hoffman's apparatus.
   B. place a sample of the compound in a Bunsen flame and determine if any water vapor is produced.
   C. heat the compound to incandescence and analyze the light produced with a pyrometer.
   °D. vaporize some of the material in a flame and use a spectroscope to analyze the light produced.
   E. pass some light through a solution of the compound and analyze the spectrum produced with a spectroscope.
4. See also Item 8 under Analysis

6. Evaluation

Evaluation includes the process of making judgments concerning the extent to which ideas, solutions, methods, and material satisfy criteria. It involves the use of criteria as well as standards for ap-

---

° It is extremely difficult to write objective items to measure synthesis and evaluation Bloom provides several examples in science. The Physical Science Study Committee tests published by Educational Testing Service also have examples.

praising the extent to which particulars are accurate, effective, economical or satisfying. The judgments may be either quantitative or qualitative and the criteria may be either those determined by the student or those which are given to him.

Some Objectives
1. Detects the logical fallacies in arguments.
2. Discerns the inconsistencies and/or logical inaccuracies in data.
3. Identifies the procedural errors in an experiment and evaluates their effect on the results.
4. Compares the effectiveness of a method used to solve a problem with the best possible method available.
5. Identifies additional evidence or experimentation that is necessary to fully justify the conclusions reached.

Some Items

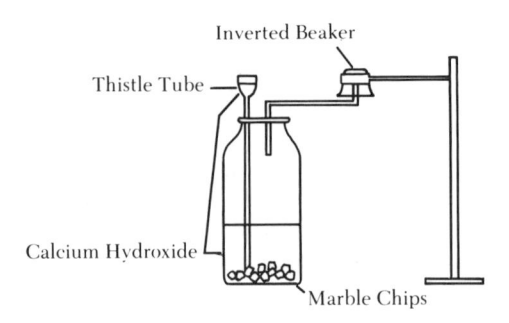

[Diagram of apparatus with labels: Inverted Beaker, Thistle Tube, Calcium Hydroxide, Marble Chips]

The above apparatus was set up to prepare carbon dioxide. The contents of the inverted beaker were tested with lime water which did not turn milky. It was concluded that the calcium hydroxide solution was not strong enough.
1. What logical inconsistencies are there in the report of the experiment?
2. Identify the procedural errors in the experiment and evaluate their effect on the results.
3. A recent popular article stated that, if a space craft were being rocketed away from the surface of the earth fast enough, its speed would offset the pull of gravity and a man in the rocket would feel weightless. This statement should be evaluated as being
   A. accurate since two forces are involved in the described situation and two forces can offset one another.
   B. accurate since the weight of an object decreases rapidly as the distance from the center of the earth decreases.
   °C. inaccurate since the floor of the man's compartment will be pushing up on the man as the rocket rises, and this push will give a feeling of increased rather than decreased weight.
   D. inaccurate since no object within the gravitational field of the earth can be weightless and so cannot seem weightless.

Evaluation

E. inaccurate since the chance that the force on the man due to the rocket moving up and the force of gravity pulling the man down will be equal is extremely minute.
4. See also Item 7 under Analysis.[1]

Constructing Test Items for Levels of Bloom's Taxonomy in Mathmatics. The taxonomy below was developed by James W. Wilson in *Handbook on Formative and Summative Evaluation of Student Learning.*[2]

A.0 Computation

Items designed to require straightforward manipulation of problem elements according to rules the subjects presumably have learned. Emphasis is upon performing operations, not upon deciding which operations are appropriate.

A.1 Knowledge of specific facts.
Example: Which of the following is not a whole number?
(a) 0   (b) 3   (e) ½   (d) 4
A.2 Knowledge of terminology.
A.3 Ability to carry out algorithms.

B.0 Comprehension

Items designed to require either recall of concepts and generalizations or transformation of problem elements from one mode to another. Emphasis is upon demonstrating understanding of concepts and their relationships, not upon using concepts to produce a solution.

B.1 Knowledge of Concepts. Knowledge of a set of related specific facts.
Example: This drawing suggests a rational number. Choose the fraction on the right which names the rational number.

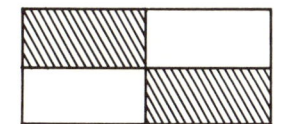

(a) 1/2
(b) 2/3
(c) 1/3
(d) 3/4
(e) none of these

B.2 Knowledge of principles, rules, and generalizations. Relationships among concepts and problem elements which the student can be ex-

---

[1] From: "Summary Description of Grade Nine Science Objectives and Test Items," Revised Edition, prepared at the direction of the High School Entrance Examinations Board, Department of Education, Edmonton, Alberta, March, 1965.
[2] James Wilson, "Evaluation of Learning Secondary School Mathematics," in *Handbook on Formative and Summative Evaluation of Student Learning* edited by Benjamin Bloom, J. Thomas Hastings, and George Madaus (New York: McGraw-Hill Book Co., 1971).

pected to know as a result of his course of study.

Example: If the decimal point in a number is moved three places to the right, we are
- (a) dividing the number by 1000
- (b) dividing the number by 100
- (c) multiplying the number by 3
- (d) multiplying the number by 1000

B.3 *Knowledge of mathematical structure.*

B.4 *Ability to transform problem elements from one mode to another.*

Example: Suppose that an operation on any numbers "a" and "b" is defined by a ° b = a + (a x b). Then 5 ° 2 equals
(a) 10 (b) 12 (c) 15 (d) 20 (e) 35

B.5 *Ability to follow a line of reasoning.*

B.6 *Ability to read and interpret a problem.*

C.0 Application

Items designed to require (1) recall of relevant knowledge, (2) selection of appropriate operations, and (3) performance of the operations. Items are of a routine nature requiring the subject to use concepts in a specific context and in a way he has presumably practiced.

C.1 *Ability to solve routine problems.* Solution of problems similar to those encountered in the course of instruction.

C.2 *Ability to make comparisons.* Requires the student to determine a relationship between two sets of information and to formulate a decision.

Example:

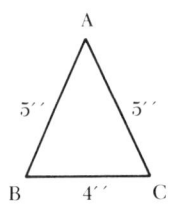

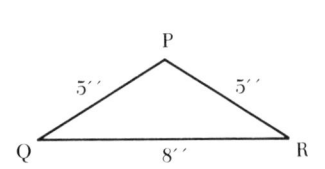

Compare the areas of the two triangles above.
- (a) ABC has the larger area.
- (b) PQR has the larger area.
- (c) The areas are the same.

C.3 *Ability to analyze data.* Analyze data and make a sequence of decisions.

Example: Interpretation of graphical data.

C.4 *Ability to recognize patterns, isomorphisms, and symmetries.* The ability to find a *familiar* relationship in data.

Example: What is the next term in this sequence?
2, 4, 6, 8, . . .

Evaluation

| D.0 Analysis |

Items designed to require a non-routine application of concepts. This behavior level includes most behavior described in the *Taxonomy* (Bloom, 1956) as analysis, synthesis, or evaluation. It involves a degree of transfer to a context in which there has been no practice.

D.1 *Ability to solve nonroutine problems.*
Example: The last digit in 4^{10} is
(a) 0 (b) 2 (c) 4 (d) 6 (e) 8

D.2 *Ability to discover relationships.* This ability differs from category C.4 in that the student must discover (formulate) a new relationship in new data.
Example: Observe the following table.

Row	Item	Sum
1	1	1
2	1+3	4
3	1+3+5	9
4	1+3+5+7	16
.	.	.
.	.	.
.	.	.

What will be the sum of the n'th row?

D.3 *Ability to construct proofs.*
D.4 *Ability to criticize proofs.*
D.5 *Ability to formulate and validate generalizations.*
Example: Prove the generalization given in Example D.2.

Several school systems encourage teachers to use a grid as shown on page 256 to insure that all levels of the taxonomy are evaluated. The chart indicates how you may use a grid to determine the sophistication of your testing procedures.

Although the chart on page 256 is designed to analyze the cognitive domain only, it can be easily modified to include the affective domain by adding a fifth category entitled Affective Domain on the left-hand side of the chart. The grid can be completely designed to evaluate this domain as indicated in the chart on page 257. Performing several analyses of tests using this grid helps to insure your growth in making better tests evaluating for the higher levels of learning. Refer to Chapter 2, Further Investigation and Study section to see how interest was evaluated on Piaget's theory.

Research indicates teachers improve tests if they use Bloom's taxonomy. Teachers who do not evaluate all their objectives or classify their test questions in a manner similar to the grid above tend to

Blueprint of World History Final Examination

OBJECTIVES	Topic or Content Area						Emphasis %
	The Development of Greek Thought	Contributions of Rome	The Medieval Period	The Renaissance	The Age of Enlightenment	The Modern Period	
1. KNOWLEDGE							40
2. COMPREHENSION							30
3. APPLICATION							20
4, 5, and 6—ANALYSIS, SYNTHESIS AND EVALUATION							10
Emphasis %							100

Analysis of Affective Domain Evaluation

OBJECTIVES	Subjects, topics, or units of study						Techniques Used to Assess: 1. Observation Inventory of Student (OI) 2. Self-Evaluation of Student (SE) 3. Student Production (SP) 4. Test Type Item (TI)	% Assessed by Instructor
RECEIVING								
RESPONDING								
VALUING								
ORGANIZATION OF VALUES								
GENERALIZED SET OF ATTITUDES AND VALUES								

evaluate for the lowest levels of Bloom's taxonomy. Scannell and Stillwagen, for example, in sampling 46 chemistry teachers' tests from four-year high schools, found that the major emphasis was on knowledge. The application, analysis, and synthesis levels were virtually neglected.[3]

General Considerations in Test Construction

This section contains some suggestions for constructing tests. These are not exhaustive, but they are fundamental for any test constructor.

True or False Test

1. If the examination is limited to true or false, 75 or more items are needed, statistically, to overcome the guessing factor.

    On a 100-question true-or-false test, students should be able to get about fifty questions right if they just guess without knowing anything about the subject. Some instructors help eliminate this problem by subtracting the number of wrong answers from the right answers to determine the score and penalize for guessing. This procedure is not recommended, because students usually think the instructor is using this technique for malicious reasons. It is undesirable also because the student is penalized for guessing. In some subjects we wish to have students make hypotheses or good guesses.

2. Avoid overbalancing the test with too many true (or false) questions. Try to have the questions fairly even in number. This prevents a student who knows little about the material from getting a high score simply by assuming that more questions are true (or false).

3. Avoid using statements that might trick students.

4. Don't use the same language found in the text. This suggests to students that they should memorize.

5. Don't use double negatives in a statement. For example, do not write "do not have no war mongers."

6. Avoid ambiguous statements. For example, do not write "Erosion is prevented by seeds."

---

[3] Dale P. Scannell and Walter R. Stillwagen, "Teaching and Testing for Degrees of Understanding," *California Journal of Instructional Improvement* (March, 1960): pp. 88-94.

Evaluation

7. Avoid using complex sentences in your statements.
8. Avoid using the following words because the questions are usually false: all, always, never, definitely, undoubtedly.
9. Avoid using the following words because the questions are usually true: some, most, should, often.
10. Don't use a pattern for ease of grading, such as TT, FF, TT because students learn these quickly and your test will loose reliability as a result.
11. Avoid qualitative language if possible. Do not write, for example, "Good plays have fewer characters," or "The better metals conduct electricity faster."
12. Arrange your statements in groups of ten to twenty. This helps to relieve tension for those taking the test.
13. Place the responses for answering the questions on one margin so that they can be easily checked by using a key.

Multiple-Choice Test

This is considered the best objective type of test because it reduces guessing and can be scored easily and objectively. A multiple-choice test should be made of items having more than three responses. If there are not at least four possible responses to each question, a correction formula should be used. A multiple-choice test differs from a multiple-response test in that only one answer is correct for each question.

1. Write your test items in question form.
2. Make all responses plausible.
3. All answers should be grammatically consistent and as short as possible.
4. Attempt to keep all responses about the same length.
5. Randomize the correct answers so that there is no pattern in the examination. Students often look for a pattern.
6. Remember that the correct response often can be arrived at by a process of elimination as well as by knowing the correct response. Try to prevent arriving at the answer this way in your phrasing of the answers.
7. Present first, in the question, the term or concept you wish to test for.
8. Test for the higher levels of understanding as much as possible.
9. Require a simple method for the response. Place the space for

the answers along one margin of a page, so that they can be easily keyed. This can be done by providing short lines on the margin.
10. Group your items in sections. This makes it easy to refer to various sections of the test and helps break monotony in taking the test.
11. Group together all questions with the same number of choices.
12. Avoid using "none of the above" or "all of the above" as possible answers.

Completion and Matching Tests

Completion and matching tests usually emphasize recall and are often tricky verbally. For this reason they should be avoided.
1. If matching questions are used they should be grouped. When there are more than fifteen matching items in a group, the test becomes cumbersome.
2. Number your questions and use letters for answers or the reverse, but be consistent.
3. Although matching tests have traditionally stressed simple recall, they can be used to test for recognition or application of principles. Three sample matching questions follow:

Questions *Answers*

_____1. A machine which would require the least amount of friction on it to move it 20 feet.
_____2. A machine which could best be used to pry open a box.
_____3. Which of the listed devices is made up of the greatest number of simple machines?

a. Pliers
b. Wheelbarrow
c. Ice tongs
d. Seesaw
e. Doorknob
f. Pencil sharpener
g. Saw

Self-Test

A self-test is similar to any other test in its construction, but it is taken by the student mainly as a learning device. It usually has questions on one side of a page and the answers on the other side. The student takes the test; then he turns over the page and checks his answers. The instructor can use the completed test as a means of stimulating discussion.

Evaluation

Teachers usually set up self-tests on Ditto masters and run off enough copies for their students. A suggested format is shown in the figure on p. 261. The back page should contain a detailed explanation for each answer so that students learn from the test. The student folds under his answers on the right side of his page. The answers then are next to the correct answers and explanations on the left margin of the back page, making it easy to correct the test.

1. Question Answer		Answer	1. Correct answer and explanation of the answer
2.		_____	2.
3.		_____	3.

A Problem Test

This kind of test presents a problem and asks the students to work on it. The test usually contains a series of questions the students are supposed to answer in solving the problem. Give the students information about the problem and have them devise their own hypotheses, research designs, or methods of collecting and recording data. A problem test can be used to involve students in critical thinking processes. The test may have an answer sheet similar to that for a self-test, or it may be used to stimulate discussion.

Some examples of problems that might be used in constructing a test of this nature are given below:

1. How would you reduce the amount of pollution from a smoke stack?
2. How could a citizen find out if the local river was polluted?
3. If a citizen wanted to improve the appearance of his community, what should he do? How would he get it done?
4. Here is a story up to this point; how would you finish it?

Diagrams or Picture Types of Tests

Many tests better evaluate reading ability than the subject matter. Often students understand the principles being tested but because they have verbal difficulties, such as reading and interpreting what they have read, they do poorly on tests. Studies have been done indicating that when a class is given tests consisting mainly of pictures, requiring only that the correct response be checked, a marked number of students do significantly better than if they were given the same test in verbal form. [4]

Practice preparing pictorial or non-verbal items for your subject area. Refer to the chapter on pictorial riddles. How could you change a riddle into an evaluation item?

Student Correction of Tests

An instructor, because of lack of time and/or having students better learn the material, may request that the students correct tests. Student correction can be done in several ways. A student can act as an aide using a key prepared by the instructor to correct tests. An instructor can pass the tests out to students at random, read the answers to the class and have them correct and compute the scores. Another approach is to give the students a key after taking a test and have them correct their own tests. For answers missed, the students are encouraged to write on the back of the test or a separate paper an explanation for their incorrect responses. These can be analyzed along with other items to determine the questions that should be modified or eliminated in future testing.

General Guidelines to Use in Testing

1. Use tests humanely as learning and diagnostic devices. Give students opportunities to demonstrate they have learned what they missed on a test and accordingly improve their grade.
2. Never use a test as a punishment.
3. *Avoid* using *completion* and *matching* questions.
4. Use tests or self-evaluational inventories to evaluate all of your objectives, including the critical thinking processes and attitudes.
5. Spend time with each student going over the questions he missed. This may be done while the class is involved in other work.
6. Remember that tests are only a sample of what has been learned and probably not a very good one. They should, therefore, not

---

[4]Leonard B. Finkelstein and Donald D. Hammill, "A Reading-Free Science Test," *The Elementary School Journal* (October, 1969): pp. 34-37.

Evaluation

be used as the only means of evaluating. Take into consideration all the things students have done in class to develop their multi-talents.

7. Test for all levels of Bloom's taxonomy and use a test analysis grid to see that this has been done.
8. Ask questions to determine how students feel about the material being used.
9. Place the easier questions at the beginning of the test so students gain confidence and minimize their frustration and nervousness.
10. Consider the time factor. How long will it take students to complete the test? Some students will finish much sooner than others. What will you do with them? If you do not have some work outlined, they are likely to present discipline problems.
11. Design the test to be easily scored. Place a space for all the answers on one margin.
12. Rather than have students write on the test, have them place their responses on an answer sheet. This insures ease of recording and saves paper since the test may be used for more than one class.
13. Endeavor to build trust in students. This may be done by having them devise, and implement, an honor system to function in their class.

 Cheating occurs usually where there is a high degree of psychological threat. For example, if students are placed in competitive situations where they know there is little opportunity of success, they will likely be more dishonest. Reducing threat by using tests mainly as diagnostic instruments rather than a means to obtain a class spread for grading should diminish cheating problems.

 If you do not feel capable of operating effectively in the above manner, and prefer to run your class in a more controlled way you will need to discourage dishonesty. You might, for example, attempt to remove the temptation to copy by spreading students out or by making two versions of the same test and alternating these when you pass out the tests. You may wish to try the honor system; some instructors in high school have used this with success. Caution the students as soon as you see anyone cheating. It generally is better not to mention the name of the culprit at the first infraction. You might just say, "I see cheating" or "Some people are stretching their eyeballs."

Evaluation of Critical Thinking Processes

One of the major goals of teaching is to develop critical thinking processes, which can be evaluated in three ways as indicated below:

Evaluation of Critical Thinking Processes

1. The student evaluates himself.
2. The instructor checks on an observational form how well a student performs certain processes.
3. An instructor tests for the attainment of the processes.

Shown below is a form that can be used as indicated in numbers 1 and 2 above.

OBSERVATIONAL OR SELF-EVALUATIONAL INVENTORY OF STUDENT BEHAVIOR

		Seldom	Sometimes	Often

A. *Creative Processes*
 1. Formulates problems
 2. Hypothesizes
 3. Designs investigations
 4. Makes inferences

B. *Other Inquiry Processes*
 1. Records accurate observations
 2. Makes comparisons
 3. Quantifies
 4. Classifies
 5. Collects information
 6. Organizes information
 7. Interprets data
 8. Graphs when needed
 9. Makes operational definitions
 10. Identifies assumptions

C. *Attitudes*
 1. Demonstrates *objective* attitude by presenting evidence *for* and *against* an idea (Ex.: drugs, alcohol, smoking, pollution)

2. Suspends judgment until he has investigated objectively the subject or states he has insufficient information to make any definite statements
3. Indicates curiosity about observations by asking questions and making investigations
4. Indicates in discussion he knows the difference between hypotheses, solutions, facts, inferences by making such statements as: My hypothesis is . . . The solution is . . . The facts are . . . One inference is . . .
5. Changes opinions when confronted with evidence
6. States in using statistical data where warranted that although there is a correlation this does not necessarily mean a cause and effect relationship
7. States cause and effect relationships
8. Evaluates his and other procedures and information in experimentation and investigation

The list above should serve as a guide to help you construct test questions to assess how well students are learning critical processes and attitudes. All tests should have some questions to evaluate these processes. Examples of questions evaluating critical thinking processes are shown below:

1. *Recognizing a problem.*
   An American contractor goes to Mexico to build a dam. He hires several local laborers and starts his project. Knowing what you do about Mexico, what problems would you anticipate if you were this contractor?

2. *Learning to make hypotheses.*
   The following questions require students to make hypotheses:
   1. If the population in our community were to double, what would this do as far as our environment is concerned?
   2. A candle is placed in a tray. Water is added to the tray so that it is two inches deep. The candle is lit and covered with a jar. What will happen and why? Which of the following hypotheses do you think to be valid?
      a. The water level will remain the same in the jar.
      b. The water level will be lower in the jar than in the tray because the heat of the candle will cause water to evaporate.
      c. The water level will rise because all the oxygen will be burned causing less gas pressure in the jar.
      d. The water level will be lower because when the candle burns it produces carbon dioxide in the jar, which will cause greater gas pressure, forcing water out of the jar.
      e. The water level will rise because the candle gives off heat. This causes expansion of gases around the candle. When the jar is placed over the candle, the candle goes out, the air cools, and has less pressure than room temperature air. The water level then rises.
   3. A new person who is very authoritarian takes over the leadership of a tribe that has a democratic leader. Which of the following do you hypothesize will happen as a result?
      a. He will get things done faster and better than the previous leader.
      b. The morale in the tribe will initially increase.
      c. The cohesion of the tribe will increase.
      d. The "satisfaction" of the individuals in the tribe will decrease.
4. *Interpretating data and making valid conclusions.*
   1. What would you say were the major concerns of the authors you have read during this period?
   2. Now that you have studied the stock market for some weeks, what does it seem to respond to?
   3. During controlled experiments, the effects of various concentrations of auxin indole acetic acid on the growth of oat coleoptiles from which the tips have been removed were measured. The coleoptiles selected from seedlings germinated in darkness were placed in sugar solution with indole acetic acid as indicated in the table below. Growth effects were observed at the end of 24 hours.

Evaluation

COLEOP- TILE	CONCENTRATION MG/L. AV. CHANGE IN LENGTH					
Initial Length	Sugar 290	IAA .01	IAA 0.1	IAA 1.0	IAA 10.	Unknown IAA Sol.
2.0	2.8	3.4	5.1	7.0	2.1	6.3
2.1	2.6	3.0	4.9	6.8	2.1	6.2
2.2	3.0	3.3	5.2	7.0	2.3	6.0
2.2	2.8	3.3	5.1	7.2	2.3	6.1
2.0	2.4	2.8	5.0	7.1	2.1	6.0

From the analysis of the experimental data which of the following are true or false?

___ a. From the data in the table it is indicated that the optimum concentration of IAA is between 0.1 mg and 1 mg/liter.

___ b. Increasing concentration from zero produces the same proportional increase in growth rate.

___ c. Concentration of IAA influences cell division but has little effect on cell growth and elongation.

___ d. Removal of the coleoptile tip removes the source of plant auxin.

___ e. Coleoptiles are selected from seeds germinated in darkness because light greatly increases the production of plant auxin.

___ f. Above a certain concentration of IAA growth is actually inhibited.

___ g. Based on the growth rate of the various concentrations, the unknown solution is about 0.05 mg/l.

4. A car has collided with another one in an intersection. One car on the main highway has skid marks of 100 feet. The other, which was entering the intersection from making a boulevard stop, has skid marks of 3 feet. From this data, what can you say about the accident? What other data do you need in order to be more certain?

5. *Devising investigations and experiments.*
   1. How would you find out what racial problems exist in our school?
   2. How would you determine how well you communicate your thoughts and feelings?
   3. You suspect that a special plastic material used to coat floors might cause lung cancer. How would you go about proving this?

4. How would you demonstrate your creative ability to someone?
5. How would you prove that?
6. If you wanted to convince someone about that, what would you do?

Quantitative Terms

Modern social sciences, business, technical fields, and sciences require mathematics. The use of mathematics insures more accurate communication and brings exactness where vagueness once flourished. When we describe phenomena, we may do so by use of *dichotomous or metrical terms*. A dichotomous explanation is of the "either-or" type, such as it is tall (or short), small (or large), heavy (or light). Better communication strives to escape from explanations of this type because they contribute to ambiguity; what may be tall to one person may be short to another. More accurate explanations are usually given in metrical terms. Instead of saying a person is tall, one says he is 6 feet, 4 inches. Instead of stating, "Place some glucose in water," say, "Place 10 grams of glucose in 100 cc of water." The use of metrical terms insures exactness.

Exactness is important not only for insuring better communication but in replicating research as in science. It is the nature of the scientific enterprise to have one scientist check the results of another. This would be impossible without the use of exact metrical terms. Compare the following and this becomes obvious.

> A non-metrical explanation: "A small amount of penicillin was injected into a human organism suffering from a bacterial infection. The infection was cured in a short time."
>
> A metrical explanation: "Sixty subjects and ten control patients infected with streptococcus were administered 500,000 units of penicillin. On the third day, forty of the patients no longer evidenced the infection in the nasal-pharyngeal passages."

The importance of metrical terms can be easily pointed out to a class by holding up an eraser and having them describe it in complete detail so that it could be produced by some African tribesman who had never seen one. Students will often write down a description without giving the dimensions, thereby emphasizing the place of math in communicating. There are other uses of mathematics aside from those discussed here, but the important point is that mathematics become a

Evaluation

part of examinations where appropriate so that students gain insights into its association with the subject under study. One way this can be done is to utilize graphs as indicated in the following section.

Three Types of Graphing Test Questions

One quantitative tool used to considerable extent in science, business, technology, and social science is graphing. Graphing has the following advantages:

1. It conveys a tremendous amount of information in a small space. Try to describe verbally all the information depicted by a curved line on a graph, and this point immediately becomes apparent.
2. It helps the viewer to quickly see relationships which are not so apparent when one looks at a set of numbers.
3. A pictorial representation of data is retained more easily by individuals than are other forms of data.

Interpreting Graphs. From the graph below answer the following questions:

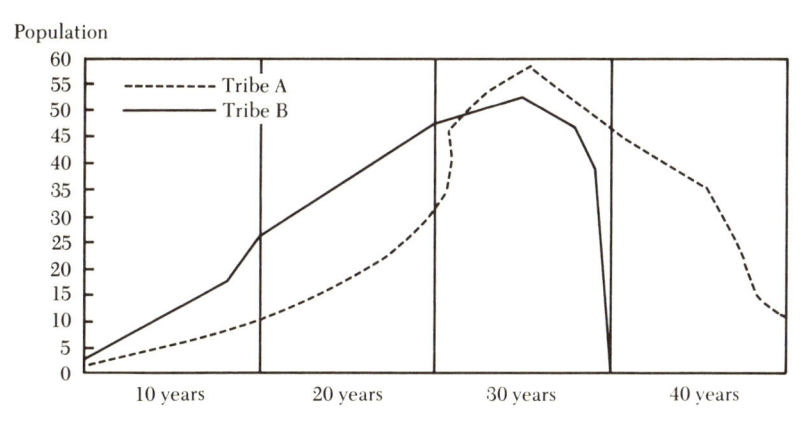

1. What information does the graph indicate?
2. What can you say about the growth of each tribe?
3. What can you say about the decline of the tribes?
4. What questions can you propose about the information on this graph?

Completion of a Graph. Another way to determine students' understanding of graphing is to have them complete a graph. They are then asked to complete it using the information they have.

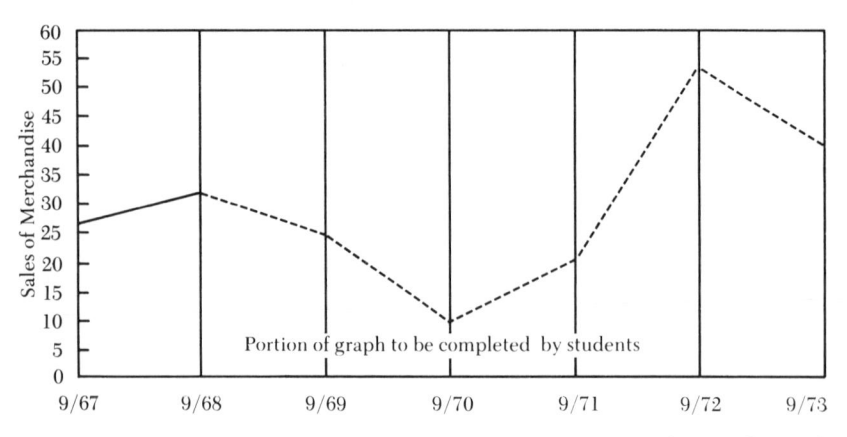

[Graph: Sales of Merchandise (y-axis, 0–60) vs. years 9/67 through 9/73 (x-axis), with label "Portion of graph to be completed by students"]

Student-drawn Graphs. Another way to test for understanding of graphs is to require students to devise one. For example, students could be given these instructions: "Given the population figures for our community over the last 50 years, prepare some way of communicating this information clearly for our local city councilmen."

Self-Evaluation Inventories

Description

A self-evaluation inventory (SEI) is an instrument enabling students to rate their progress toward attainment of cognitive and affective objectives in a course, a unit, or a daily lesson. Some curriculum projects use this form of evaluation extensively in their curriculum. The instrument consists simply of an item sheet containing behavioral objectives of a teaching unit and a response sheet. The response sheet is composed of nine-point scales, one response for each objective included on the item sheet. Three descriptions representing different levels of achievement are equally distributed along each scale.

Students evaluate their gain in knowledge and skill by placing two marks on each scale, one representing their achievement level at the beginning of the unit of instruction, and the other representing an estimate of their achievement level at the end of the unit of instruction. See the end of the chapter on Piaget for an example.

In the following example, a student has used the letter "B" to represent his knowledge level for an objective at the beginning and an "E" to represent his knowledge level for the end of the unit of instruction.

```
        Low      Moderate     High
          B                  E
   1.  1  2  3  4  5  6  7  8  9
```

The numerical difference between the two marks, called the *item gain score*, represents the gain in knowledge or skill implied by a specific objective. The sum of all the item gain scores on a self-evaluation inventory, called the *gain score*, represents the gain in knowledge perceived by the student for a particular set of objectives.

For validation of the SEI, criterion tests constructed from the same course objectives have been administered by investigators in pre-test and post-test situations. A correlation between the gain scores of the self-evaluation inventory and the gain in achievement, as measured by the criterion test, has been found to be significant (Duel, 1956; and Tillery, 1967). A significant correlation indicates students have made accurate self-judgments about their gain in achievement pertaining to the unit of instruction.

Use of Self-Evaluation Inventories

Self-evaluation inventories have many uses in education. Among those used in the past are student evaluation of teacher effectiveness, course evaluation, final grades, and teacher self-rating of effectiveness.

Only recently has emphasis been placed on allowing students to make self-judgments about outcomes that concern them individually in a course of instruction. Self-evaluation inventories can be used in daily lessons, a unit of instruction, or a course of instruction. They can be used to evaluate objectives in relation to films, field trips, laboratory exercises, and individual items contained in a multi-media approach.

Students can make self-evaluations on cognitive achievement or on a variety of dimensions within the affective domain: interest, attitudes, values, appreciations, and relevancy. Self-evaluation is only as good as the quality of the inventory.

Construction of Student Self-Evaluation Inventories

The first step in the construction of a student self-evaluation inventory is to decide what goals to evaluate for a lesson, a unit of instruction, or a course of instruction. Next, write specific behavioral objectives for goals of instruction. These objectives should include cognitive, affective and psychomotor domains.

Once the behavioral objectives have been written, place them on the item sheet. Order the objectives according to subject or cognitive level, i.e. light, sound, waves, or knowledge, comprehension . . . evaluation.

The construction of the response sheet may vary with the interests of the evaluator. If only content (achievement) is to be evaluated, place a six- or nine-point scale for each objective on the response sheet.

The scale should be on a continuum from low to moderate to high. Other scales for evaluation of interest, value, or relevancy may be included along with the content scale for each objective.

Administration of the Inventory

Two methods of administering self-evaluation inventories can be used:

1. *Same time:* The inventory is given only at the end of the period of instruction. The student rates his "before and end" achievement at the same time. This method is desirable on a daily lesson.
2. *Pre-post:* The inventory is handed out at the start of the unit of instruction and the student rates his "before" achievement on the response sheet. The response sheets are collected and the unit of instruction then takes place. After the instruction, the response sheets are handed back to the student and he makes his "end" achievement evaluation. This method may be more desirable on a unit of instruction covering a larger period of time, such as a two week unit or a ten week course. The student should be allowed to retain the list of objectives throughout the unit of instruction.

Sample SEI Illustrating Method of Same Time

STUDENT SELF-EVALUATION INVENTORY

INSTRUCTIONS: You are requested to indicate for the following series of items your opinion of the degree of skill or knowledge you possess in each case. Evaluate items in terms of the scale shown. Place two letters on the scale of the response portion for each item. A "B" should be used to indicate the amount of skill or knowledge you had at the beginning of the lesson. An "E" should be used to indicate the degree of skill or knowledge you now have at the end of the lesson.

ITEM	RESPONSE		
	Low	Moderate	High
1. *Graph* the relationship between volume, temperature, pressure of gases when one variable is held constant.	1 2 3	4 5 6	7 8 9
2. Apply volume, temperature, and pressure relationships to a balloon which moves up and down in the atmosphere to determine size relationships.[5]	1 2 3	4 5 6	7 8 9

---

[5]The above self-evaluational material has been largely prepared by Dr. Clifford A. Hofwolt of George Peabody Teachers College, Nashville, Tennessee. For further infor-

Alternatives to Traditional Grading

The evaluating process in itself is neither negative nor positive. Its function depends on how the instructor uses it. He can use it to diagnose his teaching, student achievement, or to compare one student with another.

Unfortunately, most teachers utilize the testing aspect of evaluation for obtaining a class range in which some students are identified high and others low as determined by achievement scores. These scores are then used to grade students. Presently, there are an increasing number of educators questioning the desirability of using tests for this purpose and whether grading should even be used. They argue that grading establishes a competition system which is bound to depreciate and demean the "self-concepts" of many students. True, competition may act as a motivating force for some people; however, its cost comes high because an individual will only compete if he knows he has a chance of winning. The "hierarchy game," placing one person above another, is bound to contribute to the beliefs of some students that they are trapped into a system where they seldom have opportunities for success. If this is true, no wonder the press occasionally carries stories about young vandals breaking into schools and destroying thousands of dollars worth of equipment. The general reaction of the public is that these children are bad individuals and need to be punished, but what made them bad? Why do they hate and strike out at the school? Certainly, it's human nature not to harm the things you love. The facts are that the American school system has a high percentage of drop-outs. The individuals that drop out often leave because they do not have feelings of success and thereby opportunities to enhance their self-concepts in the school environment.

It is apparent, therefore, that a teacher should seriously consider the consequences of playing the testing hierarchy game—"You're better than John, and John is better than Dick." Why do students have to be *better than?* Why can't they just be *different?* Grading, we believe, needs to be lessened or eliminated. If you are in a school where it plays a major role, endeavor to have teachers question its desirability and efficacy and strive to reduce its importance. Convey to students that you are more interested in having them achieve the goals of the class as

---

mation on the justification for using self-evaluational inventories in science consult: Clifford A. Hofwolt, "An Exploratory Study of the Effect of Self-Evaluation Inventories on Student Achievement in High School Science Courses," Unpublished Ed.D. Dissertation, University of Northern Colorado, 1971; James H. Duel, "A Study of Validity and Reliability of Student Evaluation of Training," Unpublished Ed.D. Dissertation, Washington University, 1956; Bill W. Tillery, "Improvement of Science Education Methods Courses Through Student Self-Evaluation," Unpublished Ed.D. Dissertation, Colorado State College, 1967.

best they can rather than playing "I caught you games," such as "See, you don't know this," or "You don't know this as well as. . . ." The instructor by playing this game undoubtedly conveys to the student that he is really not primarily interested in helping him to learn. We teachers are employed to help people grow as persons—not to demean nor hinder them. To look on a class as a tremendous pool of human potential striving for manifestation is an exciting perception. We believe the function of evaluation should primarily aid in the actualization of this potential.

Teachers aware of the problems in using evaluation to establish student achievement hierarchies have devised various approaches to deemphasize the importance of testing and grading. Some of these methods are:

1. *Self-evaluation* where the student evaluates himself and then decides in cooperation with his instructor where he needs to improve.
2. *Performance criteria.* The teacher outlines what material must be completed for a certain grade. The teacher may also use certain performance criteria to see whether the student has achieved a certain level; for example, in typing, 50 words a minute receives an "A".

How is this teacher using evaluation as he is teaching?

Evaluation

3. *Written evaluations.* The instructor writes a summary of the achievements and weaknesses of the student. It is suggested that this be done jointly with the student.
4. *Pass-fail.* Students are given pass or fail as a grade. This reduces competition but has the disadvantage of not recognizing excellence.
5. *Giving all students the same grade.* This eliminates competition but usually is not well received by all students, particularly if a grade less than an "A" is given.
6. *Grading secretly.* The teacher gives grades but doesn't tell the student what his grade is except that he is doing above or below average work. A disadvantage of this approach is that a student may experience anxiety over what the instructor thinks about them.
7. *Student-teacher contract.* The teacher in cooperation with the student establishes the amount of work that must be done to receive a grade of "A", "B", "C", etc.

The Contract Method of Evaluation

Dr. Arthur Combs at the University of Florida many years ago became concerned about the negative aspects of grading. As a result, he devised a contract system which he has continually modified and tested with students over the last fifteen years. A brief summary of his system is outlined below. Although his system has been tested mainly with university students, it has many components that could be modified for use in the secondary school. He says:

> The method of grading now used in my teaching is the product of 15 years of trial and error. It is the best method I have found to date for meeting the following criteria:
>
> A desirable grading system should:
> 1. Meet college and university standards of effort, performance and excellence.
> 2. Evaluate the student on his personal performance rather than in competition with his fellow students.
> 3. Permit students to work for whatever goal they desire to shoot for.
> 4. Provide the broadest possible field of choice for the student.
> 5. Challenge students to stretch themselves to their utmost.

6. Eliminate as much as possible all sources of externally imposed threat.
7. Involve the student actively in planning for his own learning and placing the responsibility for this learning directly and unequivocally on his shoulders.
8. Free the student as much as possible from the necessity of pleasing the instructor.
9. Provide maximum flexibility to meet changing conditions.

To meet these criteria my current practice is to enter into a contract with each student for the grade he would like to achieve. Each student writes a contract with his instructor indicating in great detail: (a) the grade he would like to have; (b) what he proposes to do to achieve it; and (c) how he proposes to demonstrate that he has done it. Once this contract has been signed by the student and instructor, the student is, thereafter, free to move in any way he desires to the completion of his contract. When the contract has been completed "In the letter and in the spirit" the student's grade is automatic. The procedure is as follows:

At the second meeting of the class the philosophy and procedures for this method of evaluation are carefully explained to the student. He is given two blank contracts on which to file his proposal in duplicate, and his deadline date (usually 1/4 to 1/3 of the way through the semester) is set when all contracts must be in and approved. The student is told that in proposing his contract he needs to take into consideration two things: (a) what he would like to do and (b) what the university has a right to expect of a person working for that grade. Next, the instructor discusses with the student (1) the general criteria for grades in the college and (2) the specific ways in which these may be met in this particular class. While these, of course, differ from class to class, they fall generally within this framework: For a grade of "C" —The college requirement—satisfactory completion of the basic requirements of the course. These requirements are spelled out in detail for the particular course including such things as attendance at all class meetings, required and optional readings, and such other specific requirements as the instructor intends to require of all students throughout the semester. These latter might be written reports, projects, observations, participation in research, etc.

For a grade of "B"—The college requirement—completion of all of the basic requirements for the course, plus an additional program of study above and beyond that generally expected of all students. This is interpreted for my classes to mean that a student may propose, (a) some special area of intensive study he would like to pursue, or (b) a research or action project of merit he would like to carry out.

For a grade of "A"—The college requirement—satisfactory completion of the requirements for "C" and "B" levels, plus the consistent demonstration of a high level of scholarship, interest, and excellence in the subject matter of the course. For my classes this is interpreted to mean that students working for an "A" must satisfactorily complete work at the "B" and "C" levels and take a stiff essay examination. The contract blank provides space for the student to write side by side what he proposes to do for a particular grade and how he proposes to demonstrate that he has completed that proposal. Contracts must be made out in great detail indicating precisely what is to be done and how, at every step of the way to assure that students give a good deal of thought to their contract at the time they are filed, and to make certain that there is no misunderstanding at the end of the semester when the decision must be made as to whether the contract was fulfilled or not. A long period for planning contracts is purposely given students to provide time to get the feel of the course and to make preliminary explorations concerning the problems they might like to tackle for special study or projects. As soon as a student has made out his contract, he hands it in, in duplicate, and it is discussed with him by the instructor who may suggest additions, deletions or modifications of one sort or another. Once the contract has been signed by the instructor, there are no examinations in the course except the one selected by students working for "A" grades.

During the semester if it becomes necessary for a student to make a change in his contract, he may do so by requesting its renegotiation and appropriate modifications will be made. There is one exception to this: contracts may be modified at the same level or a lesser level but a student once having decided to work for a particular grade may not decide to work for a higher one. A student who is going to work for a superior grade, after all, must begin this process at the very start of the semester. The method of demonstration the student chooses to show completion of his contract is up to him. He may put on a demonstration for the class, write a paper, run an experiment, do a tape recording, keep a log of his experiences, or whatever seems appropriate. If a student does not complete his contract at any level, his grade automatically drops back to the next level which he has satisfactorily completed. Thus a person who contracted for an "A" but decided *not* to take the final examination would automatically receive a "B" grade if his work had been complete at that level. Similarly, a student working for a "C" grade who fudged on the basic requirements of the course would move back to a "D" grade or even to an "F" grade depending upon the degree of his dereliction.

While this system of evaluation is by no means perfect, it has proven far more satisfactory than the traditional methods of grading and evaluation I formerly used. Students are sometimes upset by the procedure at first and may object to having so much responsibility placed upon them. These objections, however, quickly dissipate as the student discovers he has a brand new freedom which even permits him to disagree with the instructor with impunity. Experience has shown that students read far more under this system, work much harder and show far more originality, spontaneity and creativity. The response of students has mostly been enthusiastically favorable. From the instructor's view, it has proven eminently satisfactory. The technique is not foolproof, however, and occasionally a student misuses his privileges. But as one of my students expressed it, "I guess you know that sometimes students take advantage of your grading system —but then, I guess the old system took advantage of the student!"[6]

Summary

Evaluation involves the total assessing of a student's learning by the instructor. Just as there are levels of learning so are there levels of testing.

Teachers evaluate students mainly by tests and laboratory reports. Modern teacher-made tests should devote less time to recall questions and more to the higher cognitive levels of Bloom's taxonomy and the affective domain. Tests should be constructed from an instructor's list of objectives so that he evaluates what he considers most important in the learning process. A test is only a sample of what is being learned, and other means of evaluation should also play a major part in determining the achievement and development of the students' multiple talents.

Self-evaluational instruments should be used frequently in assessing a student's achievement. The student knows best what he is learning and how he feels about it. Teachers need, therefore, to ask students to judge their own achievement. One way to do this is to give the student a list of objectives of a unit or course and have him judge what he knew or felt about the course before, as compared to his learning after studying the material. This method has been shown to be a valid measuring technique and gives a better indication of actual growth than does the typical test.

In mathematics, social studies, business, and science, graphs are important means of communication. Their development and use should be, therefore, evaluated in these courses.

Each test should contain questions that will enable the teacher to evaluate students' critical thinking processes, values, and interests. Students should know how to recognize a problem, make hypotheses, interpret data, draw valid conclusions, devise investigations, affirm interests, and clarify values.

Certain features of each type of test must be considered before its construction. Completion and matching tests, because of their empha-

---

[6]Arthur W. Combs, "A Contract Method of Evaluation," Unpublished Paper, University of Florida (no date given).

sis on recall, are to be discouraged. Self-tests and problem tests place more emphasis on self-instruction and can be used to motivate class discussions. A teacher should consider how long a test will take and provide assignments for those who finish before the class ends, thus lessening the incidence of discipline problems. Furthermore, teachers should endeavor to indicate to students that they trust them. This has been done by some instructors through establishing honor systems or providing an atmosphere where students feel no inclination to cheat.

Good test construction requires considerable sophistication. Teachers are urged to get further training in this very important part of their professional competence.

Further Investigation and Study

1. Prepare a test to evaluate some of your objectives.
2. Classify your questions according to Bloom's taxonomy and determine the percentage of questions for each of his categories.
3. Prepare a picture type of test.
4. Prepare a self-evaluational inventory for a unit.
5. Prepare a problem test.
6. Why would you want to use a self-evaluational inventory in class?
7. Design five questions that test mainly for critical thinking processes.
8. How would you reduce threat in the evaluation process?
9. Harry Wong, a science teacher in California, says that he never gives tests to his academically poor learners. How do you think he evaluates his students?
10. What does evaluation involve?
11. Describe what you consider to be a weak test.
12. Describe what you consider to be a strong test.
13. What is meant by the statement "A test is only a sample"?
14. What do you know about a test if a student passed it by simply reading the book the night before he took it?
15. How would you evaluate laboratory work and why?
16. What are the steps you should take in writing a question requiring application of knowledge? Write three examples of this type of question.
17. Devise three questions involving understanding of graphing.
18. Write two questions requiring a student to use his creative ability.
19. What are some general considerations to be kept in mind when making a true-false, a multiple-choice, and a completion test?
20. How will you operate in the classroom to insure honesty?
21. What considerations about time and individual differences are necessary for giving a test?
22. What were the three main ideas discussed in this chapter?
23. It is said that a teacher who uses evaluation well is more scientific. What is meant by this statement?

# 12 The National Assessment of Educational Progress

What do young people in the United States know? How do they measure up with respect to certain areas of knowledge, processes, and attitudes? What are the results of the large expenditures on education for the youth of the nation? These questions are being studied in a large-scale project currently underway.

The National Assessment of Educational Progress is a survey of the knowledge, skills, understanding, and attitudes of young Americans. A sample of youngsters at ages 9, 13, and 17 and adults from ages 26 to 35 is being tested in the areas of Science, Mathematics, Reading, Writing, Social Studies, Citzenship, Literature, Art, Music, and Career and Occupational Development. Repeated measurements at approximately five-year intervals over the next decades will permit trends to be identified. The first subject areas assessed were Science, Writing, and Citizenship during 1969 and 1970. The first repeat was carried out in 1972 and 1973 with Science. The project is supported by grants from the Ford Foundation, the Carnegie Corporation, and the U.S. Office of Education. About 100,000 people are involved in the sample tested each year. While hundreds of items are administered for each subject, the total sample for each item is about 2,000.

In preparing objectives for the various subject matter areas, the National Assessment Project considered that these objectives must

1. be considered important by scholars in the field.
2. be accepted as an educational task by schools.
3. be considered desirable by thoughtful lay citizens.

In Science, four major objectives are identified:
1. To know fundamental facts and principles of Science.
2. To possess the ability and skills needed to engage in process of Science.
3. To understand the investigative nature of Science.
4. To have attitudes about and appreciation of scientists, Science, and the consequences of Science that stem from adequate understandings.

In Mathematics the National Assessment staff concluded that a three-dimensional classification scheme was the most effective and meaningful method to specify mathematics objectives. The three dimensions consider:
1. Use of Mathematics.
2. Mathematics curriculum content areas.
3. Abilities or behaviors conducive to effective utilization and understanding of Mathematics.

In Reading, the objectives are:
1. To comprehend what is read.
2. To analyze what is read.
3. To use what is read.
4. To reason logically from what is read.
5. To make judgments concerning what is read.

Additionally, in Reading, eight themes were prepared expressing behaviorally the competencies expected of students at the age levels tested. They are:
1. Word Meanings
2. Visual Aids
3. Written Directions
4. Reference Materials
5. Significant Facts in Passages
6. Main Ideas and Organization of Passages
7. Inferences from Passages
8. Critical Reading of Passages

Four Writing objectives have been prepared.
1. To write to communicate adequately in a social situation.
2. To write to communicate adequately in a business or vocational situation.

3. To write to communicate adequately in a scholastic situation.
4. To appreciate the value of Writing.

In Social Studies, five objectives are identified.
1. To have curiosity about human affairs.
2. To use analytic scientific procedures effectively.
3. To be sensitive to creative-intuitive methods of explaining the human condition.
4. To have knowledge relevant to the major ideas and concerns of social scientists.
5. To have a reasoned commitment to the values that sustain a free society.

The Citizenship objectives are ten in number:
1. To show concern for the welfare and dignity of others.
2. To support the rights and freedoms of all individuals.
3. To help maintain law and order.
4. To know the main structure and functions of our government.
5. To seek community improvement through active democratic participation.
6. To understand the problems of international relations.
7. To support rationality in communicating thought and action on social problems.
8. To take responsibility for one's own personal development and obligations.
9. For ages, 9, 13, and 17, to help and respect one's own family.
10. For adults, to nurture the development of their children as future citizens.

In Literature the objectives are as follows:
1. To read literature of excellence.
2. To become engaged in and find meanings in and evaluating works of literature.
3. To develop a continuing interest in participating in literature and the literacy experience.

In Art the objectives are:
1. To perceive and respond to aspects of Art.
2. To value art as an important realm of human experience.

3. To produce works of art.
4. To know about art.
5. To make and justify judgments about the esthetic merit and quality of works of art.

In the field of Music, the following objectives are listed:

1. To perform a piece of music.
2. To read standard musical notation.
3. To listen to music with understanding.
4. To be knowledgable about some musical instruments, some of the terminology of music, methods of performance and forms, some of the standard literature of music, and some aspects of the history of music.
5. To know about the musical resources of the community and seek musical experiences by performing music.
6. To make judgments about music and value of personal worth of music.

In the field of Career and Occupational Development, the objectives are as follows:

1. To prepare for making career decisions.
2. To improve career and occupational capabilities.
3. To possess skills that are generally useful in the world of work.
4. To practice effective work habits.
5. To have positive attitudes about work.

Examples of Exercises

Exercises were prepared for each of the objectives in each of the subject areas. For example, in the area of Science under Objective 1 "Know the fundamental facts and principles of Science," the exercises were largely paper and pencil multiple-choice questions which were read to the respondents. Some of the examples of representative exercises under Objective 1 are as follows (the percent of 9-year-olds correctly answering these exercises is given for each example):

1. A human baby comes from its mother's body. 92%
2. You brush your teeth to keep them from decaying. 91%
3. Bees get their food, nectar, from flowers. 88%
4. Day and night occur because the earth rotates. 81%

5. To see something, light must reach one's eyes. 79%
6. The sun is seen only during daytime because the earth is turning. 70%
7. Most scientists think the center of the earth is very hot. 58%
8. A different substance is formed from a candle when it burns. 46%
9. After a cold front passes, it is common to have clearing skies. 34%
10. Coal is formed from dead plants. 15%

For 17-year-olds, representative exercises for Objective 1 were as follows:

1. An example of a balanced meal is steak, bread, carrots, and milk. 95%
2. Among five animals that have been found as fossils in rocks, only dinosaurs have never been seen alive by man. 89%
3. An electric current in a copper wire involves mainly the movement of electrons. 69%
4. The idea of natural selection is usually associated with Darwin's theory of evolution. 68%
5. Research into the nature of matter shows that it is made up of individual moving particles. 58%
6. The temperature of two pints of water at 40° F mixed with one pint of water at 100° F will be about 60° F. 57%
7. A boat traveling at five miles per hour down a river which flows at five miles per hour will take 60 minutes to go 10 miles downstream. 54%
8. C above middle C has a higher frequency and shorter wavelength than middle C. 46%
9. On the average, in human females the egg is released 14 days after menstruation begins. 29%
10. A substance synthesized in one part of a cell and then later broken down in other parts with the resulting release of energy is ATP. 17%

In the exercises used with young adults on Objective 2 "Possess the abilities and skills needed to engage in the processes of Science," most young adults responded correctly to:

1. Very few people in the United States today get smallpox because most people have had smallpox vaccinations. 95%

Many young adults were able to perform the following tasks:

1. Interpret tabular data to correctly determine which series of four weights best establishes that one object is heavier than another. 63%
2. Use a watch to determine the total time it takes a pendulum to swing 10 times. 49%
3. Balance a beam balance with a weight. 74%

To illustrate the exercises used on Objective 3 in Science "To understand the investigative nature of science," most 13-year-olds were able to correctly:

1. Select from a variety of skills (music, magic, marketing, mathematics, and manufacturing) the one, mathematics, which is most useful to scientific research. 79%
2. Recognize that the statement, "My dog is better than your dog" is not a question amenable to scientific inquiry. 73%
3. Recognize that repeated measures of the same thing will usually yield successive results which are close to each other but not exactly all the same. 69%
4. Recognize that the basic purpose of a scientific theory is to explain why things act as they do. 56%

In Reading, the following exercises illustrate for age nine the median percentage of success for the reading themes designated as Word Meanings. The exercise was:

> Complete the sentences with the words that make the most sense.
> The boy wanted (a) a new ball, (b) under dinner, (c) rode his bike, (d) to the circus, (e) stopped raining, (f) I don't know.

The correct answer was (a) a new ball and the national percentage of success was 83 percent on this exercise.

For the reading theme Visual Aids a picture of a boy with a dog on a leash and another dog resting nearby was presented, and the instructions were:

> Look at the picture and fill in the oval beside the sentence which tells best what the drawing shows: (a) The boy has two dogs on a leash. (b) The boy is walking behind his dog. (c) The dog on the leash has spots on it. (d) The dog sitting down has spots on it. (e) I don't know.

The National Assessment of Educational Progress

The correct answer was (c) and the national percentage of success was 85 percent.

For the reading theme Picking Significant Facts From Passages, at age nine, instructions were to read the passage and answer the question which followed it. The passage was:

> Helen Keller was born in 1880 in Tuscombia, Alabama. When she was two years old, she lost her sight and hearing as a result of an illness. In 1886 she became the pupil of Anne Sullivan who taught Helen to "see with her fingertips," to "hear with her feet and hands" and to communicate with other people. Miss Sullivan succeeded in arousing Helen's curiosity and interest by spelling the names of objects into her hand. At the end of three years, Helen had mastered both the manual and Braille alphabet and could read and write.
>
> Miss Sullivan's method of teaching chiefly made use of what? (a) writing, (b) gestures, (c) pictures, (d) sound waves, (e) sense of touch, (f) I don't know. The correct answer was (e) sense of touch, and the national percentage of success was 54 percent.

In the reading theme Picking Inferences From Passages for age seventeen, the student was instructed to read the passage and complete the sentence which followed it. The passage was:

> Between April and October, the Persian Gulf is dotted with small boats of pearl divers. Some 75,000 of them are busy diving down and bringing up pearl-bearing oysters. These oysters are not the kind we eat. The edible oyster produces pearls of little or no value. You may have heard tales of diners who discovered pearls and sold them for great sums of money. These stories were entertaining but not accurate.
>
> The Persian Gulf has many: (a) large boats of pearl divers, (b) pearl divers who eat oysters, (c) edible oysters that produce pearls, (d) non-edible oysters that produce pearls, (e) edible oysters that do not produce pearls, (f) I don't know.

The correct answer is (d) and the national percentage of success on this exercise was 68 percent.

Examples of writing exercises in the four objectives are as follows: For Objective 1, To Write to Communicate Adequately in a Social Situation, 9-year-olds were asked to:

1. Write a thank-you note to their grandmother for the birthday gift of a puppy. Eighty-eight percent of the 9-year-olds wrote a ledgible letter expressing their thanks for the gift.

2. Address an envelope giving all the information which should be placed on a properly addressed envelope. Six bits of information were required for the task to be scored acceptably. Twenty-eight percent of nines did the task successfully.

For Objective 2, To Write to Communicate Adequately in a Business or Vocational Situation, 13-year-olds were given all the information necessary to order a pair of seahorses. The product was mentioned by 88 percent, but only 49 percent included the place to send the seahorses. Only 46 percent provided all the necessary information to complete this task successfully.

Thirteen-year-olds were asked to write an invitation to the mayor to speak to a seventh grade class about his work. The invitation had to include four bits of information in order to be judged acceptable. This task was completed successfully by 27 percent of the 13-year-olds, although much larger percentages succeeded in mentioning several parts of the information but not all needed.

For Objective 4, Appreciate the Value of Writing, adults were:

1. Asked what they ordinarily read during the week. Ninety-seven percent stated that they read at least one of the following: books, business letters, recipes, etc. Only three percent did not indicate reading of any of them.

2. Fifty-five percent of adults said that they had written a letter to order something through the mail during the past 12 months.

In the area of Citizenship, Objective 1, To Show Concern for the Well-being of Others, is exemplified by the following exercise: 9-year-olds and 13-year-olds were asked in interviews, "Have you ever helped another boy or girl do something outside of school because he or she needed help?" Fifty-nine percent of the nines and 78 percent of the thirteens reported that they have helped another boy or girl outside of school within the past year.

In another exercise they were asked to state actions that they could take to help stop public park discrimination. Eighty-one percent of the thirteens, 92 percent of the seventeens and 82 percent of the adults stated one or more actions they could take.

In Objective 2, Support Rights and Freedoms of All Individuals, one exercise presented to 13-year-olds was an interview as follows: Suppose the police arrest someone they think steals things. The person arrested may or may not be guilty of stealing things. What decides if a person is guilty and has to go to prison for stealing? Eighty-one percent of the 13-year-olds stated that a jury, trial, judge, or court decides whether or not a person is guilty.

The National Assessment of Educational Progress

For Objective 3, To Recognize the Value of Just Law, an exercise to assess the understanding of the need for law and order was presented to 9-year-olds. The results showed that 99 percent of 9-year-olds indicated that we need rules on the playground and 88 percent indicated that grownups also need rules. Sixty-three percent additionally were able to give at least one reason.

In Objective 4, To Know the Main Structure and Functions of Government, 49 percent of 9-year-olds, 17 percent of 13-year-olds, 78 percent of 17-year-olds, and 89 percent of adults stated that the President does not have the right to do anything affecting the United States that he wants.

In Objective 6, To Understand Problems of International Relations, 97 percent of 13-year-olds, 94 percent of 17-year-olds and 98 percent of adults could name at least one country where fighting has been going on during the last 12 months. Only 30 percent of adults could name four countries.

How well are the youth of our country able to use library skills?

In Objective 8, To Take Responsibility For One's Own Development, 24 percent of 13-year-olds and 58 percent of 17-year-olds reported that they have talked about their plans for education or jobs with a teacher or school counselor. About 82 percent of 13-year-olds and 86 percent of 17-year-olds reported that they have talked about their plans for education or jobs with their parents or guardian.

A final example of an exercise is given for Objective 9, To Help and Respect Their Own Families. In this exercise 91 percent of 9-year-olds reported that they worked around home about five hours or more each week.

The previous examples have shown the great variety of objectives and exercises presented to four age levels in the National Assessment Program. The data obtained to this date in the subjects assessed have been analyzed according to five major categories and breakdowns within these categories: sex, region, size and type of community, parental education, and color. Wide disparities were found when the results among these categories were compared. In general, inner-city, black, and southeastern United States pupils of parents with limited education fared least well on almost all of the assessments to date. Table 4 on page 296 shows the comparisons of average percentage deviations from national medians in three subject areas by six analysis categories.

Interrelationships Between Subject Areas

Certain interrelationships exist between the findings in the NAEP surveys of science, reading, and citizenship thus far reported. School learning is not unilateral. Students experience a wide spectrum of learnings at all levels. The typical educational experience is a blend obtained by exposure to and selection from a variety of separate disciplines presented in greater or lesser measure.

Considering this state of affairs, it is inevitable that interrelationships between the various disciplines will develop. This must be considered as a normal result of the systems and patterns of education extant in the United States. This section deals with interrelationships between the results obtained in national assessment surveys of Science, Reading and Citizenship.

The Reading and Literature assessment was conducted from October, 1970, through August, 1971. This followed by approximately eighteen months the assessments of Science, Writing, and Citizenship which were conducted between March, 1969, and February, 1970. Populations assessed were similar in categories—9-year-olds, 13-year-olds, 17-year-olds, and young adults (ages 26-35). Data presented in each of the surveys were likewise categorized according to region, sex, size and type of community, race, and parents' high school education.

The objectives of the Reading survey do not contain items comparable to the first objective in the Science survey—Know Fundamental Facts and Principles of Science—mainly because reading is itself a process and a skill rather than a body of knowledge.

In comparing the second objective of the Science survey—Possess the Abilities and Skills Needed to Engage in the Processes of Science—with the first five objectives of the Reading survey, it is apparent that many similarities exist. The skills and processes of comprehending, analyzing, using, reasoning logically, and making judgments require essentially the same kinds of mental operations whether they involve science materials, reading materials, social studies materials, or those of any other subject.

When one compares the number of exercises written for the national assessment surveys in science and reading in the respective objective categories, the disparity of emphases becomes apparent. The distribution of exercises for the science objectives is shown in Table 1.

Table 2 shows the distribution of objectives in the Reading survey. It can be seen in Table 1 that Science devoted 68 percent of its exercises to Objective I, "Know Fundamental Facts and Principles of Science." Reading, by comparison, had no exercises of a comparable type. Science devoted approximately 27 percent of its exercises to Objectives II and III, "Possesses the Abilities and Skills Needed to Engage in the Process of Science" and "Understand the Investigative Nature of Science." Reading, on the other hand, devoted all of its exercises to Objectives 1-5 which dealt with processes and skills of comprehending, analyzing, reasoning, using what is read, and making judgments. Both the Science and Reading surveys essentially omitted exercises purporting to assess objectives dealing with attitudes, interests, and appreciations (e.g., Science 5.2%, Reading 0.0%).

TABLE 1. Categories of Science Objectives

Age	Objective	Released	Unreleased	% of Total
9	I (Know fundamental facts and princi-	40	57	
13	ples of science)	28	47	
17		38	51	
Adult		34	51	
Totals		(140)	(206)	(346) 68%

Age	Objective	Released	Unreleased	% of Total
	II			
9	(Possess the abilities and skills	12	16	
13	needed to engage in the processes of	12	19	
17	science)	10	14	
Adult		11	13	
Totals		(45)	(62)	(107) 21%
	III			
9	(Understand the investigative nature	5	6	
13	of science)	4	4	
17		3	3	
Adult		2	3	
Totals		(14)	(16)	(30) 5.8%
	IV			
9	(To have attitudes about and apprecia-	1	8	
13	tions of scientists, science, and the con-	3	5	
17	sequences of science that stem from ade-	3	2	
Adult	quate understandings)	2	3	
Totals		(9)	(18)	(27) 5.2%

TABLE 2. Categories of Reading Objectives

Objective	Number	Percent
1	145	34.9
2	40	9.7
3	106	25.6
4	43	10.4
5	5	1.2
6	0	0.0
1 & 2	1	0.2
1 & 3	54	13.0
1 & 4	3	0.7
2 & 4	1	0.2
Unknown	18	4.1
Total	416	100.0

Study of the results of the Science and Reading survey reveals certain similarities and dissimilarities. "Participants—fared best on exercises which required them to read to gain factual information and less well on critical and interpretive reading."[1] In Science, for the 13-year-old groups, the exercises causing students least difficulty were those requiring them to form a simple hypothesis employing elementary scientific knowledge. It may be that similar skills are employed in these two types of problems, thus producing comparable results.

In reading, "highest scores were made on tasks such as reading a TV guide from a newspaper, a road map, directional signs, store labels, recipes, and answering factual questions about them. These questions were considered the 'day to day' or functional types of reading."[2] In Science, "most 13-year-olds answered correctly when asked about simple scientific facts, many of which are close to everyday experience."[3]

From these results, it appears that children perform similarly in Science and Reading on tasks requiring basically similar skills and knowledge.

The reading and science data showed many apparent similarities regarding the performance of children in the two disciplines. For example, one is more likely to find a child having reading difficulties in one of the economically depressed areas of a large city or in a sparsely settled rural area than in an affluent suburb. In science, data showed that all of the sampled age groups in large cities and small rural areas had performance medians below the national medians on all exercises. In Reading:

> the difference between the typical performance of students in the nation as a whole remained relatively constant regardless of whether the reading ability being measured involved some of the simpler activities (like reading signs) or activities considered more difficult and complex (like extracting the main ideas from passages or the critical reading of a literary work).
>
> The relative consistency of this difference between subgroups did not occur in the National Assessment survey of science. There the black subgroup, for example, generally did best on exercises tied in to daily experience and fell behind national performance as the exercises grew more complicated and abstract. But in reading, the difference seemed relatively little altered by the increasing difficulty of the exercises.[4]

Concerning regional results, it was found in the Reading survey that those students in the first three age groups (9, 13, and 17) who were located in the northeast and central regions did best on all types

---

[1] *NAEC Newsletter*, No. 4 (June-July, 1972), p. 1.
[2] *NAEC Newsletter*, 1972.
[3] *NAEP, Science National Results*, 1970, Report 1.
[4] *NAEP*, 1970.

of reading tasks. Adults in the west showed the best performance. This differs from science results only in that 17-year-olds in the west, in addition to adults, exceeded northeast and central performance. This exhibits once again the strong positive correlation among all groups between Reading and Science results.

Home environment and parental education appear to be highly influential factors in children's success in reading and science. In reading, students with at least one parent educated beyond high school generally succeeded about 30 percent better than students with parents who had not gone beyond grade school. Comparable results are evident in science with children or parents who had not graduated from high school performing about 1 to 7.5 percent below the national median for all students.

When one examines the Reading themes used in the survey, it is evident that several of them may require competencies similar to those needed for success in science, particularly for higher level operations such as critical analysis, drawing inferences, or making judgments. To study this hypothesis, three of the reading themes were identified as having possible elements of commonality with the science objectives: Using Visual Aids, Following Written Directions, and Picking Significant Facts From Passages. The released science exercises were scrutinized for the employment of these particular skills. The average percent of success was computed and compared with the average percent of success on the reading exercises employing the same themes. Results of this investigation are shown in Table 3.

TABLE 3. Comparison of Science and Reading Results on Exercises Requiring Similar Skills (9-, 13-, and 17-year-olds)

Skill	Age Level	Science % Success	Science No. of Exercises	Reading % Success	Reading No. of Exercises
Using Visual Aids	9	69	5	79	14
	13	65	5	78	19
	17	75	2	83	14
Following Written Directions	9	68	10	78	6
	13	43	3	76	28
	17	75	1	73	16
Picking Significant Facts from Passages	9	41	8	51	13
	13	54	6	74	22
	17	35	11	84	22

For the 9-year-olds a high degree of similarity exists with Reading percentages being only slightly higher than Science. For 13-year-olds, some disparity begins to appear, and for 17-year-olds, wide variations are evident, particularly in the ability to pick significant facts from passages. Since the correlation between Science and Reading results on this particular investigation seems to diminish from 9-year to 13-year to 17-year age levels, it may be that in science, the exercises chosen as exemplifying particular skills were complicated by other factors such as knowledge, reasoning ability, or familiarity with the problem of the exercises. Results for older children might be influenced more than those for younger children because of these factors.

To further document the general similarities discerned in the results of the surveys conducted to date, Table 4 shows the comparisons of average percentage deviations from the national medians in Science, Reading, and Citizenship. With only two exceptions (Males vs. Females in Reading and Inner-City Fringe in Reading), the directions of the deviations from the national medians in all categories were identical. That is, all categories in which pupils performed better than the national median in Science showed similar results in Reading and Citizenship. Similarly, in all categories in which pupils fell below the national median in Science, they also performed below the median in Reading and Citizenship. In the case of Reading, however, females performed better than males, and pupils in the Inner-City Fringe performed slightly better in Reading when compared to the national median than they did in Science and Citizenship.

Implications

The interrelationships between subjects may permit schools to improve their teaching effectiveness by capitalizing on certain synergistic effects. For example, schools might use science narrative material at the appropriate level to develop reading skills. Reading interest may increase through exposure to science narratives. The intrinsic interest and excitement of a well-written science story may encourage young readers to develop their reading competencies more rapidly than use of other less interesting material. Thus, two learnings might be gained for the price of one. At the same time improved reading skills may produce better science learning, particularly in areas of critical analysis, reasoning, recognizing and choosing significant information from reading material. It appears that certain skills necessary for good reading are also necessary for good performance in science.

The correlation between Science and Reading results of the National Assessment surveys seems to diminish from 9- to 13-year to 17-year age levels. Since the types of exercises designed for upper age

TABLE 4. Comparisons of Average Percentage Deviations From National Medians in Three Subject Areas By Six Analysis Categories°

Category		1969-70 Science	1970-71 Reading	1969-70 Citizenship
Sex	Male Female	+ 3.7°°	− 2.2	+ 1.2°°
Region	Northeast Southeast Central West	+ 1.8 − 4.9 + 1.0 + 0.9	+ 2.1 − 3.4 + 1.5 + 0.0	+ 1.4 − 4.1 + 0.7 + 0.9
SCO	Big Cities Urban Fringe Middle Size Cities Smaller Places	− 3.6 + 3.0 + 0.8 − 1.8		− 1.3 + 1.8 + 0.7 − 1.7
Parental Education	1 8th Grade 2 Some High School 3 Completed High School 4 High School	− 9.1 − 5.4 + 0.5 + 6.1	−12.2 − 4.4 + 1.1 + 8.3	− 5.7 − 3.0 + 2.3 + 6.6
Color	White Black	−14.3°°°	+ 3.2 −20.1	−8.8°°°
STOC	Extreme Affluent Suburbs Suburban Fringe Medium Sized Cities Inner-City Fringe Small City Extreme Rural Extreme Inner-City	+ 7.6 + 1.8 + 1.1 − 2.2 − 0.7 − 5.1 −11.6	+ 7.7 + 2.4 + 1.0 + 0.8 − 0.7 − 5.0 −17.1	+5.6 +1.1 + 0.7 −0.5 −1.0 −4.3 −6.1

° Figures are averages for all age levels
°° Shows Male advantage over females
°°° Shows Black deviation from national average

levels appear to employ higher levels of thinking such as analysis, reasoning, and evaluation, perhaps more practice should be given to children both in reading and science in the skills of drawing inferences, reading critically, selecting pertinent information from data, and making interpretations. Practice in these higher level thinking processes, if carried out in two or more school subjects simultaneously, might bring about the desired result of improved competencies among children at all age levels.

The similarity of assessment results in five subject areas when analyzed for the categories of sex, region, size and type of community, parental education, and color indicates a high degree of consistency that deserves further study. It appears that education of youth in the nation displays a remarkable homogeneity among designated subject categories. Large differences appear when socioeconomic, racial, and geographical categories are compared. The prospects of alleviating the differences across these categories presents formidable challenges to educators. The National Assessment of Educational Progress represents a significant step in recognizing and identifying the problems that face professional educators today.

Further Investigation and Study

1. What forseeable impact will the National Assessment project have on classroom teachers at the secondary level?
2. What might account for the similarities between the assessment results in science, reading, and citizenship, with respect to the performance by various groups and subgroups?
3. List five implications for classroom teachers as an outcome of the national assessment (a) present results and (b) probable future results.

13 Competency-Based Teacher Training

Introduction

One approach to defining good teaching is in terms of teacher competencies. For years we have attempted to identify those skills, competencies and characteristics that make good teachers. The thinking is that if these traits and characteristics can be identified, we will be able to train and prepare good potential teachers in the secondary schools. As a result of this thinking, in recent years there has been a considerable amount of research into what traits good teachers have and how they apply and use these traits in their methods of teaching.

Traditional programs for the training of teachers are often criticized for a number of faults which may be remedied by the competency-based approach. One criticism directed to traditional programs is that all education courses are alike and that there is a great deal of duplication from course to course. Another criticism is that instructors in education courses often talk about individualization as a method of teaching but do not practice it. A frequent criticism is that instructors in education speak at a theoretical or philosophical level but are unable to or do not apply these philosophies and ideologies to common classroom problems; there is too little application of principles and the student is unable to make the transfer to the real situation he finds in the schools. Education instructors are also accused of insufficient use of the media and technology methods about which they speak; consequently, students do not see the material in operation and again are unable to see how it can be applied in the classroom. Educational innovations are often discussed but frequently instructors using these educational innovations provide poor models after which prospective teachers can pattern their teaching methods. A system of teacher preparation based on competency measures can help to alleviate these criticisms and produce teachers more adequately prepared for their tasks.

Teacher Education

Henderson and Lanier have commented on the tasks of teaching and competency-based training.[1] A definition of teaching suggested by the authors is "Teaching is manipulating the variables of instruction to produce intended changes in learner behavior." This definition lends itself to breakdown into three parts, namely the means, the givens, and the ends. "Teaching is manipulating" refers to the means. "Variables of instruction" refers to the givens, and these include human, environmental and curricular variables. "To produce intended changes in learner behavior" represents the ends.

There are four major tasks of teaching: assessment, establishing objectives, preparing strategies, and evaluation. The teacher begins the first task of teaching by assessing the givens present in the unique instructional situation. The second major task becomes that of specifying intended changes or goal setting. The third task is that of selecting, preparing, and implementing strategies for producing the intended changes. The fourth and last task that must be mastered is evaluation which includes knowing how to design, prepare and implement evaluation instruments and procedures.

The skill areas needed by a teacher for performing goal setting include goal identification skills, objective specification skills, and communication and/or negotiation skills. In the third task, the skill areas for planning and implementing strategies include decision-making skills, preparation skills, and implementation skills. In the evaluational task, the skill areas needed by a teacher for performing successfully are decision-making skills, preparation skills, data collection skills, data analysis skills, and communication skills.

In an article entitled "Specifying Teacher Competencies" by Cooper, Jones and Weber, certain assumptions are made concerning why teacher competencies should be specified.[2] These assumptions are:

---

[1] Judith E. Henderson and Perry Lanier, "What teachers need to know and teach: (for survival on the planet)," *Journal of Teacher Education*, Vol. XXIV, No. 1 (Spring, 1973).

[2] James M. Cooper, Howard L. Jones, and Wilford A. Weber, "Specifying Teacher Competencies," *Journal of Teacher Education*, Vol. XXIV, No. 1 (Spring, 1973): 17.

Competency-Based Teacher Training

1. A person learns significantly only those things which he perceives as being involved in the maintenance or the enhancement of the structure of self.
2. Education should provide for the development of the personal qualities of the individual learner; it should provide opportunities for him to establish his self-identity; and it should help him pursue his personal objectives.
3. A supportive, non-evaluative environment reduces external threat and facilitates learning.
4. One cannot teach another person anything meaningful that will have significant influence on behavior; one can only facilitate his learning.

Following are some teacher competencies that are consistent with and derived from the role of the teacher as a facilitator of learning.

1. The teacher will clarify students' attitudes by reflecting them back to the learner.
2. The teacher will guide pupils through processes which will help them to clarify values that they hold.
3. The teacher will guide pupils in using a systems approach to solving problems identified by the pupils.
4. The teacher will create a supportive learning environment that provides learning resources in response to the needs and desires of the pupils.

There are three kinds of teacher competencies specified in the competency-based program:

A. Knowledge competencies that specify cognitive understandings the teacher education student is expected to demonstrate
B. Performance competencies which specify teaching behaviors and attitudes the student is expected to demonstrate
C. Consequence competencies specifying pupil behavior which are taken as evidence of the teacher's teaching effectiveness. While all three are found in a competency-based program, it is believed there should be a major emphasis on performance

Blanton lists several tenets undergirding performance based programs.[3] Among these are:

1. There is no performance model for a "good" teacher. Thus many models should be constructed.

---
[3] B. Blanton, "Performance Based Teacher Education," *Reading Teacher* 25 (March, 1972): 579.

2. Objectives for the trainee should be determined prior to instruction and should be well defined, made public, and used for evaluation.
3. Individual differences should be recognized. The rate of progression through a given program should be determined by a demonstration of competencies rather than by time.
4. Evaluation should focus on what the student knows and how he performs.

Several problems are implicit in a performance based program including the fact that programs will tend to overemphasize isolated elements of performance at the expense of a total teaching performance. Many more instruments are needed to assess performance. Questions of who should assess and how the results of assessment will be used are potent.[4]

Some of the features of the competency-based program purported to overcome the criticisms of teacher education programs are that material is replicated only when reinforcement seems necessary; the student's work is entirely self-paced; the student works from instructional objectives which tell him exactly what is expected of him; resource materials, much wider in variety and number, are made available to the individual student; students are allowed to take self-tests or qualifying tests whenever they feel that they are ready; and advisors are available to assist students to work on a one-to-one basis. Instead of grades, a student receives a specified number of merit points upon completion of his instructional package and credit when the total requirements are met.

Numerous lists of competencies have been prepared by various groups, one example of which is entitled "Teacher Competency Development System" by W.J. Popham and Eva Baker. The list follows:

1. Deciding on Defensible Goals
2. Using Modern Measurement Methods
3. Selecting Appropriate Instructional Tactics
4. Analyzing and Sequencing Learning Behaviors
5. Making Better Lesson Plans
6. Planning and Setting Up Teaching Units
7. Motivating Learners
8. Humanizing Educational Objectives
9. Teaching Reading
10. Defining Content for Objectives
11. Opening Classroom Structures

---

[4] One example of a competency-based teacher education program has been tried out at Illinois State University. Howard Getz, Larry Kenedy, Walter Pierce, Cliff Edwards, and Pat Chesebro "From Traditional to Competency Based Teacher Education," *Phi Delta Kappa* (January, 1973), pp. 300-302.

Competency-Based Teacher Training

12. Establishing Performance Standards
13. Avoiding and Dealing With Discipline Problems
14. Planning, Grading, and Interpreting Tests
15. Using the Most Effective Instructional Tactics
16. Providing Appropriate Practice
17. Individualizing Instruction
18. Generating Effective Objectives[5]

Another list of competencies required of a good teacher has been designed by the authors of this book.

1. Questioning and Discussion
   A. Asks divergent questions of peers, self, and instructor
   B. Uses adequate wait-time when questions are asked
   C. Waits for multiple responses after correct answers are given
   D. Promotes student interaction
   E. Is able to lead brainstorming sessions
2. Use of Inquiry Discovery Methods
   A. Is able to construct an inquiry lab situation requiring higher level thought processes
   B. Is able to construct invitations to inquiry
   C. Is able to construct an inquiry bulletin board
   D. Is able to construct an inquiry quiz board
   E. Can devise questions for pictorial riddles and audio riddles
   F. Uses films and filmstrips in an inquiry way
3. Application of Piagetian Theory in Practice
   A. Is able to administer Piagetian interviews and record proper data
   B. Is able to administer Piagetian tasks
   C. Can determine the cognitive level of students
   D. Can diagnose cognitive problems or insufficiencies with respect to Piagetian levels and is able to suggest activities to remediate
4. Curriculum Knowledge
   A. Can state the philosophies, objectives and knows the authors of modern curriculum projects
   B. Can identify the strengths and weaknesses of such projects and be able to evaluate them
   C. Can teach lessons from the curriculum projects and be able to demonstrate his competencies in this skill

---

[5] W.J. Popham and Eva Baker, "Teacher Competency Development System,"

5. Behavioral Objectives
    A. Can write cognitive psychomotor and affective objectives for a course he is teaching
    B. Can evaluate the achievement of such objectives by various methods
    C. Is able to classify objectives according to Bloom's taxonomy of educational objectives

The following list is a checklist for administrators or supervisors on the qualities of a good teacher. Among the following statements one can discern many traits which characterize a good teacher.

1. Is he enthusiastic about what he is doing and does he show it?
2. Is he dynamic and does he use his voice and facial expression for emphasis and to hold attention?
3. Does he use illustrative devices extensively to make each new learning experience as concrete as possible?
4. Does he show originality in securing teaching materials from simple objects?
5. Does he have a functional knowledge of his subject so that he can apply what he knows to everyday living?
6. Does he possess the ability to explain ideas in simple terms regardless of how extensive his knowledge may be?
7. Does he stimulate actual thought on the part of his students or does he make parrots out of them?
8. Is he a "have to finish the book" type of teacher or does he teach thoroughly what is accomplished?
9. Does he maintain calm poise in the most trying of classroom circumstances?
10. Does he use a variety of teaching techniques or is it the same thing day after day?
11. Does he exhibit feelings of confidence and are the students confident about his ability?
12. Does he encourage class participation and questions and does he conscientiously plan for it?
13. Does he maintain a good instructional tempo so that the period does not drag?
14. Does he use techniques to stimulate interest at the beginning of new material or does he treat it merely as something new to be learned?

15. Does he concentrate on key ideas and use facts as a means to an end?

Criticism of Competency-Based Programs

R. J. Nash is critical of performance based teacher preparation programs and proposes that four questions should be asked before embarking on this method of teacher education.[6]

1. To what extent is the curriculum confronting the education student with the realities of the school and the society in which he will be spending his professional and personal lifetime? To what degree does it "train teachers to be futurologists"?
2. To what extent are we including educational experiences which help students to get from the realities of the school to what they would like the school to be?
3. To what extent are we preparing the student to take his place in the classroom, the administrative office, or the counseling situation as a critic of the educational status quo rather than as a conformist in the name of professionalism?
4. To what extent are we as teacher educators becoming models for educational and social change?

Chambers and Graham state,

There is a justifiable feat that the specification of competencies and subsequent analyses of related behavioral objectives will produce a tyranny worse than before and will constrain rather than free a student. Manipulation of students with highly prescriptive and non-negotiable behavioral objectives would be a perversion of the intent."[7]

The competencies approach to teacher education encounters some difficult problems and cannot be conceived to be a panacea in the area of teacher education. One problem is that the nature of a teaching task appears to be much more complicated than can be adequately described by lists of competencies or attributes. There is ample evidence that what constitutes a good teacher is disputed by the recipients of that teacher's efforts, the students. Frequently, students critical of a particular teacher's methods and personality will report on how much they have learned from that teacher; the ultimate result is

---

[6] R.J. Nash, "Commitment to Competency: The New Fetishism in Teacher Education," *Phi Delta Kappa*, Vol. 52 (December, 1970): 240.

[7] M. A. Chambers and R. A. Graham, "Competence: The Measure of Tomorrow's Teacher," *Peabody Journal of Education* (April, 1971).

positive. Teaching is an extremely personal matter and deals with highly personal interrelationships between teacher and student.

How can prospective teachers be educated in the skills of discussion and discourse?

The development of long lists of competencies to present to potential teachers may have a deleterious effect in that it will provide a vision of insuperable tasks to be completed to become an effective teacher and to be certified. The beginner as a general rule is apprehensive about his role as a prospective teacher and he lacks confidence about his ability to handle subject matter, pupil-teacher problems, matters of organization, contacts with administration and many other matters of concern. It is necessary for him to mature gradually and slowly and build a firm base of confidence and skill in order to move forward into larger vistas of work. Presenting him with long lists of competencies may be threatening. It is necessary for each teacher to work out his best plan of action and to build on his successes day by day in the classroom. There is a tremendous amount of self-feedback and self-correction that takes place in every teaching situation and each is unique in that it requires the best use of mature judgement. Many times there are no precedents that can be followed and the course of action depends upon assessing the situation and making the best judgement on the matter at the time that it occurs.

The preceding remarks are not intended to diminish the value of competencies and skills in the preparation of teachers. Certainly, it is important to recognize that teachers must develop such competencies in order to be effective, but it must be equally recognized that teaching is a much more complex art than simple rote handling of discrete skills and competencies. If teaching were only this it could be done by a computer. It is important in the teacher training program to avoid giving the impression that following a number of known rules, gathering a bag of tricks and dispensing these skills and procedures without reference to the child is a successful way to become a teacher. This is absolutely not true. Critics of the competency-based approach to teacher education have emphasized the dangers inherent in such a mechanical method of teacher preparation.

Further Investigation and Study

1. As a prospective secondary teacher, what competencies would you like to have to feel secure in your forthcoming tasks? Make a list of these and compare your list with that of a classmate. As an additional challenge, try to rank the desired competencies in order of importance from greatest to least. Be prepared to defend your rankings.
2. Try to recall the two "best" teachers you have encountered in your educational experience. What exemplary traits stood out? Were these traits similar in the two teachers you selected? What kind of teacher preparation program would you recommend to produce the traits you have identified? Are good teachers "made" or "born"?
3. Write to three institutions of higher education that have teacher training programs. Ask them to send you descriptive material about their programs. Assemble the information you receive and prepare a class discussion on the relative merits of the programs as judged in the light of material in this chapter on competency-based teacher education.

14 A Positive Approach to Discipline

For the beginning teacher, anticipating problems in handling his class and controlling the discipline is probably one of the most serious considerations. He has more apprehension about this aspect of teaching than almost any other area of preparation. Students in methods classes frequently express this apprehension even after having visited classes in which experienced teachers were in charge of the class, and in many cases, were able to sensitively handle the problems of discipline and allow the class to proceed in a normal manner. On other occasions, students may observe a beginning teacher or student teacher for whom discipline has not yet become a controlled situation. In some of these cases, classes may seem to be out of hand, the teacher distraught, and evidence of learning at a minimal level. These situations are frightening to the prospective teacher.

Before discussing the techniques for controlling discipline in a high school class, we should consider the purposes of a good disciplinary procedure. Why is it necessary to have discipline? What constitutes good discipline? Does this mean total absence of noise? Does it mean students sitting like sticks in straight rows without looking to the right or left? Does it imply that any kind of student activity can take place?

Certainly, one of the major reasons for having good discipline is to be able to achieve the objectives of the class. Without good discipline there is not much point in developing learning objectives. A second purpose, and perhaps most important of all, is the objective of developing self-discipline in students. It is to be hoped that students who graduate from their secondary school experience will have gained a certain degree of maturity and self-discipline. It is quite likely that unless they have had practice in developing self-discipline, they will not achieve it. Therefore, it is doubly important to provide opportunities in which self-discipline can be developed.

A third purpose is consideration for the student's time and worth. The presence of a few students or a large number for whom time-wasting is a way of life and disruption of the class a standard procedure is an infringement on the time of those who are seriously attempting to acquire an education. Therefore, the teacher has an obligation to maintain the best possible discipline, if for no other reason than to protect those who are seriously engaged in a learning experience.

Good discipline promotes efficiency in learning and helps to develop positive attitudes toward learning. Certainly, these are worthwhile objectives. The provision for good discipline enhances communication and provides for two-way exchange between students and teachers. Discipline is a two-way problem, and the basis for communication is a strong mutual feeling of respect between teacher and student. Not only does the teacher insist that students respect him, but he merits it by his behavior, his treatment of students, and his humanitarian concern for them. This is what is meant by mutual respect. As a result, teachers and students are able to see the intrinsic worth of each other and are capable of benefiting from the contributions that each can make to the learning experience.

Without suitable discipline, no class can be a success. With good discipline, the teaching objectives can be realized and the discipline measures can be considered as tools and media for better learning. This is a positive view and does not imply using discipline as a threat or punishment tool. The latter can only result in negativistic effects and the development of poor attitudes among the students.

Understanding the Secondary Student

Why should a student want to learn? Does he want an atmosphere of good discipline? Generally, the junior high school and senior high school student wants freedom, but freedom within known boundaries or constraints. He does not want to feel that he is the object of authoritarian control and that he does not have a say in how he responds to the learning process. Rather, he wants to know to what extent he can operate. Nevertheless, it is important that he know the boundaries and limitations of his actions. Not only is this desirable from the teacher's point of view, but it is also desired by the student himself.

A Positive Approach to Discipline 311

The secondary student wants to appear an adult. He is impatient for the freedoms that adults enjoy. Yet, he knows that these freedoms carry with them a degree of responsibility. Generally, he is attempting to mold his behavior in such a way that he will be able to enjoy the freedoms and to understand the responsibility that goes along with them.

The secondary student is generally full of vigor and enthusiasm. He is likely to be uninhibited and vocal. Many times he views adults as obstructionists and may view his teacher as a symbol of an authoritarian rule-making society. Sometimes he does not understand the reasons for the limits within which he is expected to operate.

The secondary student in this modern day is subject to many pressures both from within and without. He is undergoing certain physiological changes of adolescence—physical growth, changes in the chemistry of his body, and other physical manifestations of these changes. He is subject to pressure from his peers, he desires acceptance and popularity, and he is conscious of school and parent constraints. The secondary student is reaching toward maturity and in so doing needs practice in assuming responsibility. Once given responsibility, he is given the opportunity to perform under conditions of self-discipline which is the objective being sought.

How Does a Teacher Gain Respect?

A teacher, most importantly, should display himself as a mature, functioning, satisfied human being with aspirations that involve improvement of himself as a teacher and dedication to the teaching profession. He should attempt to be friendly and civil and should dispense humane treatment to all of his students impartially. He should treat students as adults and expect the best from them. These kinds of expectations will, in all likelihood, bring forth a favorable response from the students. The teacher should be impartial, treating all students alike in terms of meting out punishment, giving grades, and showing a genuine interest in their activities. He should be punctual and keep his promises. The good teacher will avoid disparaging remarks about students or other teachers. He should show enthusiasm for school work and activities and demonstrate sincere enjoyment of his job. He should show personal concern for the students, occasionally inquiring into their activities and interests.

The teacher who fails to consider these points and to make a sincere effort to communicate with his students may find himself with numerous discipline problems. Each teacher must develop his own style of discipline and control. In the final analysis, control of discipline is a matter of careful planning of class work and anticipation of problems that might arise. It can probably be said that many discipline problems occur because of laziness on the part of the teacher—that is, the failure to take adequate measures in anticipation of the teaching task.

Setting the Stage for Discipline

When conducting a class avoid long lists of disciplinary rules. These put a negative cast on the whole matter. For some individuals such lists provide a challenge, especially to those who would dare to test you. Once rules are made, it is necessary to follow through; the rules must be adhered to. It is somewhat like setting up targets for marksmen to shoot at. If a rule is broken, it is necessary then for the teacher to punish the person who breaks the rule or in some way demonstrate that a breach of discipline has occurred. Therefore, it is a better policy to make only the rules that are obviously needed as time goes on and as situations develop. The same conditions must be upheld and the rules that are made must be adhered to, but at least the reasons for the rules will then be known and understood by the students.

Be forthright in taking charge of your class. Show clearly that you are in charge, not by bullying or threats, but by a businesslike demeanor. Impress upon the students the importance of the time that they have available to learn the subjects at hand and expect that everyone will make his best effort. Be observant of incipient problems and nip them early. Clues to such problems are boredom, bullying of one student by another, boy-girl relationships that are disruptive in the class, and other types of observable behavior. Have your lesson plans well made. Know what you are going to do at all times. Be prepared to make changes as circumstances require. Plan for flexibility, but not to the extent of doing no planning. This is the surest way to incur disciplinary problems. You are then losing the battle by default.

There is a technique which can assist you in learning your class effectiveness. It involves having an observer assist you. This could be another teacher, a principal, or a student teacher in your charge. His job would be to monitor the class attention at regular intervals, for example, every three minutes. He would simply make a count of the class at these intervals attempting to determine how many students were paying attention to the learning activity. The learning activity might be a lecture, a demonstration, a student report, laboratory work, or some other activity. The monitor's judgment must be used in order to decide what

A Positive Approach to Discipline

students are paying attention. It is true this is not an infalliable judgment, but it is sufficiently valid to make this a useful technique.

After the class period is over, calculate the percent of attention and plot the information on a graph with the ordinate representing percent of attention and the abscissa representing time intervals for the duration of the class period. The following is an example of the technique.

Education 441

Observation Data Sheet Number _____

Name _____   Class Observed   Physics _____
Date   February 24, 1972   Time   8:10 a.m. _____

Instructions: (a) At intervals of three minutes, count the class and determine the number of students who are actively paying attention to the lesson or activity. Use your best judgment as to whether a student is paying attention. (b) Keep a record of the types of activities engaged in by the teacher and/or class, e.g., lecture, discussion, demonstration, experiment, film, student report, or other. Note the time of transition from one type of activity to another. Note any major occurrences such as disciplinary action, P.A. system coming on, entrance of a visitor, or any unusual or distracting event. Plot a graph of percent attention versus time for each class observed.

Total attendance on day observed? 13 at 0, 15 at 3, 14 after 50

Time	Class count		Time	Class count	
0 min.	1	7.7%	30 min.	15	100%
3 min.	10	66.5%	33 min.	12	80%
6 min.	13	87%	36 min.	15	100%
9 min.	7	46.5%	39 min.	10	66.5%
12 min.	10	66.5%	42 min.	13	87%
15 min.	10	66.5%	45 min.	13	87%
18 min.	14	93%	48 min.	8	53.5%
21 min.	12	80%	51 min.	10	71.5%
24 min.	11	73%	54 min.	10	71.5%
27 min.	15	100%	55 min. end	12	86%
			57 min.	7	50%

Record and time of events: 0-lecture, 4-teacher leaves, 6-demonstration, 8-asked Darrel to put chess set away, 9-lecture, 18-joke, 21-lecture, 27-demonstration, 28-class to hall for demonstration, 31-return to room, 53-lecture, 36-discussion of lecture by students, 39-lecture, 42-student discussions, 43-lecture, 45-discussion, 51-lecture, 55-lecture continues on after time, 50-class member leaves

Attention Curve
12th grade physics

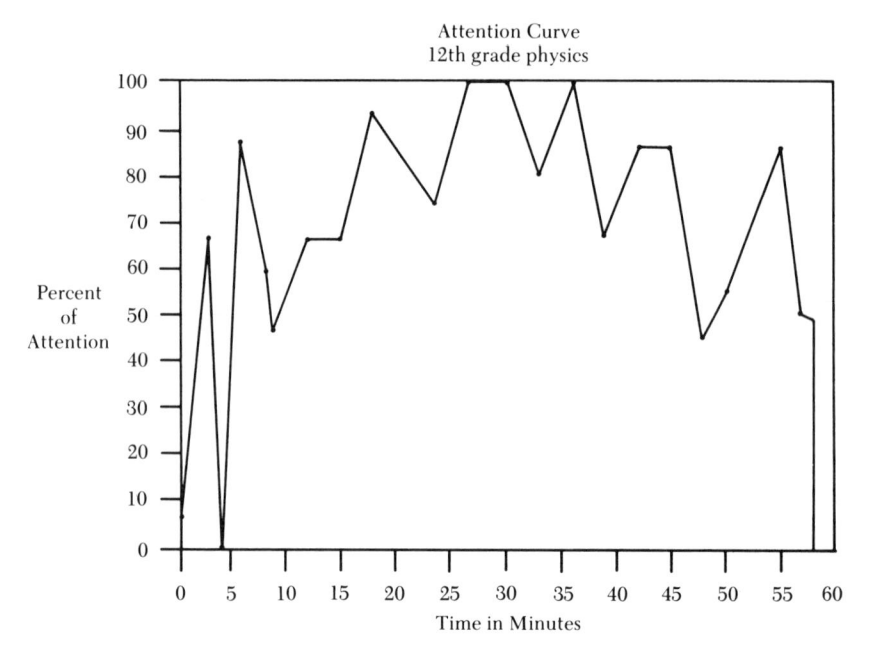

Total Attendance
 0 min. 13
 3 min. 15
 50 min. 14

Legend
Basically the teacher lectured on Newton's Second Law. At the following times these special events occurred:

4 min.	teacher leaves
6 min.	demonstration
8 min.	disciplinary action
18 min.	teachers joke
27-30 min.	demonstration in hall———Attention counted every 3 minutes.
36 min.	student discussion
42 min.	student discussion
45 min.	student discussion
50 min.	one student leaves
55 min.	period should end
57 min.	class dismissed

Making Your Class Exciting

A busy class does not find time for creating discipline problems. Make students want to come back to class the next day. Make them look for-

A Positive Approach to Discipline

ward to attending your class and engaging in the educational experiences there. To do this, show enthusiasm yourself, demonstrate that you love your subject and that you appreciate the wonder and significance of learning. Maintain a good active pace with much participation by the students, not necessarily physical participation at all times, but encourage mental alertness and conscious participation of a mental sort. Good discipline is good teaching and good teaching maximizes good learning.

One important consideration is to provide success experiences for all in the class. Anyone who succeeds wants more of it. The satisfaction enjoyed needs to be repeated. This is the key idea behind all learning and motivation. To provide these success experiences, make sure that everyone has the opportunity to do well on a quiz, that he gets frequent commendations from you as the teacher, and that he senses his real worth as a participating member of the class.

Another technique that is sometimes used to maintain a high level of interest is to pose puzzling problems. Have a variety of these available so that you can use them when the circumstances warrant. Use them as interest getters or as real content learning devices.

Thought Problem

1. There are five houses.
2. The Englishman lives in the red house.
3. The Spaniard owns a dog.
4. Coffee is drunk in the green house.
5. The Ukranian drinks tea.
6. The green house is immediately to the right of the ivory house.
7. The Old Gold smoker owns snails.
8. Kools are smoked in the yellow house.
9. Milk is drunk in the middle house.
10. The Norwegian lives in the first house.
11. The Chesterfield smoker lives next door to the man with the fox.
12. Kools are smoked in the house next to the house with a horse.
13. The Lucky Strike smoker drinks orange juice.
14. The Japanese smokes Parliament.
15. The Norweigian lives next door to the blue house.
16. In each house there is one nationality, one pet, one cigarette smoked and one liquid drunk.

Who drinks water?
Who owns the zebra?

The following grid may be of assistance in solving this problem.

	House #1	House #2	House #3	House #4	House #5
House Color					
Nationality					
Pet					
Cigarette					
Drink					

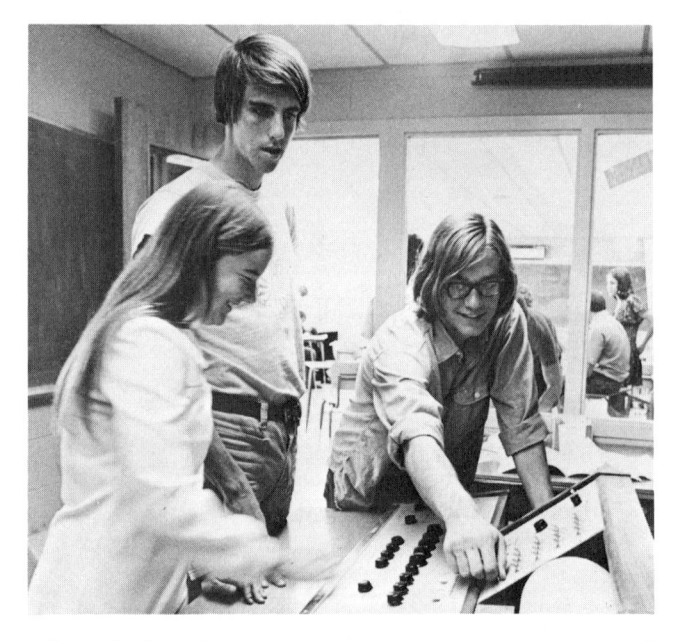

What role does the teacher play in developing students who can discipline themselves?

Self-Discipline Procedures

Junior High Level

In the junior high school, we want to give students an opportunity to practice self-discipline whenever possible. It is important that they have these experiences and that they have options in selecting their own learning and teaching materials such as books, tapes, encyclopedias, slides, or films. These options are best provided in a resource center setup. Allow the students to select their own seats in the classroom or in the assembly hall. Along with this, however, demand responsible behavior and make them understand that the privilege of selection of one's seating partner carries with it the responsibility for good discipline. Individualize your instruction as much as you can. This provides for self-pacing, self-selection of time to be spent in the resource center, and optional choices of activities and exercises. The exercise of these selections and choices provides the needed self-discipline we are striving for. Give the students responsibilities, then check on their progress frequently. Allow them to evaluate themselves.

Whenever possible, send students out on short-term field assignments, individually or in pairs, rarely in large groups. Make their responsibilities specific such as: "Interview Mr. Smith to find out how he feels about the new wage-price laws," or "Collect data relating to the amount of traffic at the intersection of Sixteenth and Eighth Avenue during the noon hour," or "Construct a chart that shows the rate of growth of the plants in the greenhouse during the Christmas vacation." The above examples should provide some means by which junior high school students can exercise self-discipline with a minimum of supervision. This, of course, does not mean abdicating responsibility for supervision, but rather allowing the students to control themselves within certain limitations and restraints.

Senior High Level

Senior high school students are approaching maturity and adulthood. They strive for this and are pleased when they are treated in an adult manner. They should be given adult responsibilities in order to bring out self-discipline opportunities. Examples include: "Attend the city council meeting and bring back a report on the discussion concerning the sewage disposal system," or "Order the materials listed here in the catalog and arrange to have the school billed," or "Devise a procedure to secure the needed information from the city council, and then go out and collect it."

Other means of developing self-discipline might be activities such as placing the senior high student in charge of a younger group such as an elementary or junior high school group of students. Put him in charge of a resource room on a regular schedule, or a library, laboratory, or stockroom. Have frequent opportunities to talk with him about the responsibilities involved in carrying out his tasks. Have the student take a group of younger pupils on a field trip, with him making all the necessary arrangements for permission, transportation, and conduct of the students during the field trip. Have the student present a paper at a youth meeting, or a PTA meeting, council meeting, or other type of group function. Have him take over the regular high school class for a period or a portion thereof. Make the student responsible for the discipline in the class during the time he is in charge. Give the class to understand that the student is now the teacher under your authority and that you expect the same type of response as you would receive if you were teaching. Suggest he arrange for a speaker

How did these students achieve the self-discipline to engage in this activity?

A Positive Approach to Discipline

for the class or for an assembly program; have the student make the initial contact, the follow-up reminding letter, meet the speaker on the day of the assembly, and send a thank-you note at the conclusion.

All of the above examples illustrate the reaching toward maturity and adult functions that students in the senior high school are striving for. Students at this level should not be deprived of the opportunity to develop these skills and responsibilities. One can only diminish the development of self-discipline by treating young adults as children who cannot be trusted or depended upon.

Handling Discipline When the Need Arises

In the classroom when it becomes obvious that a strong measure such as asking the student to leave the room or to go to the principal's office arises, be sure to act forthrightly and without hesitation. Control your anger and take whatever action is necessary with a cool head. Do not set the punishment immediately. Think over the situation calmly and decide what measures will be most beneficial for the student. Generally, some form of remedial treatment is better than a straight out and out punishment, in terms of the educational value to the student. Remember, the purpose of discipline is largely for rehabilitation of a student who is not able to discipline himself. Be completely impartial, treat all offenders with the same rules, firmness, and dispatch. Students will recognize a sense of fairness on your part and will be quick to take advantage of any evidence of partiality. If a student is requested to come in after class or school to talk with you, see that he does. Do not let it slide. If necessary, write yourself a note to help you remember, then check up on the student either on the day in question or at the first opportunity thereafter. If he fails to appear, do not jump to the conclusion that it was a deliberate skip, but try to ascertain fairly and impartially what his excuse is. This will indicate once again that you value the person as a person, but that you recognize that discipline is a necessary part of one's school work and of his development.

Be sure you know the policy of the school concerning discipline and matters involving sending students to the principal's office. Do you use a referral slip? Must you personally escort the student to the office? Can it be done during, or before, or after class?

Ascertain what the principal's attitude is toward students being sent to him for disciplinary treatment. Does he look upon this as a sign of weakness on the part of the teacher? Does he support the teacher one hundred percent with respect to the disciplinary measures invoked? It is a wise idea to talk with the principal concerning this matter before the need for it arises.

Classroom Management

Every junior high school and high school teacher is inevitably faced with the problem of discipline. This will be a vital, daily concern of the teacher, and yet discussion of the proper use of discipline is dealt with so briefly during teacher preparation.

The key to teaching is the ability to instill the desire to learn. Teaching methods are learned and practiced to do this, but methods of discipline so often are ignored. Discipline handled incorrectly causes three effects:

1. It produces a negative attitude in the student toward the teacher. This attitude erases all the desire to learn previously instilled by the teaching methods.
2. Freedom of communication is hindered. An intangible barrier arises between the student and the teacher and destroys the principle of teaching by inquiry. This barrier will keep the student from asking questions or responding on his own initiative because of recollections of the teacher's previous disposition.
3. The student may lose respect for the teacher. This kills any desire for the student to want to learn.

The following suggestions may add to your set of teaching tools. These do not constitute a recipe for the complete elimination of disciplinary problems, but they break the huge theory of discipline down into some practical applications.

1. Learn the names of pupils quickly and call them by name.
2. Be prompt. A good teacher gets to class on time. He calls the roll immediately and sets the proper instructional attitude for the day. Meeting students at the door usually contributes to better discipline.
3. Be well prepared. A good teacher always has a lesson plan. He has an alternate plan to use in case the original does not achieve the desired results.
4. Be businesslike. Have materials ready for class. Provide the widest variety of materials possible. Idle groups or individuals awaiting their turns are the starting points for disciplinary problems.
5. Never read the lesson from the manual or text in class or have it read by other students. This type of teaching is inexcusable. This does not preclude certain excerpts being read.
6. Expect no problem; do not be looking for them. Assure by your manner that there will be none.

A Positive Approach to Discipline

7. Be enthusiastic about your subject. A good teacher radiates enthusiasm for his subject. He feels that his subject is the most important in the curriculum.
8. Use your voice to advantage. Your voice can radiate enthusiasm, soothe a troubled situation or command respect.
9. Consider the physical comfort of the pupil. If there is evidence of excessive yawning and a general restlessness, a good teacher looks for the causes.
10. Maintain a certain reserve between yourself and the students. Never accept any manner of address except Mr., Mrs., or Miss and your last name. Never permit students to refer to other teachers in any other way.
11. Let the students know that you are a good-natured, cheerful and happy individual, capable of laughing with them and at yourself.
12. Be fair, firm and consistent. If behavior is considered unacceptable one day, this same behavior must be unacceptable every day.
13. Don't threaten anything you can't carry out. Words mean little to children. Give them the security of knowing exactly where they stand—a certain behavior brings a certain result. There is no need to talk about it—act!
14. Uphold school policies. Enforce school policies but don't argue about them. Overlooking a school policy is as bad as defying it.
15. Sarcasm has no place in your dealings. Be just and fair. Forced apologies are useless. Make no threats. Offer no bribes.
16. Watch your voice. Do not try to talk over the noise of the class. They can *always* talk louder!
17. Use social disapproval whenever possible.
18. When dealing with a case, be impersonal. Focus on the cause. Realize that the act is an outward manifestation of a maladjustment.
19. When the case is closed, draw the curtain. Let all parties know it.
20. Never punish the whole class for the act of one.
21. Displaying your best teaching ability is likely to win the respect of your pupils. Avoid ostentation. Speak in simple language.
22. Never dismiss a student from class without supervision. A

student should never be permitted to wander aimlessly in the school building because he has been a discipline problem in class.
23. The principal can help. There is a stigma attached to being sent to the principal's office. However, a good teacher does not send youngsters so often that this effect is lost. It is better to confer with the principal about discipline problems and let him call the offenders to the office for a talk.
24. Remember, behavior is learned. Students act the way they do because of the environmental conditions under which they live.
25. Busy, interested children are seldom control problems. Observe, diagnose, treat and observe again. Most of the cases disappear.
26. Be human. Do your best—no one asks more. Recognize that we all have good and bad days.

Developing Self-Discipline

The goal of all discipline training should be the development of responsible self-discipline. Students should reach a point where they have inner motivation to complete the learning tasks of their own volition. Discipline of this type is positive and self-rewarding; accomplishment of the task is reward in itself. To reach this goal, numerous opportunities must be provided for students to practice self-discipline or peer-group discipline, and as with the development of any skill, there must be time to practice. Self-disciplined students are not likely to emerge from autocratic classrooms.

Teaching by inquiry methods provides a setting for development of self-discipline. Individual work in the laboratory or projects carried out in the classroom or at home give many opportunities to develop good work habits and qualities of self-reliance, persistence, and reliability. Students engaged in a task for which they have a high degree of motivation are less likely to create problems of discipline requiring action by the teacher.

The following suggestions may assist the teacher in providing an environment in which student self-discipline can be developed:
1. Capture interest through activities, experiments, projects, and other student-oriented learning methods.
2. Allow a degree of unstructured work commensurate with the maturity and experience level of the students in the class.

A Positive Approach to Discipline

3. Give suitable guidance to students who require direction and external control, until it is no longer needed.
4. Treat students as adults from whom you expect mature behavior and evidence of self-discipline.

Developing self-discipline is as much a matter of concern for the teacher as for the students. In carrying out this task, it is as important to know what not to do as to know what positive steps to take. David Welch and Wanda Schutte express the "Do's and Don't's of Discipline" effectively in the following list:[1]

DOs

1. Do accept choices if you give them.
2. Do accept feelings.
3. Do earn respect.
4. Do enforce the rules you set.
5. Do earn affection.
6. Do act when it is necessary and think about it later.
7. Do realize there are reasons why children can't express why or won't express why they did something.
8. Do respect the 5th and 6th amendments to the Constitution for children.
9. Do give children responsibility. If you give them a job and they fail, don't take it away from them. Give them a second chance.
10. Do learn what is reasonable to expect from a child.

DON'Ts

1. Don't give children a choice unless you are willing to accept their decision.
2. Don't deny a child's feeling.
3. Don't demand respect.
4. Don't demand a behavior you can't or don't intend to enforce.
5. Don't try to buy a child's affection.
6. Don't be afraid to make mistakes.
7. Don't always expect children to tell you why they did something.
8. Don't demand a confession of guilt.
9. Don't teach children to be responsible by taking responsibility away from them.
10. Don't expect children to behave like adults.

---

[1] Reprinted from *Discipline: A Shared Experience*. Copyright 1973 by Shields Publishing Co., Inc. 155 N. College Ave., Ft. Collins, Colorado 80521

Summary

The matter of class control is of primary concern to the beginning teacher. The multiple problems of class preparation, devising suitable teaching methods, and keeping the class under control are frequently overwhelming.

Real disciplinary control comes from the development of mutual feelings of respect between students and teacher. When this rapport is developed, discipline problems largely vanish, and the mode of control becomes student self-discipline. The beginning teacher should strive to create such rapport by taking a sincere interest in the students. At every opportunity he should give assistance generously, be fair and impartial, stress the values of learning, and demonstrate positive attitudes toward discipline. Students in junior and senior high school respond to adult treatment. The teacher's expectations in this respect will influence student response.

In the handling of discipline, the application of common sense and a positive approach will satisfactorily solve most of the problems which arise. It is well to assume the attitude that discipline problems will be minimized by careful planning of daily work, use of a variety of techniques, keeping students busy, and treating them like adults. Problems that remain unsolved may require specially trained personnel; the classroom teacher should know to whom these cases may be channeled for treatment.

Further Investigation and Study

1. Make a list of ten typical discipline problems that might occur in a class. For each, describe the measures you would use to solve the problem if you were the teacher of the class.
2. Prepare a brief annotated bibliography of recent books and articles that deal with the problems of discipline.
3. Observe a high school class for a week. Keep a record of the events which in your opinion represented discipline problems. How did the teacher handle the situation?
4. Interview a secondary school teacher and raise questions concerning the following:
    a. Discipline in activity-oriented classes, e.g., laboratories, shops, home economics kitchens, etc.
    b. Preventive technique for minimizing discipline problems.
    c. Use of peer pressure to solve problems of discipline.

15   Student Teaching

Students preparing to do their student teaching after having spent many years in preparation for this event are naturally apprehensive and somewhat anxious about the prospects. In some cases, individuals may be looking forward with anticipation to "trying their wings" as a teacher in the classroom. Other students, however, may feel considerable trepidation at the prospects of facing a room full of students. Will he be prepared? Will he be able to control his nervousness? Will he be able to handle discipline problems? What will he do about questions from the class? These concerns face every prospective teacher. They are important concerns and deserve attention in preparing to meet the new challenges posed by being a teacher rather than a college student.

    Why engage in student teaching? This experience is designed to smooth the transition from the role of a student to that of a teacher. It is an opportunity for the student to test his liking for the teaching role; he will have an opportunity to find out whether he really enjoys this career choice. He will learn whether he is capable of establishing rapport with high school students and whether he is capable of talking their language. It is important for him to find this out before fully committing himself to a teaching career, since he must reflect a genuine enthusiasm for teaching which will enable him to be an effective teacher and to engender a similar enthusiasm in his students.

    The practice teaching assignment will also provide the training institution with an opportunity to evaluate the student's progress and teaching capabilities. This culminating experience in the preparation

Student Teaching

program for a prospective teacher is a very important one and will, if done successfully, enable the training institution to place its stamp of approval on the student teacher's work with confidence and assurance that he will be successful in the classroom.

Some of the following advantages can be expected in the student teaching experience. The responsibilities for acquiring these values and competencies lies with the student teacher.

1. Actual experience with a class will remove the fear of the unknown which everyone experiences when faced with a new situation. This will be an opportunity to build up one's confidence and to see for oneself whether he is able to meet the challenge of teaching high school students.

2. This is an opportunity for the new teacher to test out some of the things that he has learned in his classes in methods in curriculum, in adolescent psychology and others. It will provide a stage in which to test out methods of handling individual differences and discipline problems, techniques of presenting material, techniques of working with small groups and other normal teaching procedures.

3. The student teaching experience will provide the prospective teacher with opportunities to learn about high school students firsthand. He will find that they have individual and group characteristics which are not different from groups of other age levels. He will be able to observe them under a variety of conditions both within the classroom and without. He will be able to learn of their motivation; their enthusiasm, or lack of it; and many other factors which make up the "climate" of a typical classroom.

4. The student teaching experience provides a chance to test one's knowledge of subject matter. Regardless of the neophyte teacher's self-assurance and confidence, it is necessary to find out through actual practice the degree to which one understands the subject he is teaching. The opportunity to transmit his knowledge to a group of learners will tell him in short order whether he has this capability. Should he find himself weak in this regard, it is not a time for discouragement or frustration, but a time for accepting the challenge. Facing a class of expectant and sometimes critical students with the responsibility to teach them can sometimes be an unnerving experience, and it is almost certain to convince the student teacher of the necessity of knowing his subject very thoroughly

and the need to prepare well for his contact with the class. A frequently heard statement by experienced teachers is, "I really learned my subject when I had to teach it."

5. Student teaching provides an opportunity to gain the benefits of constructive criticism. Perhaps there is no other time in the teacher's career when he will have the benefit of prolonged, intensive observation of his teaching by an experienced teacher or supervisor in a position to help him constructively. This is an important value and should be made use of to the maximum extent. If the criticisms and suggestions are taken in a receptive fashion by the student teacher with an intention to put them into practice, if at all possible, this experience can be a valuable part of the student teacher's assignment. The importance of this aspect of student teaching makes locating an excellent and helpful supervising teacher imperative. The chance to observe and be observed by a master teacher is an atmosphere of mutual respect and helpfulness is immeasurably worthwhile.

6. This is an opportunity to discover one's teaching strengths and weaknesses. Not every individual has equal capabilities in the various aspects of a teaching situation. Some have excellent use of vocabulary and a good speaking voice and can make use of these effectively. Others may have strengths in working with individual students or in small groups and should capitalize on this particular advantage. Others may be exceptional organizers or directors of learning in laboratory situations and should capitalize on this particular strength. It is important to recognize that one must develop his own style and be alert for methods and techniques that work for him. At the same time, it is necessary to be aware of a great variety of teaching methods and to be willing to try them out for clues as to still better ways of teaching. It is certainly advantageous for a teacher to be highly competent in many methods of teaching, but it is equally important to recognize that individual teachers have certain innate teaching strengths and should make use of the technique which capitalizes to the maximum on these strengths.

7. Finally, the student teaching experience should provide an opportunity to gain poise and finesse in working with a group of individuals, students as well as other teachers. Teaching is more of an art than a science and requires constant attention to small and subtle effects that help to make a classroom effec-

tive. Such fine points of handling classes as anticipating student questions and problems, timing, exploiting enthusiastic and dramatic classroom events, sensing the proper time for introducing a new activity, and commending good work are techniques that the new teacher should become aware of quickly. These factors will contribute to smoother functioning of class activities and generally more effective learning. While this is only the beginning, it is true that improvements in these factors and others can continue throughout the teacher's life and that rarely, if ever, does a teacher reach complete perfection in the art of teaching.

Selecting Your Supervising Teacher

Frequently, a certain amount of latitude is allowed the prospective student teacher in his choice of school, subject, and teacher under whom he wishes to work. The extent of this freedom will vary with the institution and circumstances in which the practice teaching program is operated, and it is entirely possible that assignments may be made arbitrarily. However, it is more likely that, within certain limitations, the wishes of the student will be taken into consideration.

It is, therefore, to the advantage of the student teacher to make a careful selection of school, subject, and supervising teacher. It is quite frequently the feeling of new teachers that their practice teaching assignment was the most valuable experience in their training program. This may be entirely true if the selection was well made and the experience fulfilled its potential.

The prospective student teacher ought to obtain the maximum advantage by teaching in his major field. It is this area for which he is best prepared and in which he will probably feel the greatest confidence. If the situation permits, teaching in his minor field at the same time under a different supervising teacher may be advantageous. This will give him the benefit of constructive help from two experienced teachers and may be analogous to an actual situation as a full-time teacher in a small or medium-sized school system.

It would be wise to visit several classes in a number of different schools in the quarter or semester before the practice teaching assignment. Arrangements can be made through the principal of the school, and advance notice can be given to the teachers involved. If the purpose of the visits is explained, it is quite likely that the prospective student teacher will be favorably received, particularly if it is a school in which student teachers have customarily been supervised.

The advantage of the visit can be manifold. The student will be able to refresh his memory of the atmosphere and activities of a high school classroom. He will be able to observe an experienced teacher in action. He will mentally attempt to project himself into an equivalent situation as a teacher in charge of a class—a desirable step in preparation for his actual practice teaching assignment. He may be able to talk briefly with the teacher at the close of class to gain further insight into the teaching situation. After several such visits to a variety of classes, the prospective student teacher will be able to choose more intelligently the kind of teaching situation he wishes to select for his practice teaching experience.

Some suggestions of criteria to look for in the teaching situation are:

1. Is the teacher well prepared, and is he teaching in his major field?
2. Does the teacher have good control of the class?
3. Do the students appear to be alert and interested in the activities carried out?
4. Is there a genuine atmosphere of learning present?
5. Do the facilities and materials appear to be adequate for the kind of subject being taught?
6. Does it appear that the teacher is a person from whom one can learn valuable teaching techniques?
7. Is there opportunity for a certain degree of flexibility in carrying out one's teaching plans?
8. Does the teacher have a moderate work load, thus affording time for constructive help for a student teacher?
9. Does the teacher appear to be interested in serving as a supervisor for a student teacher in his or her charge?

Meeting Your Supervising Teacher

Once the assignment is made for a particular school, class, and teacher, it is imperative that the student teacher arrange for a short interview before attendance at the first class. This can be brief but preferably should be a day or two in advance, and by appointment. This will avoid incurring the displeasure of the supervising teacher by intruding upon his last-minute preparation for class and will give an opportunity for an interchange of questions and answers by both parties.

Student Teaching

At the interview, the student teacher should be punctual, interested, enthusiastic, and in tasteful attire. The purpose of the interview is to become acquainted and to exchange ideas and information. The supervising teacher is interested in knowing the background and preparation of the student teacher. In addition, he is interested in any special qualifications the student teacher may have, such as ability to handle audio-visual equipment, take charge of a club, or talk on travel experiences. The student teacher is interested in learning what his role is to be in the classroom, what meetings he should attend, and what text materials are in use.

It is likely that the supervising teacher will suggest a period of class observation, perhaps a week or two, at the outset. There may be certain room duties to perform such as roll taking, reading announcements, and distributing materials. Each of these tasks will enable the student teacher to learn the names of pupils quickly, a necessary step in establishing good rapport with members of the class. The student teacher will probably be encouraged to prepare a seating chart immediately. Text materials may be discussed and the teacher's long-range objectives clarified. The student teacher will probably be asked to read certain assignments in order to be intimately acquainted with what the pupils are presently studying. He will find it imperative to do this regularly, so as to be of maximum assistance to pupils who call upon him for help.

Materials available for teaching the class may be shown to the student teacher during the interview. Location of the library and special preparation rooms may be pointed out. The place in the classroom where the student teacher may observe the activities of the class may be designated. (In one school, it was customary for the student teacher to sit next to the teacher's desk, facing the class. In this way, it was possible to learn to recognize pupils more quickly; but, more importantly, this arrangement enabled the student teacher to see the expressions on the faces of the pupils as they responded to questions, watched a demonstration, showed perplexity, or registered insight into problems under discussion.)

Students who intend to teach in urban areas or inner-city schools are advised to seek out practice teaching experiences that will give them the the best possible preparation for such an assignment. This might involve student teaching in a school similar to the type they wish to teach in ultimately.

As an example of an assignment providing the type of relevant experience needed in this situation, the University of Northern Colorado has developed an innovative plan for qualified juniors and seniors who are preparing to teach in the secondary schools of the inner city. In the materials announcing this plan, the following descriptions are given:[1]

> Participants in the program spend much of the first four weeks of the quarter engaged with concentrated study in areas of concern related to specific course offerings. Emphasis throughout the program is on preparing prospective teachers for working in urban schools whose populations are composed of children from culturally diverse backgrounds. At the same time, it is recognized that there is more to developing teachers for inner-city schools than simply making them aware of the cultural differences among the children they will be teaching. The teacher's positive self-concept and feelings of adequacy to meet his own needs and those of his students form the basics from which he can function effectively as a teacher, and must be taken into consideration in any program for teacher preparation.
>
> Other activities which are included in the field experiences include the following:
>
> 1. A six-week live-in experience which is one of the most important aspects of the program. Whenever possible, and with the consideration of the students' needs and wishes, housing for the participants is arranged in the city with a family whose life style is significantly different from that of the student.
> 2. At least one-half of each day for a six-week period is spent working with children as a teacher-assistant in an urban-deprived school of the participant's choice. Work in the school is under the supervision of experienced, highly qualified school personnel.
> 3. Additional time is spent actively participating in the work of public and private agencies within the community so that the students can gain a greater understanding of the social groups that make up the community.
> 4. Seminars coordinated with both types of field experiences in an effort to provide a basis for solutions to the sociological, psychological, and educational problems encountered.

Your First Days in the Class

Observing pupils in the class can be a profitable experience the first few days or weeks. The student teacher has an advantage in this situation because he is not preoccupied with teaching plans and conduct of the class as is the regular teacher. The alert student teacher can, in fact, be of assistance to the regular teacher in recognizing incipient

---

[1] "Teacher Training Experience for Inner-City Schools," mimeographed materials, University of Northern Colorado, 1970.

Student Teaching

discipline problems, lack of interest, or special conditions which might lead to better teaching if recognized early.

The student teacher may wish to engage in a systematic program of observation in order to gain familiarity with all members of the class. For this purpose, a checklist of individual differences is suggested:

Recognizing Individual Differences in a New Class
During the First Few Weeks

DOES THE PUPIL APPEAR TO (BE):	PUPILS 1 2 3 4 (etc.)
Health	
1. Pale	
2. Tired and listless	
3. Sleepy	
4. Nervous	
5. Often absent	
6. Of normal health	
7. Of robust health	
Physical Defects—Differences	
8. Left-handed	
9. Wear glasses	
10. Need to wear glasses	
11. Wear a hearing aid	
12. Need to wear a hearing aid	
13. Possess a leg defect	
14. Possess an arm/hand defect	
15. Possess a weak speaking voice	
16. Possess a nasal difficulty	
17. Free from physical defects	
Personality	
18. Happy with a ready smile	
19. Quiet	
20. Shy	
21. Easily embarrassed	
22. Cynical	
23. Passive	
24. Effusive	
25. Appreciative	
26. Conscientious	
27. Persistent in face of difficulties	
28. Give up easily	
29. Set high standards	
30. Worry excessively	
31. Indifferent	
32. Average of any teenager	

DOES THE PUPIL APPEAR TO (BE): PUPILS
1 2 3 4 (etc.)

Basic Skills
33. Low in basic reading mechanics
34. Read slowly but carefully
35. Gain little understanding from reading
36. Outline or underline as an aid to reading understanding
37. Write in a fashion difficult to read
38. Write slowly
39. Encounter difficulty in expressing his thoughts orally
40. Encounter difficulty in expressing his thoughts on paper
41. Possess basic spelling difficulties
42. Low in basic math processes
43. Careless in spelling
44. Careless in working with numbers
45. Very neat (written work)
46. Disorganized in laboratory and other work involving procedure
47. Systematic in laboratory and other work involving procedure
48. Normal or above average (in) math skills
49. Normal or above average (in) writing skills
50. Normal or above average (in) spelling skills
51. Normal or above average (in) reading skills
52. Possess little recall of concepts previously studied
53. Have lower-than-normal ability to reason out solutions to problems involving numbers
54. Have poor mastery of problem-solving reasoning with ideas
55. Have excellent reasoning ability
56. Have average reasoning ability
57. Think slowly
58. Possess the ability to apply learning to everyday situations

Relationships with Fellow Pupils
59. A leader
60. Easily influenced by others in group

Student Teaching 335

DOES THE PUPIL APPEAR TO (BE):	PUPILS
	1 2 3 4 (etc.)

    61. Anxious to be accepted by others
    62. Attempt to impress others with knowledge
    63. Have few friends
    64. Oblivious of what others think of him
    65. Liked and respected by others
    66. Critical of others
    67. Cooperative/helpful to others

Relationship with Teacher
    68. Resent suggestions
    69. Disregard suggestions
    70. Disregard specific requests
    71. Show lack of respect of teacher
    72. Deliberately "test" teacher's patience
    73. Make it difficult for teacher through leadership of the group
    74. Assist the teacher through leadership of the group
    75. Respect teacher
    76. Friendly with teacher
    77. Rely too much on teacher for help

Class Participation
    78. Frequently show lack of preparation in class responses
    79. Only volunteer answers when specifically called upon
    80. Jump to conclusions without sufficient thought
    81. Always anxious to volunteer
    82. Often ask questions of a more complicated nature than the material at hand
    83. Ask questions which would indicate not having paid attention in class
    84. Ask questions when there is lack of understanding
    85. Pay attention to the answers given by others
    86. Indifferent to the contributions of others
    87. Unable to grasp important ideas developed in a class discussion
    88. Regulate participation so as to be a real asset to class

DOES THE PUPIL APPEAR TO (BE):	PUPILS
	1 2 3 4 (etc.)

    89. Afraid of making a mistake _____
    90. Argue about accuracy of conclusions _____
    91. Attempt to be humorous to gain attention _____

Class Attitude and Cooperation
    92. Listen attentively _____
    93. Take notes _____
    94. Have a short span of attention _____
    95. Bored _____
    96. Break into contributions of others _____
    97. Work on other class assignments during discussion periods _____
    98. Daydream _____
    99. Not hear questions directed to him _____
    100. Talk or argue with others while another "has the floor" _____
    101. Make noises, etc. to interfere with the class _____
    102. Show marked interest in the subject _____
    103. Respond when corrected _____
    104. Show indifference when majority are interested _____
    105. Draw on paper or look out of window often _____
    106. Seem disturbed when another student is interfering with class _____
    107. Ask for special help when there is lack of understanding _____
    108. Appear at general "help" sessions _____

Dependability
    109. Submit written assignments on time _____
    110. Give oral reports on time _____
    111. Occasionally misinterpret assignments _____
    112. Give alibis for assignments not done _____
    113. "Give-up" easily _____
    114. Complete assigned work in a sketchy manner _____
    115. Volunteer for extra tasks _____
    116. Appear for extra help sessions on time _____
    117. Appear at class without the necessary materials for work _____
    118. Leave laboratory desk in an unsatisfactory condition at the close of the period _____

Student Teaching

DOES THE PUPIL APPEAR TO (BE):	PUPILS
	1 2 3 4 (etc.)

119. Work with average dependability and thoroughness on assignments _____
120. Quality of work on assignments excellent _____

Probable Ability Combined with Effort _____
121. Possess low ability and be discouraged _____
122. Possess medium ability and be discouraged _____
123. Possess low ability but make a conscientious effort _____
124. Possess medium ability but encounter difficulty due to having no previous experience with subject field _____
125. Possess medium ability and make conscientious effort _____
126. Possess medium ability but not motivated _____
127. Possess high ability but not motivated _____
128. Possess high ability but not challenged _____
129. Possess high ability but not sufficiently thorough _____
130. Memorize well but not able to apply it to new situations _____
131. Possess high ability and perform in a very capable manner _____

The first days in the practice teaching class should afford opportunities to give individual help to pupils who need it. Do not answer questions directly but use inquiry methods—ask guiding questions. It is wise to confer with the supervising teacher about the extent of such help permitted. There may be some reason to withhold assistance on certain assignments. At the same time, contact with students on an individual basis is an excellent way to gain confidence in one's ability to explain, teach, or convey information. The student teacher should capitalize on every possible opportunity to develop this skill.

Because the initial period of observation may be rather brief—perhaps only a few days or a week—the student teacher will do well to begin thinking about the choice of a teaching area or unit. Such choice may have already been made in conference with the supervising teacher. It will most certainly be dependent on the subject-matter goals of the course during the semester or quarter of the assignment. In anticipation of the beginning of teaching, the student teacher will wish to gather appropriate materials and to prepare general plans. Some of the details of the preliminary planning are considered in the next section.

How does a student teacher develop rapport with his pupils?

Preparing to Teach a Lesson

A teacher facing a class for the first time may be inclined to expect far too much to be accomplished in a given amount of time. Although it is not necessarily wasteful to overplan a lesson, it is a mistake to attempt to teach everything on the lesson plan just because it is there, or when the learning pace of the pupils does not warrant it. One must constantly be in tune with his class, sensing the proper pace and modifying his presentation as the situation demands.

A second common fault of the beginning teacher is the tendency to teach at a level above the comprehension of the class members. This may be a result of his recent contact with college courses, in which the level is very high, or of the inability to place abstract ideas into concrete terms for comprehension by secondary school students. The problem is important enough that it is worth extra consideration by the beginning teacher to make certain his presentation is at the appropriate level for the class involved. Perhaps a few "test trials" with individual students

Student Teaching

to acquire a realistic sense of the proper difficulty level might be carried out before teaching the entire class.

Construction of unit and daily lesson plans is an important task at this stage. The important thing is to have a clear idea of what one wishes to accomplish in the allotted time and what specific objectives are to be met. The student teacher should attempt to place himself in the position of a pupil who is learning about the material for the first time. He should consider factors of interest, motivation, individual differences, time limitations, facilities, and equipment; he should try to anticipate the kinds of problems which may occur and prepare possible solutions to them. After he has done this, the more secure he will be and the less discipline problems he will have.

A further item of planning for the beginning teacher involves anticipation of questions from the class. First attempts at planning tend to neglect preparations for handling these questions and fail to provide sufficient time for dealing with them in the class period. Yet the frank interchange of ideas between teacher and pupils which is provoked by questions can be an effective teaching technique and should not be ignored. In planning, it is advantageous to try to anticipate the kinds of questions pupils may ask. If one remembers that the pupils may be encountering the subject matter for the first time, it is not too difficult to foretell what questions may come to their minds. These probable questions should be jotted down on the lesson plan with suitable answers or with suggested procedures for finding the answers if the questions come up. Time spent in this manner is not wasted, even if the specific anticipated questions do not arise. The beginning teacher will gain confidence in his own understandings of the subject matter and in his ability to provide suitable answers.

A final point for consideration is that of proper pacing and timing of the class period. The written lesson plans may have suggested time allotments for various activities, but the actual class is certain to deviate to some extent from these plans. The important thing is to be organized flexibly enough to accommodate minor variations within the class period. However, to avoid gross miscalculations of time requirements for certain activities, it is well to rehearse the activities in advance. A short lecture, for example, can be tried out on one's roommate, who will be able to give critical comments on clarity and organization, as well as on timing. In the case of student activities or laboratory work, it is usually advisable to allot about fifty percent more time than appears adequate for the teacher himself to perform the activity. This is also recommended in the giving of written tests.

At all stages of planning for the first day of teaching, it is imperative that the student teacher keep the supervising teacher informed of his plans, solicit advice and assistance, and in general plan in such a way as to make the transition from regular teacher to student teacher as smooth as possible.

Discipline

Of major concern to the beginning teacher is the problem of how to handle discipline when the need for it arises. More has been said about this in Chapter 14, and a few summarizing statements will suffice for review here:

1. The major responsibility for discipline measures within the class lies with the supervising teacher; however, by previous agreement, the student teacher may have certain responsibilities in the matter when directly in charge of the class. From the standpoint of class respect for the student teacher and future harmony and cooperation, it is to his advantage to handle discipline matters himself, without requiring assistance from the supervising teacher.

2. An atmosphere of mutual respect between teacher and pupil should be cultivated if possible. This precludes the use of sarcasm or intimidation by the teacher in order to secure discipline. If pupils are treated as adults, they will in all likelihood respond favorably in an adult manner.

3. Avoid the tendency to begin the class by enumerating a list of "don'ts" in regard to possible infractions of classroom rules. It is better to maintain the attitude that the goals of the class are to teach—that discipline problems are not to be tolerated and will be handled summarily if the need arises.

4. In most classes, the majority of pupils are seriously engaged in pursuit of an education, and it is a relatively small minority which is disruptive. Thus, it frequently is possible to allow peer pressure to exert its influence on individuals who create problems in the classroom. Open expressions of distaste by one's peers for unruly behavior frequently have beneficial effects.

5. Assignments of classwork or homework should never be used as punishment for discipline problems. At all times, the activities of the class should be made to appear interesting and exciting. The surest way to destroy interest is to assign extra work or give tests as punishment for misbehavior.

The First Day of Teaching

If the student teacher has had frequent opportunities to work with individuals and small groups before his first day of actual teaching, he will find the new experience a natural extension of these tasks and a challenging opportunity for growth in the art of teaching.

A good introduction will get the class off to an interesting start. A brief explanation of the purpose of the lesson and the work at hand, followed immediately by plunging into the class activities, will convey to the students an appreciation of the tasks to be accomplished. A forthright and businesslike manner by the student teacher will elicit cooperation of the class and leave no doubt about who is in charge.

Attention should be given to proper speech and voice modulation. A good pace should be maintained, and, above all, genuine enthusiasm must be displayed. This enthusiasm will normally be infectious and will secure an enthusiastic response from the class. If possible, pupil participation should be employed. Questions from pupils should be encouraged, and a relaxed atmosphere maintained for free interchange of ideas.

It is usually advisable, especially with junior high school classes, to arrange to vary the activity once or twice during the class period. Perhaps a short lecture can be followed by a brief film and the period concluded with a summarizing discussion. Or a demonstration by the teacher might be followed by a period of individual experimentation. It is true that planning and execution of a varied class period requires more work on the part of the teacher, but it will pay dividends in the form of enthusiasm, alert attention, and better learning by the pupils.

The last five or ten minutes of a class period are frequently used for summarization of the major points of the lesson and for the making of appropriate assignments. It is important to recognize that pupils need to have a feeling of accomplishment and progress in order to keep their motivation high. A final clarification of what is expected of them in preparation for succeeding lessons is worth a few minutes at the close of a class period.

Completion of the first day of teaching by the student teacher should be followed as soon as possible by reflection on the successes and failures of the class period and an effort to diagnose any problems which may have arisen. This can usually be done profitably in conference with the supervising teacher and can be a useful follow-up to the day of teaching. Any required adjustments in the future plans can be made at this time, necessary additional materials can be gathered, and the stage can be set for a new day of teaching to follow.

Your Responsibilities as a Student Teacher

The opportunity to practice teach in a given school system under a competent supervising teacher should be deemed a privilege by the student teacher. Contrary to an apprentice in a typical trade situation, the "apprentice teacher" is not working with inanimate materials such as wood and metal but with live human beings of infinite worth. One must never forget his responsibility to provide the best possible education for the pupils in the classroom and to avoid possible harmful measures.

It is, therefore, of extreme importance to make one's lesson plans with care, to consider individual differences in interest and ability, and to conduct the class in an atmosphere of friendly helpfulness. Each pupil should be considered a potential learning organism with capabilities for infinite growth. The teacher's responsibility is to develop this potential to the maximum extent.

The student teacher's responsibility to the supervising teacher rests in the area of recognition of authority and respect for experience. It is certain that disagreements about teaching methods or approach may exist, but the final authority in the matter is that of the supervising teacher, who is officially responsible for the class. At the same time, an alert student teacher can be of infinite help by anticipating the needs of the class, suggesting materials, preparing materials, and in general earning the title of "assistant teacher" which is used in some school systems. The varied backgrounds of student teachers and willingness to share experiences and special talents which they may have can make the classroom more interesting and educationally effective than it would be without these resources.

The responsibility of the student teacher toward himself and his potential as a teacher is important as well. It would be relatively easy to sit casually by, waiting for things to happen in the practice teaching assignment. The student teacher who gains the most, however, from the standpoint of personal growth, will be the one who enters into the experience with a dynamic approach, intent on learning everything he can in the time allotted. He will participate, when permitted, in meetings of the school faculty, in attendance and assistance at school athletic events, in dramatic and musical productions of the school, and other functions relating to school life. He will in this way see his pupils in a variety of roles outside of the classroom and will gain insight into the total school program. He will be able to achieve a balanced perspective of his own role as a teacher of his subject among the other academic disciplines and curricular activities of the school. Such experience will enable him to become a mature teacher and complete the metamorphosis from the role of college student.

Tips for the Student Teacher

The committee on student teaching of the University of Northern Colorado has summarized the experience considered essential for the student teacher.[2] A partial list follows:

All-School Involvement
1. The student teacher should assist in organizing the school at the opening of the school year.
2. The student teacher should take part in the program of the faculty in the school. This includes committee work, faculty meetings, etc.
3. The student teacher should take part in conferences with parents and have some direct relation with the home.
4. The student teacher should have experiences leading to an understanding of the operation of the total school.
5. He should have experiences leading to an increased understanding of education as a profession.

Observation
6. Much opportunity should be provided to observe master teachers in the classroom.
7. An opportunity should be provided to observe the work of other teachers during student teaching.

Lesson Planning
8. The student teacher should have instruction in lesson planning.
9. The student teaching experience should provide an opportunity to plan, and to carry out, the ideas gained in college methods classes.
10. The prospective teacher should have experience in planning a program or a curriculum in his field.

Supervision
11. Student teachers should be provided with specific instruction in how to construct and administer tests, and to assign grades.
12. The student teacher needs directed experience in classroom speaking and in discussion techniques.

---

[2]Report of the Student Teaching Committee, University of Northern Colorado, Greeley, June 1, 1962.

13. The student teacher must have an opportunity to work under the supervision of a master teacher in his field.
14. He must have a supervisor who can give criticism followed by constructive ideas.
15. He should have an opportunity to consult jointly with the college supervisor and supervising teacher.
16. The student teacher should be assigned to teach where he is wanted.
17. He should have a supervisor who stays in the classroom most of the time.
18. His supervisor should not criticize him in the presence of the pupils.
19. He should work under the supervision of a teacher who is well-qualified in his subject and has a broad perspective of the area.

Work With Students.

20. The student teacher should be prepared for, and have experience in, the instruction of both the gifted and the slow learner.
21. The student teacher should have some opportunity to have complete responsibility for the class.

Self-development

22. The student teacher should understand, and know how to plan for, developmental growth and learning extending over a period of time.
23. The student teacher should be provided with means for self-evaluation.
24. He should have a "special problems" seminar either at the close of student teaching or between a split in the teaching assignment.
25. He should become aware that it takes time to develop the skills and understandings essential to effective teaching.

Miscellaneous

26. The student teacher should be prepared for teaching in such a manner that he is capable of carrying out instruction in his field with limited equipment and materials.
27. There should be no full-time teaching assignment the final quarter before graduation.
28. In some areas the student teaching experiences should be extended over more than one quarter.
29. The student teacher should be instructed in how to dress appropriately.
30. He should have a student teaching handbook which guides him in the effective planning and carrying out of instruction.

Summary

Practice teaching is the most important phase of the prospective teacher's training. Entered into with enthusiasm and a willingness to learn, the experience will be for the student teacher a valuable culmination to college preparation for teaching.

The selection of subject, school, and supervising teacher is enhanced by visits to schools before the semester or quarter of practice teaching. It is advisable to do one's practice teaching in the major field of preparation in order to capitalize on one's strength of subject-matter competency.

The usual pattern of preparation is to spend several days or a week observing the class one is going to teach. Such observation can be done on a systematic basis and may enable one to achieve real insight into the individual differences present in the class. The student teacher can be an "assistant teacher" in the truest sense if he is alert to developing problems, anticipates future activities of the class, and prepares himself accordingly.

Taking over the class to teach a lesson or a unit will be completely successful if the student teacher plans adequately in consultation with the supervising teacher and makes his preparations carefully. Advance rehearsal for the first day of teaching is an advisable procedure, particularly if the time budget is questionable or if class questions are anticipated. An immediate follow-up of a day of teaching with a brief conference with the supervising teacher is advisable. Necessary changes in lesson plans can be made at this time.

A desirable arrangement is to follow the practice teaching quarter with a final quarter on the college campus before graduation. At this time, seminars in special problems of teaching can be most profitable, and the student teacher can reflect upon the practice teaching experience to good advantage. The opportunity to give maximum attention to the very important choice of a first teaching position in the light of the recent experience in practice teaching is thus afforded.

Further Investigation and Study

1. In your observation of a high school or junior high school class, use the checklist on pp. 333-37 to discover the individual differences present in the class. At the end of a week, discuss your observations with the teacher. How do the students' achievements appear to correlate with your observations of study habits and classroom behavior?

2. Make a list of the traits you would like to see in the supervising teacher with whom you wish to do your practice teaching. Using this list as a guide, objectively analyze your own traits and compare. Do you think similar or opposite traits are preferable, or that a judicious blend of both is preferable?

16 The Professional Educator

The teacher today is a member of a dedicated group of professional educators which includes supervisors, coordinators, administrators, and other educational specialists. This group, which numbers in the millions, has the responsibility for developing curriculum plans and carrying out the teaching process for the youth of the nation, at a time when the need for high-quality education is unsurpassed.

If the average class size is considered to be twenty-five students, the average daily contact load of these teachers is 125 students. Students spend an average of five hours per week in the direct charge of a teacher whose job it is to instill knowledge and develop skills, interests, and attitudes.

The younger teacher of today cannot help but feel pride in being a part of the teaching profession. It is an exciting time to be a teacher and the rewards are abundant. Along with favorable attitudes toward teaching comes responsibility for dedication to the task and for self-improvement. It is for this reason that attention is directed in this chapter to the preparation of the professional educator.

The New Teacher

The prospective teacher in an undergraduate program at a college or university is nearing his goal of becoming a qualified specialist in his subject. In most cases his decision to prepare himself as a teacher of a particular subject was made early in his college career—on the basis of interest, environmental background, previous training, and prospective rewards in the teaching field. As he approaches the end of his training, the prospective teacher looks forward to an interesting and productive career as a professional educator in a challenging field of teaching. He is concerned that his training has been adequate for the task and that he will be successful in meeting the challenges ahead.

Securing a Teaching Position

Recent years have showed a somewhat discouraging job market for teachers of most subjects. The situation that existed a short time ago no longer is present. We now are in a buyers market with many more applicants for positions than there are jobs available. In this respect, the prospects are not as bright as they were a few years ago. It is necessary for the prospective teacher to work diligently in finding a suitable position. Competition is high and he needs to use all of the available avenues to secure a satisfactory teaching job.

Getting ready to look for a job. As one prepares to enter the job market there are several steps necessary to get ready. The prospective employee of a school system will wish to secure a number of recommendations from his college instructors in his major and minor fields, his methods instructors, and perhaps others of his own choosing. To get these recommendations, be sure to obtain permission to use an instructor's name for a reference and request the recommendation personally, either by letter or by personal conversation. One should remember that instructors are asked by many individuals to write recommendations and a thoughtful instructor will put in a reasonable amount of time in writing a good recommendation. In order to make the job as easy for him as possible supply information of a specific nature about yourself. For example, give him information on your hobbies, on the experiences that you have had in working with children such as coaching, camp counseling, summer recreation programs, Sunday School teaching, and others. Inform him about any special competencies that you have such as the ability to handle a club, or special knowledge of Melville, or model airplane building, or any other relevant experiences. Give specific evidence of the kinds of experiences that would qualify you to be a good teacher. This kind of information will pay dividends and will secure for you the immediate attention of a thoughtful school administrator.

When requesting a recommendation, if the contact with the instructor is several months old, it is a good idea to supply him with a snapshot of yourself which will refresh his memory as to your presence in his classes. The following is a sample recommendation request form used by a methods instructor, on which you might supply the kind of information that your instructor needs to do a thorough job.

Personal Recommendations

Name _____
Classes From Me _____
Grades _____

Because many of you will be applying for teaching jobs (or other in the near future), you will be required to obtain letters of recommendation for your files at the Office of Appointments. If requested to write such a recommendation, I shall be happy to oblige, but I should like to have some further information about you to include in the recommendation. It is my belief that the following types of information can be very meaningful to a prospective employer and may make the difference between being hired and not being hired.

Please give information on the following points, if possible.

1. Any experience you have had working with young people in any other capacity besides practice teaching, such as scout leader, Sunday School teacher, swimming instructor, camp counselor, or other. Give specific information.

2. Any hobbies you may have (past or present) such as specimen collecting, special reading in a topic, etc.

3. Any travel you have done which may have been broadening or educational, such as Carlsbad Caverns, Grand Canyon, Yellowstone Park, or any others.

4. Any other experience information which may be important for a prospective employer to know.

Using placement services. You will probably wish to make use of one or more teacher placement services in order to secure a satisfactory position. Most teacher training institutions have placement offices.

There may be an enrollment fee of five or ten dollars for this service. You would be well advised to get all of your required materials in early, usually by January 1, because the placement offices begin to make appointments with school administrators early in the new year for the purpose of interviewing applicants for positions. If you are conscientious about getting all of your requirements in, you will be eligible to meet with prospective employers.

Secondly, many state departments of education have placement bureaus. It is wise to contact them and give them the necessary information so that they can assist you in locating vacancies within your state.

A third type of agency is the commercial variety which will send you notifications of vacancies. They usually require an enrollment fee plus a certain percentage of your first year salary if you secure a job through their services. The percentages range from seven to ten percent of one's first year salary. One should give serious thought to the value of spending this large fraction of income to secure an initial teaching position.

Letters of application. Once you have been notified of a suitable vacancy for which you wish to apply, it is necessary to prepare a letter of application in good form so that it will be looked upon favorably by the recipient. It is a good idea, if you plan to type your own application letter, to check with a secretary to refresh your memory on style and form. In many cases, your letter of application will merely bring forth a standard application form from the school to which you apply. In this case, give the complete information required by the school.

If possible, it is a good idea to have your letter of application typed by a secretary. This adds quality and dignity to the correspondence and will impress the recipient. A poorly constructed letter with typographical errors, erasures, and other evidence of carelessness is almost certain to be tossed into the reject file.

In your letter of application, be sure to include all of the necessary information to give a clear picture of your qualification for the job for which you are applying. This includes your major and minor teaching areas, information on special competencies such as ability to handle specific types of clubs, etc., your marital status and size of the family, and information on your familiarity with new teaching trends such as inquiry teaching, team teaching, individualized instruction, new curriculum projects, open school concepts, and other current trends.

You might conclude the letter by volunteering your willingness to meet the superintendent for an interview at a mutually convenient time. Following is a sample letter of application which you might use as a guide:

May 15, 1973

Dr. Floyd Smith
Superintendent of Schools
Wichita Falls, Missouri

Dear Dr. Smith:

I wish to apply for the position as teacher of Junior High School Social Studies announced as a vacancy in your school system. The placement office at Webster State College, Webster, Kansas, will send my complete credentials.

My major teaching area is junior high school social studies and my minor is mathematics. In addition, I have secured a teacher's permit for driver education and am qualified to give the driver education course for the state of Missouri.

Photography has been a hobby and avocation of mine for many years and I would be interested in supervising a junior high school photography club.

I shall be happy to come for a personal interview at your convenience.
Sincerely yours,

John Tryst

The job interview. If you secure the opportunity to interview the principal or superintendent of schools you will wish to present yourself in the best possible manner. Be sure to arrive on time, dress conservatively for the occasion, be properly groomed in hair and clothing. Allow the employer to conduct the interview at his own pace and in his own manner. Supply information about yourself as requested. If asked, discuss your philosophy of teaching briefly, tell about your training and special competencies, and inform him of your professional memberships, and other organizations to which you belong. He will probably request certain family information, such as whether you are married and whether you have children. These questions are asked in order to give you the best possible evaluation for the job for which you are applying and in recognition of the fact that one's professional career life depends a great deal upon satisfactory home life and living conditions.

You will have the opportunity, also, to ask questions. You will want to know some of the details of the position, such as the level of the class, its probable size, the text materials that are used, and the availability of supplies. You perhaps will want to ask questions about the community such as the availability of housing, churches, and recreation facilities. Let the interviewer supply you with information on the prospective salary and other fringe benefits associated with the job.

After obtaining the job. Securing a position as a new teacher is a major accomplishment and it may give you the feeling that your teaching career is set for all time. But this would be a shortsighted view. Of course it should be your intention to remain on the job with the expectation of doing excellent work but it should be recognized also that you may want to move upward professionally as the years go by. Therefore, it is a good idea to keep your placement file up-to-date. Keep in contact with the placement office by informing them of any new course work that you have taken such as institutes, or summer school attendance. Have updated transcripts supplied to the placement office which may include the completion of a new degree or additional course work. When you are ready to apply for a new position, be sure to get recommendations from your principal and supervisor in the school system in which you work.

Characteristics of a Good Teacher

Administrators and supervisors are faced with evaluating teachers constantly, for purposes of salary increments, promotions to department chairman, differentiated staffing and other reasons. Unfortunately, many evaluations are made on the basis of superficial characteristics or personal qualities that happen to please or displease the evaluator, rather than on more basic characteristics that exemplify good teaching. Following is a question checklist that can be used by an administrator, supervisor, or by the teacher himself for self-evaluation:

Question Checklist

1. Is he enthusiastic about what he is doing and does he show it?
2. Is he dynamic and does he use his voice and facial expression for emphasis and to hold attention?
3. Does he use illustrative devices extensively to make each new learning experience as concrete as possible?

The Professional Educator

4. Does he show originality in securing teaching materials from simple objects or "junk"?
5. Does he have a functional knowledge of his subject so that he can apply what he knows to everyday living?
6. Does he possess the ability to explain ideas in simple terms regardless of how extensive his knowledge is?
7. Does he stimulate actual thought on the part of his students or does he make parrots out of them?
8. Is he a "have to finish the book" type of teacher or does he teach thoroughly what is accomplished?
9. Does he maintain calm and poise in the most trying of classroom circumstances?
10. Does he use a variety of teaching techniques or is it the same thing day after day?
11. Does he exhibit a feeling of confidence and are the students confident about his ability?
12. Does he encourage class participation and questions and does he conscientiously plan for them?
13. Does he maintain a good instructional tempo so that the period does not drag?
14. Does he use techniques to stimulate interest at the beginning of new material or does he treat it merely as something new to be learned?
15. Does he concentrate on key ideas and use facts as means to an end?

Of a more formal nature is the Stanford Teacher Competence Appraisal Guide.[1] It may be used to assist the individual teacher in assessing his strengths and weaknesses, or it may be used for formal evaluation purposes. For rating, each item may be evaluated on the basis of eight points and totalled for a cumulative score. The ratings are:

0 Unable to observe	4 Strong
1 Weak	5 Superior
2 Below average	6 Outstanding
3 Average	7 Truly exceptional

---

[1] "Stanford Teacher Competence Appraisal Guide," Stanford Center for Research and Development in Teaching, Stanford, California. This Guide is no longer used on a regular basis by the Stanford Secondary Teacher Education Program and copies are no longer available from Stanford.

STANFORD TEACHER COMPETENCE APPRAISAL GUIDE

AIMS

1. Clarity of Aims — The purposes of the lesson are clear.
2. Appropriateness of Aims — The aims are neither too easy nor too difficult for the pupils. They are appropriate and are accepted by the pupils.

PLANNING

3. Organization of the Lesson — The individual parts of the lesson are clearly related to each other in an appropriate way. The total organization facilitates what is to be learned.
4. Selection of Content — The content is appropriate for the aims of the lesson, the level of the class, and the teaching method.
5. Selection of Materials — The specific instructional materials and human resources used are clearly related to the content of the lesson and complement the selected method of instruction.

PERFORMANCE

6. Beginning the Lesson — Pupils come quickly to attention. They direct themselves to the tasks to be accomplished.
7. Clarity of Presentation — The content of the lesson is presented so it is understandable to the pupils. Different points of view and specific illustrations are used when appropriate.
8. Pacing of the Lesson — The movement from one part of the lesson to the next is governed by the pupils' achievement. The teacher "stays with the class" and adjusts the tempo accordingly.
9. Pupil Participation and Attention — The class is attentive. When appropriate the pupils actively participate in the lesson.
10. Ending the Lesson — The lesson is ended when the pupils have achieved the aims of instruction. Tie together chance and

		planned events and relate them to long-range aims of instruction.
11.	Teacher-Pupil Rapport	The personal relationships between pupils and the teacher are harmonious.

EVALUATION

12.	Variety of Evaluative Procedures	The teacher devises and uses an adequate variety of procedures, both formal and informal, to evaluate progress in all of the aims of instruction.
13.	Use of Evaluation to Provide Improvement of Teaching & Learning	The results of evaluation are carefully reviewed by teacher and pupils for the purpose of improving teaching and learning.

PROFESSIONAL

14.	Concern for Professional Standards and Growth	The teacher helps, particularly in his specialty, to define and enforce standards for 1) selecting, training, and licensing teachers, and 2) for working conditions.
15.	Effectiveness in School Staff Relationships	The teacher is respectful and considerate of his colleagues. He demonstrates awareness of their personal concerns and professional development.
16.	Concern for the Total School Program	The teacher's concern is not simply for his courses and his students. He works with other teachers, students, and administrators to bring about the success of the program.
17.	Constructive Participation in Community Affairs	The teacher understands the particular community context in which he works and helps to school's program to the community.

An additional excellent Self-Evaluation Inventory for Teachers, originally produced by the National Science Teachers Association, is found in Appendix 1.

Opportunities for Professional Growth

Among the opportunities for professional growth while on the job are graduate work in a subject field or in education during the summer or at night, depending upon the available opportunities; inservice workshops and institutes; government- or industry-sponsored summer institutes; committee activity on curriculum revision or evaluation; membership in professional organizations, with accompanying attendance at regular meetings and participation in committee work; reading professional journals and current books in teaching; writing for professional publications; keeping up to date on new materials, teaching resources, education aids, etc.

Graduate Work

The opportunities for graduate work are abundant. The usual requirement for completion of a master's degree in education is one year or four summers of course work. Theses are generally not required, but comprehensive examinations in a major and minor field usually are. The monetary rewards for teachers with master's degrees are well worth the time and expense involved in obtaining the degree. Most school systems have a salary differential of $300 to $500 for holders of master's degrees; furthermore, opportunities for higher-paying jobs are greater and better selection of teaching positions is available for the applicant who holds a master's degree.

It is becoming increasingly apparent that a year of graduate work beyond the bachelor's degree is a worthwhile investment. Consider a hypothetical example: Student A earns his bachelor's degree and obtains a teaching position in a small school which pays $6,000 per year. Student B stays in school an extra year and obtains a master's degree. This year costs him $2,000. At the conclusion of his work, he accepts a position which pays $7,000 per year. (This is a reasonable expectation because he will be attractive to larger school systems, whose salary scales are significantly higher than those of small school systems.)

In this example Student B is able to recoup the additional expense of $2,000 in two years of teaching, furthermore, he is a much more desirable candidate for higher-paying jobs and perhaps will be in a larger school system with better teaching facilities, more classes in his major field, and higher annual salary increments. This example expresses quite accurately the prevailing situation with reference to training and job seeking. It merits thoughtful consideration by the undergraduate prospective teacher as he considers his future in teaching.

Inservice Training

Inservice workshops and institutes are usually sponsored by public school systems for improvement of the teachers within that system. Degree credit may or may not be offered, depending on the arrangements with the colleges or universities from which consultant services are obtained. Such workshops and institutes frequently have objectives designed to stimulate curriculum improvement or to improve teacher competencies in subject-matter understandings and teaching techniques. The new teacher is encouraged to avail himself of these opportunities in order to familiarize himself with broad problems of curriculum improvement and in order to benefit from the experience of older teacher in the system.

Committee Work

Committee activity while on the job is an excellent way to develop a professional attitude and become cognizant of the manifold problems facing the teacher. Active school systems frequently have a curriculum committee, a professional committee, a salary and grievance committee, a textbook-selection committee, or other committees of temporary nature as the need for them arises. Participation on one or more of these committees can be enlightening and can contribute to the professional growth of the new teacher; however, committee responsibilities mean extra work, and the new teacher should consider his total work load and weigh carefully the ultimate benefits of participation.

Professional Organizations

Membership in a professional organization brings benefits which are proportional to the member's active participation in the organization. Attendance at periodic meetings develops a sense of cohesiveness and shared objectives; the stimulation of meeting professional coworkers and the absorption of new ideas from meetings attended bring many rewards. Voluntary participation as a panel member or speaker at a discussion session is a highly beneficial experience. It is not necessarily true that a teacher must have many years of experience before he can be considered worthy of a presentation at a professional meeting. A young, enthusiastic new teacher with a fresh approach to a problem can make a definite contribution to a meeting of this type.

Professional journals provide another source of teaching ideas. A teacher should personally subscribe to one or two and make it a habit to peruse regularly others which may be purchased by the school library. Occasional contribution of teaching ideas for publication in a professional journal is highly motivating and is to be encouraged. The professional benefits of such a practice, because it helps one to become known in teaching cirlces and to make valuable contacts, are unlimited.

Professional journals usually contain feature articles on subject-matter topics or educational topics of current interest; ideas for improvement of classroom teaching techniques; information on professional meetings; book reviews; information on teaching materials, apparatus, and resource books; information on career opportunities for secondary school students and information on scholarships and contests for students and teachers.

This is an exchange teacher from Mexico. How does teaching in a foreign land contribute to one's professional growth?

Summary

Today's teacher is in a position of respect and responsibility. The demand for well-prepared teachers has never been greater, and the rewards are exceptional.

The Professional Educator

Proper education of the teacher in this fast-moving age is a matter of increasing concern. A suitable balance of general education, subject-matter preparation, and professional training must be achieved. The current trend is toward strengthening all of these areas, particularly subject-matter preparation. Attainment of a bachelor's degree does not end the teacher's education. More and more, demands for graduate work, up to and beyond the master's level, are being heard. From a financial standpoint, it is generally to the teacher's advantage to obtain this advanced training as soon as possible. Better-paying jobs with other attractive features frequently await the applicant who has additional training.

Professional growth of the teacher can occur in a variety of ways. Graduate course work, inservice institutes and workshops, summer institutes, committee involvement, membership in professional organizations, a program of reading, participation in meetings, and writing for professional journals are but a few. It is important to realize that continual growth and experience are necessary if one is to be an enthusiastic, productive teacher.

The professional educator of today faces a challenging future. Investment in superior preparation and recognition of the need for continual professional growth can return rich dividends: a citizenry better educated for the complex society of today.

Further Investigation and Study

1. Write to the department of education in your state and obtain a summary of the current salary schedules in the major cities or school districts. Compare the starting salaries for teachers with bachelor's degrees and master's degrees. Compare the annual salary increase and the number of years required to reach maximum salary.
2. Prepare a critical analysis of two professional journals in the field in which you are preparing to teach. Examine the feature articles, the classroom teaching helps, the articles contributed by teachers in the field, the book reviews, and other parts of the publication.
3. Prepare a critical review of two research-oriented professional journals in your field. Report on the results of one research study published in each of the journals reviewed. How can the results of educational research be made more available and meaningful for the classroom teacher?

Appendix 1

Self-Evaluation Inventory for Teachers[1]

A. The Professional Teacher is well educated in his subject and the liberal arts

   A teacher needs a thorough understanding of his subject, therefore, his education includes

   Penetrating deeply into the content, conceptual framework, and methodology of his subject

   Studying his subject on a broad front by having taken, regardless of his teaching major, courses involving concepts and processes from a wide variety of subjects including the humanities, sciences, and the arts

   Becoming acquainted with the interrelatedness of education by taking at least one integrated, interdisciplinary course

   Teachers, above all, should be liberally educated human beings, therefore, their academic preparation should include substantial study in

   The natural sciences and mathematics

   The social and behavioral sciences

   The graphic, performing, or industrial arts

   Literature and philosophy, for the insights they give into values and human condition

---

[1] This form is modified from the *Annual Self-Inventory for Science Teachers in Secondary Schools* produced by the National Science Teachers Association, July, 1970.

B. The Professional Teacher possesses a functional philosophy of education and the technical skills of teaching

Based on information and insights gained from formal study, personal reading, and discussion with scholars and practitioners, he has formulated a working philosophy of education—continuously modified by experience—that includes explicit assumptions about

> Students: What they are like. How they learn. What their goals are. How they can benefit by studying his subject.
>
> Teachers:
> a. What their responsibilities are for setting goals, motivating students, keeping order, judging performance, and giving rewards and punishments.
> b. How they stand in the educational enterprise in relation to students, school administrators, parents, college teachers, and each other
> c. What balance they should strike between the interests of the individual and the desires of the community, and between serving the local community and the larger ones
> d. What balance they should seek between transmitting the existing values of the culture and fostering change
>
> Schools:
> a. Their responsibilities to the students, individually and collectively
> b. Their responsibilities to local, state, national, and world communities
> c. Their relationship to other levels and kinds of schools
>
> His subject: What it is, how it functions, its relevance, its relation to the humanities and social sciences, its relation to technology, its impact on society; the moral and social responsibilities of its practitioners

By the time he has completed his training (university courses on methodology, supervised practice or intern teaching, and two or three years of apprenticeship on the job) the teacher should have acquired the basic knowledge and technical skills of his job, having

> Familiarized himself thoroughly with the materials of instruction, how to evaluate them, where they can be obtained, and when and how they can best be used
>
> Mastered varied techniques, styles, and strategies of instruction, such as how to manage multi-media instruction, individualize learning, organize meaningful laboratory investigations, and evaluate learning and motivate reluctant students
>
> Demonstrated in competent observers an ability to conduct learning effectively and wisely

C. The Professional Teacher continues to grow in knowledge and skills throughout his career

Self-Evaluation Inventory for Teachers

He examines his teaching critically at least every two or three years by such methods as

Inviting a professionally competent person (the department chairman, a teacher from another school, an educator from a nearby university) to observe his teaching and to help find ways for improving it

Making audiotapes or videotapes of real teaching episodes and analyzing them with the aid of a competent colleague

Soliciting thoughtful student feedback

He makes up deficiencies in his academic preparation and keeps up-to-date in teaching, education, and the interaction of his subject and society, by

Utilizing appropriate journals

Reading several books each year on education and his subject

Attending professional conferences periodically

Taking advantage of professional days to observe teaching in other schools and to visit universities and agencies related to his teaching field

Enrolling in summer, inservice, or correspondence courses

Keeping informed on, and applying for admission to, appropriate programs of study for teachers, such as those supported by the National Science Foundation and other agencies

Utilizing a sabbatical leave period to carry through a study plan especially tailored to his own needs

He tries to improve his opportunities for professional self-improvement by

Informing his department chairman and principal in writing of specific ways in which the school's professional growth policies and practices must be changed to bring them up to high standards

Requesting, if necessary, his local teachers organization to take up the issue of school support for teacher professional improvement with the superintendent and school board

Seeking, if there has been no real progress toward an acceptable policy after several years of effort, a teaching position where there are better opportunities for professional growth

D. The Professional Teacher insists on a sound educational environment in which to work

He presses for the provision by the school of those services, facilities, and learning materials necessary for effective teaching by

Participating in any planning for new or renovated facilities that may be under way

Annually informing the department chairman and principal in writing of the particular ways in which the school services and facilities fall below acceptable high standards and recommending specific changes

Urging his local teachers organization to fight for better teaching conditions and offering help in that effort

He safeguards the lives and health of his students by

Familiarizing himself with school emergency procedures, state safety regulations, and National Safety Council recommendations

Informing his students of emergency procedures and of any special laboratory hazards

Forbidding students to indulge in activities or experiments that will endanger themselves or their fellow students

Making a thorough safety check each year to see that the rooms in which he teaches and the equipment he expects his students to use meet modern safety standards and that emergency equipment is on hand and in working order

Notifying the department chairman and principal in writing of unsafe conditions and requesting the necessary repairs, replacements, and changes

Refusing (with a full written explanation of his action to the department chairman and principal, and a copy to his local teachers organization) to teach in any facilities or to use any materials or follow any procedures that present an immediate and grave danger to his students

He believes that there must be no school policies or teacher or administrator practices that are unfair, inhumane, or degrading to any students, whatever their individual abilities, goals, family background, appearance, race, or religion; and that he must work toward the elimination of any such policies or practices by such means as

Periodically making a penetrating appraisal of his own attitudes and behavior toward his students

Bringing to the attention of the faculty, school administrators, and local teachers organization any continuing violations he perceives of the educational interests and human rights of any group or category of students

Trying to persuade his local teachers organization to form a high-level committee of sensitive and respected teachers to oversee continuously this dimension of the total school environment and to take valid issues to the superintendent and school board, to the community and state teachers organization

If the educational environment seriously mitigates against good learning and teaching and shows no signs of improvement in spite of his conscientious efforts over several years, he demonstrates his own professional integrity by

Seeking employment in a school where the educational environment is healthier and where he can serve students better

Apprising university and teacher organization placement agencies of the situation so that prospective job applicants can be informed

Self-Evaluation Inventory for Teachers

E. The Professional Teacher maintains his professional status

He is an active member, sometimes serving on committees or holding an office, in appropriate professional organizations, such as

    Local, state, and national organizations for teachers of all subjects and all levels

    Organizations of special relevance for his subject

He takes other positive steps to increase his knowledge and influence

    Reading several teaching, subject, and education journals

    Seeking a significant role in one or more educational matters that go beyond his own classroom teaching (such as curriculum, budget, policy, professional standards, and inservice programs), becoming informed on those matters and requesting meaningful responsibilities related to them

    a. Within the department itself
    b. Within the school or school district

In order to protect the educational interests of students

    He refuses to accept teaching assignments outside of his area of preparation

    He protests to his department chairman and principal (and to his local teachers organization if the practice persists) the assignment of non-science teachers to the teaching of science

F. The Professional Teacher contributes to the improvement of teaching

Because the general improvement of teaching depends upon the accumulation from many sources of new and improved learning materials, techniques, and approaches, and because his own classroom teaching will profit from it, he

    Uses some of his time and energy to develop projection visuals, audio-tapes, test questions, reading lists, demonstrations, student experiments and project ideas, club activities, etc.

    Participates from time to time in the critical classroom testing of new materials and approaches developed by other teachers, national curriculum groups, Regional Laboratories, and educational publishers

    Occasionally accepts invitations (with administrative approval, and after careful consideration of the welfare and rights of his students) to serve as an experimental or control teacher in thoughtful educational experiments

In order to share his ideas, developments, and concerns with colleagues, he may

    Submit articles, book reviews, apparatus notes and letters-to-the-editor to appropriate professional journals

    Give papers or demonstrate new materials and techniques at regional or national meetings, or other appropriate professional conferences

Willingly permit teachers from other schools to visit his classes

G. The Professional Teacher takes a vital interest in the quality of future teachers

He encourages his outstanding students to consider careers as teachers by

Himself teaching in a way that emphasizes the creative, challenging, socially significant, and personally rewarding aspects of the profession

Permitting likely candidates (his own or other high school students, or nearby college students) to tutor, serve as assistants, or otherwise learn by direct experience some of the difficulties and pleasures of teaching

Accepting opportunities to speak with students from nearby colleges and universities (and with their faculty advisers) about the realities and trends in teaching

He contributes to the improvement of teacher preparation by

Informing the institution where he received his own training of the strengths and weaknesses of his preparation in the light of experience

Serving periodically as a supervising teacher of teacher interns

Recognizing that the first year or two on the job is a crucial period in the training of a teacher and, therefore, helping the local teachers organization to secure special working conditions for beginning teachers (including adequate professional supervision, a reduced teaching load, and a limited number of preparations and out-of-classroom assignments)

Supporting efforts of state and national teacher organizations to gain a stronger voice for teachers in the setting of standards for entry into the profession of teaching

Appendix 2

An Analysis and Checklist on the Problem-Solving Objective[1]

Achieving the Problem-Solving Objective

Problem solving, or scientific thinking, is a widely accepted outcome of teaching in schools over the country. In the past much attention has been given to this objective in education literature and there appears to be an interesting increase in it at present.

Very little reliable evidence is available to indicate the extent to which the problem solving objective is provided for in day-to-day classroom activities. Still less evidence is available on the extent to which the objective is achieved with young people.

Among other difficulties in reaching the fullest attainment of the objective is the failure, on the part of many teachers, to recognize that problem-solving behavior is a complex ability made up of elements which can be identified. Some of these elements are quite simple manipulative skills but many more are of a highly intellectual character.

Regardless of the category in which these skills fall, it is very important to recognize that they are developed by recurrent practice. Just as any skill re-

---

[1] Prepared by Ellsworth S. Obourn, Specialist for Science, U.S. Office of Education (Science Teaching Service Circular). Modified for general use by Leslie W. Trowbridge.

lated to problem solving, such as learning how to locate information in a library, the skill must first be taught thoroughly and then practiced until achieved. In a similar way, if the teacher wishes to develop the ability to analyze problems, or interpret evidence, the skills must first be taught and then the teacher must provide classroom situations, day after day, when the pupil will have to use them. There is no easy way of teaching children to use the abilities of problem solving other than by setting classroom situations which call for their repetitive use.

Some authorities have characterized the steps in problem solving as a complete act of thought. This has led many teachers to believe that the act of problem-solving thinking, beginning with the recognition of a problem and ending with a conclusion, must always be practiced in its complete cycle. This is not necessarily true. Scholars rarely ever use the method in its complete cycle. In fact, they are more likely to use it in other ways.

For example, it is quite possible, in fact even desirable, to use the lesson of a given day for practicing whatever elements of the total problem-solving pattern it may best be directed toward. In the development of a topic the teacher may plan to do a demonstration on a given day. This demonstration might provide material especially useful for practicing, among other things, the ability to interpret data. It should be used fully for this purpose and the teacher should see to it that all aspects of data interpretation afforded by the demonstration are carefully identified, clearly understood, and thoroughly practiced by the class.

On another day the teacher might find that a laboratory exercise could provide opportunities for resting a hypothesis or evaluating assumptions. This experience should be used to yield whatever practice for these purposes it might possess. The important thing to remember is that almost every classroom situation can in some way contribute opportunities for pupils to practice certain elements of problem solving. The teacher must be alert to recognize these opportunities and to make the fullest use of each one. This discussion provides an analysis of the attitudes of mind that accompany problem-solving behavior and also an analysis of each of the major elements in problem solving. Such an analysis is essential first to suggest guides for teachers in planning classroom situations that will call for the practice of essential skills and second, to provide a basis for developing tests to evaluate the degree to which the skills have been attained.

Problem-Solving Behaviors[2]

I. Attitudes which can be developed through good teaching.
The program should develop the attitude which will modify the individual's behavior so that he:

---

[2] This analysis was prepared by Dr. Darrell Barnard, Professor of Education and Head of the Department of Science Education, New York University, and Dr. Ellsworth Obourn, U.S. Office of Education.

Appendix

A. Looks for the natural cause of things that happen
   1. Does not believe in superstitions such as charms or signs of good or bad luck.
   2. Believes that occurrences which seem strange and mysterious can always be explained finally by natural cause.
   3. Believes that there is necessarily no connection between two events just because they occur at the same time.
B. Is open-minded toward work, opinions of others, and information related to his problem
   1. Believes that truth never changes, but that his ideas of what is true may change as he gains better understanding of the truth.
   2. Bases his ideas upon the best evidence and not upon tradition alone.
   3. Revises his opinions and conclusions in light of additional reliable information.
   4. Listens to, observes, or reads evidence supporting ideas contrary to his personal opinions.
   5. Accepts no conclusion as final or ultimate.
C. Bases opinions and conclusions on adequate evidence
   1. Is slow to accept as facts any that are not supported by convincing proof.
   2. Bases his conclusions upon evidence obtained from a variety of dependable sources.
   3. Hunts for the most satisfactory explanation of observed phenomena that the evidence permits.
   4. Sticks to the facts and refrains from exaggeration.
   5. Does not permit his personal pride, bias, prejudice, or ambition to pervert the truth.
   6. Does not make snap judgments or jump to conclusions.
D. Evaluates techniques and procedures used, and information obtained
   1. Uses a planned procedure in solving his problems.
   2. Uses the various techniques and procedures which may be applied in obtaining information.
   3. Adapts the various techniques and procedures to the problem at hand.
   4. Personally considers the information obtained and decides whether it relates to the problem.
   5. Judges whether the information is sound, sensible, and complete enough to allow a conclusion to be made.
   6. Selects the most recent, authoritative, and accurate information related to the problem.
E. Is curious concerning the things he observes
   1. Wants to know the "whys," "whats," and "hows" of observed phenomena.
   2. Is not satisfied with vague answers to his questions.

II. Problem-solving abilities which can be developed through teaching.
The program should develop those abilities involved in problem solving which will modify the individual's behavior so that he:
- A. Formulates significant problems
    1. Senses situations involving personal and social problems.
    2. Recognizes specific problems in these situations.
    3. Isolates the single major idea in the problem.
    4. States the problem in question form.
    5. States the problem in definite and concise language.
- B. Analyzes problems
    1. Picks out the key words of a problem statement.
    2. Defines key words as a means of getting a better understanding of the problem.
- C. Obtains information regarding a problem from a variety of sources
    1. Recalls past experiences which bear upon his problem.
    2. Isolates elements common in experience and problem.
    3. Locates source materials.
        a. Uses the various parts of a book:
            (1) Uses key words in the problem statement for locating material in the index.
            (2) Chooses proper sub-topics in the index.
            (3) Uses alphabetical materials, cross references, the table of contents, the title page, the glossary, figures, pictures and diagrams, footnotes, topical headings, running headings, marginal headings, an appendix, a pronunciation list, and "see also" references.
    4. Uses sources materials.
        a. Uses aids in comprehending material read.
            (1) Finds main ideas in a paragraph.
            (2) Uses reading signals.
            (3) Formulates statements from reading.
            (4) Phrases topics from sentences.
            (5) Skims for main ideas.
            (6) Learns meanings of words and phrases from context.
            (7) Selects the printed material related to the problem.
            (8) Cross-checks a book concerning the same topic.
            (9) Recognizes both objective and opinionated evidence.
            (10) Determines the main topic over several paragraphs.
            (11) Takes notes.
            (12) Arranges ideas in an organized manner.
            (13) Makes outlines.
        b. Interprets graphic material.
            (1) Obtains information from different kinds of graphic material.
            (2) Reads titles, column headings, legends and data recorded.

Appendix

      (3) Formulates the main ideas presented.
      (4) Evaluates conclusions based upon the data recorded.

5. Uses experimental procedures appropriate to the problem.
   a. Devises experiments suitable to the solution of the problem.
      (1) Selects the main factor in the experiment.
      (2) Allows only one variable.
      (3) Sets up a control for the experimental factor.
   b. Carries out the details of the experiment.
      (1) Identifies effects and determines causes.
      (2) Tests the effects of the experimental factor under varying conditions.
      (3) Performs the experiment for a sufficient length of time.
      (4) Accurately determines and records quantitative and qualitative data.
      (5) Develops a logical organization of recorded data.
      (6) Generalizes upon the basis of organized data.
   c. Manipulates the laboratory equipment needed in solving the problem.
      (1) Selects kinds of equipment or materials that will aid in solving the problem.
      (2) Manipulates equipment or materials that will aid in an understanding of its function to the outcome of the experiment.
      (3) Recognizes that equipment is only a means to the end results.
      (4) Determines the relationship between observed actions or occurrences and the problem.
      (5) Appraises scales and divisions of scales on measuring devices.
      (6) Obtains correct values from measuring devices.
      (7) Recognizes capacities or limitations of equipment.
      (8) Returns equipment clean and in good condition.
      (9) Avoids hazards and consequent personal accidents.
      (10) Practices neatness and orderliness.
      (11) Avoids waste in the use of materials.
      (12) Exercises reasonable care of fragile or perishable equipment.
6. Solves mathematical problems necessary in obtaining pertinent data.
   a. Picks out the elements in a mathematical problem that can be used in its solution.
   b. Sees relationships between these elements.
   c. Uses essential formulae.
   d. Performs fundamental operations as addition, subtraction, multiplication and division.

e. Uses the metric and English system of measurement.
f. Understands the mathematical terms used in these problems; i.e., square, proportion, area, volume, etc.
7. Makes observations suitable for solving the problem.
   a. Observes demonstrations.
      (1) Devises suitable demonstrations.
      (2) Selects materials and equipment needed in the demonstration.
      (3) Identifies the important ideas demonstrated.
   b. Picks out the important ideas presented by pictures, slides, and motion pictures.
   c. Picks out the important ideas presented by models and exhibits.
   d. Uses the resources of the community for purposes of obtaining information pertinent to the problem.
      (1) Locates conditions or situations in the community to observe.
      (2) Picks out the essential ideas from such observation.
8. Uses talks and interviews as sources of information.
   a. Selects individuals who can contribute to the solution of the problem.
   b. Makes suitable plans for the talk or interview.
   c. Appropriately contacts the person who is to talk.
   d. Selects the main ideas from the activity.
   e. Properly acknowledges the courtesy of the individual interviewed.

D. Organizes the data obtained
  1. Uses appropriate means for organizing data.
    a. Constructs tables.
    b. Constructs graphs.
    c. Prepares summaries.
    d. Makes outlines.
    e. Constructs diagrams.
    f. Uses photographs.
    g. Uses suitable statistical procedures.

E. Interprets organized data
  1. Selects the important ideas related to the problem.
  2. Identifies the different relationships which may exist between the important ideas.
  3. States these relationships as generalizations which may serve as hypotheses.

F. Tests the hypotheses
  1. Checks proposed conclusion with authority.
  2. Devises experimental procedures suitable for testing the hypotheses.
  3. Rechecks data for errors in interpretation.

Appendix

G. Formulates a conclusion
 1. Accepts the most tenable of the tested hypotheses.
 2. Uses this hypothesis as a basis for generalizing in terms of similar problem situations.

An inventory of problem-solving practices can be used by a teacher in making an appraisal of the extent to which he provides for the suggested items under the various elements in problem solving. By making a self-analysis of practices in regard to this objective, a teacher should be able to locate his strengths and weaknesses. This would provide a reliable basis for improving classroom practice.

Inventory of Problem-Solving Practices

Directions: Check your response to each of the following items in the proper space at the right.   Often   Occasionally   Seldom   Never

A. *Sensing and Defining Problems:*
To what extent do you:
 1. help pupils sense situations involving personal and social problems?
 2. help pupils recognize specific problems in these situations?
 3. help pupils in isolating the single major idea of a problem?
 4. help pupils state problems as definite and concise questions?
 5. help pupils pick out and define the key words as a means of getting a better understanding of the problem?
 6. help pupils evaluate problems in terms of personal and social needs?
 7. help pupils to be aware of the exact meaning of word-groups and shades of meaning of words in problems involving the expression of ideas?
 8. present overview lessons to raise significant problems?
 9. permit pupils to discuss possible problems for study?

	Often	Occasionally	Seldom	Never

10. encourage personal interviews about problems of individual interest?

B. *Collecting Evidence on Problems:*
   To what extent do you:
   1. provide a wide variety of sources of information?
   2. help pupils develop skill in using reference sources?
   3. help pupils develop skill in note taking?
   4. help pupils develop skill in using aids in books?
   5. help pupils evaluate information pertinent to the problem?
   6. provide laboratory demonstrations for collecting evidence on a problem?
   7. provide controlled experiments for collecting evidence on a problem?
   8. help pupils to develop skill in interviewing to secure evidence on a problem?
   9. provide for using the resources of the community in securing evidence on a problem?
   10. provide for using visual aids in securing evidence on a problem?
   11. evaluate the pupils' ability for collecting evidence on a problem as carefully as you evaluate their knowledge of facts?

C. *Organizing Evidence on Problems:*
   To what extent do you:
   1. help pupils develop skill in arranging data?
   2. help pupils develop skill in making graphs of data?
   3. help pupils make use of deductive reasoning in areas best suited?

Appendix

		Often	Occasionally	Seldom	Never

   4. provide opportunities for pupils to make summaries of data?
   5. help pupils distinguish relevant from irrelevant data?
   6. provide opportunity for pupils to make outlines of data?
   7. evaluate the pupils' ability to organize evidence on a problem as carefully as you evaluate their knowledge of facts?

D. *Interpreting Evidence on Problems:*
   To what extent do you:
   1. help pupils select the important ideas related to the problem?
   2. help pupils identify the different relationships which may exist between the important ideas?
   3. help pupils see the consistencies and weaknesses in data?
   4. help pupils state relationships as generalizations which may serve as hypotheses?
   5. evaluate the pupils' ability for interpreting evidence as carefully as you evaluate their knowledge of facts?

E. *Selecting and Testing Hypotheses:*
   To what extent do you:
   1. help pupils judge the significance or pertinency of data?
   2. help pupils check hypotheses with recognized authorities?
   3. help pupils make inferences from facts and observations?
   4. help pupils devise controlled experiments suitable for testing hypotheses?
   5. help pupils recognize and formulate assumptions basic to a given hypothesis?
   6. help pupils recheck data for possible errors in interpretation?

	Often	Occasionally	Seldom	Never

7. evaluate the pupils' ability for selecting and testing hypotheses as carefully as you evaluate their knowledge of facts?

F. *Formulating Conclusions:*
   To what extent do you:

   1. help pupils formulate conclusions on the basis of tested evidence?

   2. help pupils evaluate their conclusions in the light of the assumptions they set up for the problem?

   3. help pupils apply their conclusions to new situations?

   4. evaluate the pupils' ability to formulate conclusions as carefully as you evaluate their knowledge of facts?

Index

Abstraction processes, 28
Academic talent, 109
Acting, in creativity, 231
Action, representation by child, 24
Advanced Placement Program, for gifted students, 197
Affective objectives, 62, 83
  continuums of, 99-100
  evaluation of, 110-12
  hierarchy of, 95-96
  overt and covert, 96-97
  samples of, 97-99
  two strategies, 134
  writing objectives, 100
Affective Self-Report Instrument (Likert Scale), 111
American Association for Advancement of Science, 29
Analogies, in creativity-synectics, 219-21
Animistic views, by child, 22
Art, National Assessment Project objectives, 283
Association for Supervision and Curriculum Development (ASCD), 8
Assumptions, contrary to fact, 28
Attention, centering, 20
Authority, and values, 113

Baker, Eva, 302
Barron, Frank, 209

Behavior-content grid, 88-89
Behavioral objectives
  affective, 83
  analyzing and evaluating techniques, 88-89
  cognitive, 82
  criticisms of, 101
  evaluating, 245
  psychomotor, 83
  teachers' competencies, 304
  two measurement instruments, 111
Biological Sciences Curriculum Study, 29
  Comprehensive Biology Test, 51
  invitation to inquiry, 127, 151, 152
Blanton, B., 301
Bloom, Benjamin, 95
  taxonomy, 61-62, 75, 82
  test questions for, 246-57
British open classroom instruction, 175-76
Bruner, Jerome, 41
  four reasons for discovery approach, 42
Business and industry programs for gifted students, 195

Career Occupational Development, objectives in, 284
Carnegie-Mellon University, 52
Chambers, M.A., 305
Cheating, 263

Child, four stages of mental development
   abstract reflexive thinking, 25-29
   concrete operations, 22-25
   discriminating and labeling, 17-19
   intuitive stage, 19-22
Citizenship
   exercises for objectives, 288-90
   interrelationship with other subjects, 290-96
   National Assessment Project objectives in, 283
Clark, John M., 181
Classes, making exciting, 314-16
Classifying concepts, by a child, 23
Classroom management
   discipline, 320-22
   rewarding creativity, 214
   stimulating creative environment, 212-14
Cognitive development, four stages, 16-35 (*see also* Mental development)
Cognitive objectives, 62, 82
   action verbs, 89-90
   skill development, 90-95
   steps in writing objectives, 84
      establishing acceptable performance, 87
      hypotheses, design, and infer, 85-86
      writing conditions, 86
      writing extent of achievement, 87
Combs, Arthur W., 8
Commerical tests, 243
Committee work for teachers, 357
Communication, free, 212, 213
Communication talent, 109
Competencies, of good teachers, 300-7
Competency-based programs, criticism of, 305-7
Concepts
   attaining, 132
   classifying and relating, 23

Concepts (Continued)
   developing, 131
   as discovery activity, 39, 40
Continuous progress instruction plan, 174
Control, and creativity, 213, 214
Cooper, James M., 300
Cost, for individualized instruction, 180
Cox, Benjamin, 125
Craig, Richard, 204
Creative abilities
   categories of, 206
   predictions of, 207-9
Creative individuals, characteristics, 206
Creative questioning, 215
Creative talent, 108
   methods for developing, 215-19
   listening, 218
   questioning, 216
Creativity
   defined, 205
   developing (other ways), 232-37
   development of potential, 211-12
   and modern curricula, 237
   morphological analysis approach to problem solving, 227-30
   research findings, 209-10
   rewarding, in classroom, 214
   stimulating class environment, 212-14
   time rating form, 237-39
Creativity -synectics, 219-27
Critical thinking, 130
   evaluation of process, 264
      examples of questions, 265-68
   objectives for inquiry roles, 154-55
   in questioning process, 62, 63
Curriculum, and creativity, 237
Curriculum knowledge, and teachers' competencies, 303
Curriculum projects, 29

Dance, in creativity, 231
Day, William, 51

Index

Decision-making talent, 109
Democratic methods in teaching, 124
  conflict of public issues, 126-30
  democratic process involvement, 125
  Dewey on, 123
  investigative group appraoch, 125
Denver, Colorado, Manual High School, 196
Dewey, John, and democratic processes, 123-24, 126
Dichotomous terms, 268
Discipline
  and classroom management, 320-22
  handling when need arises, 319
  purposes of, 309-10
  self-discipline
    developing, 322
    in junior and senior high, 317-19
  setting stage for, 312-14
  and student teachers, 340
Discovery activities defined, 39
Discovery learning, guided vs. free, 46-48 (see also Inquiry teaching)
Discovery teaching
  four reasons for using, 42
  research findings, 51-53
Discrepant event, 138, 139
Discussions
  student-centered, 68-72
  and teacher competency, 303
Disraeli, on theory, 4
Downs, Gary, 111
Durkin, Mary C., 130

Earth Science Curriculum Project, *Investigating the Earth*, 180
Edmonton, Alberta, Department of Education, 247
Educational objectives, 61-63
Egocentricity, 22, 113
Elementary Science Study, 29
Elkind, David, 24, 38
English syllabus, 187-93
"Environmental Studies" project, 166

Essay tests, 245-46
Evaluation (*see also* Tests)
  Alternatives to grading, 273
  contract method, 275-78
  of critical thinking process, 264-68
  self-evaluation inventories, 270-72
  for teachers, 361-66
  testing for objectives, 245
Evaluation instruments, types of, 243
Expectancy level, of student, 44
Extrinsic rewards, 42

Facilities in schools, for individualized instruction, 177
Feelings, exploring in inductive approach, 134
Forecasting talent, 109
Fort Lauderdale, Flroida, Nova High School, 178, 181, 187, 193
Fraenkel, Jack R., 130

Generalizations, in inductive approach, 132, 133, 136
Genetic and Epistemology Institute in Geneva, Switzerland, 16
Gibbs, Jack R., 212-14
Goals
  defined, 81
  examples, 82
Gordon, William J. J., 219, 221, 227
Grades, 214
  alternatives to, 273-75
  contract method, 275-78
  and creative ability, 208
Graduate work for teachers, 356
Graham, R.A., 305
Graphs, and test questions, 269-70
Guilford, J.P., 10, 110

Hackett, Jay, 110-11
Harmin, Merrill, 116
Henderson, Judith E., 300
Henkel, Omar T., 51
Hess, Robert D., 211-12
Hofwolt, Clifford A., 272n5
Horn, Paul, 219

Human Science, 29
Hutchinson, 208
Hypotheses
 and deductive thinking, 27, 32, 41
 limited, of a child, 23

Illinois Studies in Inquiry Training, 29
Individualized instruction
 achievement recognition, 201
 advantages of, 176
 continuous progress plan, 174
 for gifted students, 194-98
 large or small group, 193-94
 open school, 175
 problems of implementing, 177-80
 resistance to, 174
 for slow learners and culturally deprived, 198
 syllabuses for, 180-93
 teaching activities for, 199-201
 term oriented, 175
Inductive approach, 130 (see also Inquiry approach)
 analyzing values, 135-36
 concepts
  attaining, 132, 133
  developing, 131-32
 exploring feelings, 134
 generalizations
  applying, 136-37
  developing, 132, 133
 interpersonal problem solving, 134
Infralogical operations, 20
Inner-city programs, for gifted students, 196
Inner-city teaching, 164
 and the new teacher, 167-68
 humanizing teaching, 168-70
 and student teachers, 331-32
Inquiry approach
 dividing class period, 158-61
 invitations to inquiry, 151
  example of, 156-58
  student-prepared, 158
 role approach, 152-56, 231
 and teacher competencies, 303

Inquiry strategies, for problem-solving abilities, 123-24
Inquiry teaching, 40
 free inquiry, 49-50
 guided vs. free, 45-48
 mental processes chart, 41
 reasons for using, 42-45
 research findings, 51-53
Inservice training for teachers, 357
Instructional theories, foundation for, 4-9, 13
 main tenets of, 8
 principles of learning, 6
 teaching principles, 7
Intellectual potency, 42
Intrinsic rewards, 42
I.Q., 239
 testing, 110, 207-8

Jones, Howard L., 300
Joyce, Bruce, 128
Judd, Charles H., 125
Junior high self-discipline, 317

Kapfer, P., 99
Kelley, Earl C., 8
Kilpatrick, William H., 125
Kohlber, Lawrence, 113, 115, 116
Krathwohl, David R., 95, 99

Labeling, in sensori-motor stage, 18
Lanier, Perry, 300
Learning, principles of, 6-7
Learning process
 as complex, 1-3
 three steps, 106
Listening, sensitive, techniques, 75-76
Literature, National Assessment Project objectives in, 283
Logical operations, 19
Logical thinking, 31-35

McNaughton, Anthony H., 130
Madison Project, 29
Makato State College, Wilson School, Makato, Minnesota, 175
Masia, Bertram B., 95

Index

Maslow, Abraham H., 8, 9, 204-5, 239
Massialas, Byron, 125
Materials, for individualized instruction, 179
Mathematics, 268
   graphs, 269-70
   National Assessment Project objectives in, 282
Mathematics nights/days, 196
Memory retention, 42
Mental development, four stages, 17, 31
   concrete operational, 22-25
   formal operational, 25-29, 32
   pre-operational, 19-22
   sensori-motor, 17-19
Metaphors, in creativity-synectics, 219
Metrical terms, 268
Michaelis, John U., 125
Mid-Continent Regional Educational Laboratory (McREL), 152, 153-56
Montean, John, 51
Morals (*see* Value clarification)
Morphological analysis approach, 227-30
Mueller, Richard J., 208
Multiple-talent approach, 10-14
   chart, 12
   questioning for, 66
   six talent areas, 107, 108-9
Music, National Assessment Project objectives in, 284

Nash, R.J., 305
National Assessment of Educational Progress, 281-97
   examples of exercises, 284-90
   interrelationship between subjects, 290-95

Objectives, in National Assessment Project, 281-84
Observed Affective Behavior Checklist, 111
Oliver, Donald W., 125, 126-28, 138
Open school instruction, 175-76

Organization, in child development, 18

Pacs (learning materials), 200
Physical operations, in sensori-motor stage, 18
Piaget, Jean, 41, 45, 53, 67, 115
   theory of cognitive development, 16-35
Piagetian theory, and teachers' competencies, 303
Pictorial riddle approach, 140-51
Planning talent, 109
Play, and reality, 22
Popham, W.J., 302
Principles
   discovery activity, 39, 40
   of learning, 6-7
   of teaching, 7-8
Probability, understanding of, 22, 26
Problem-solving, 123-24
   interpersonal, 134-35
   morphological analysis approach in creativity, 227
Problem-solving objectives
   achieving, 367-73
   inventory of practices, 373-76
Progressive Education Movement, 124
Professional groups, programs for gifted students, 197
Professional organizations for teachers, 357-58
Psychomotor objectives, 83

Quantitative terms, 268-70
Questioning (*see also* Inductive approaches)
   teachers' competencies, 303
   creative, 215-17
   for good discussion
      amplifying and pursuing thought, 71
      clarifying material, 71
      constrictive thinking, 70
      emotional overtone of material, 72

Questioning (Continued)
  halting time, 69
  multiple questions, 69
  over-generalizations, 71
  over-reacting to replies, 70
  paraphrasing, 72
  rewarding responses, 70
  summarizing, 71
Questions
  area of instruction involved, 58
  classifying, 62
  convergent and divergent, 63-65
  for critical thinking processes, 62, 63
  for an inquiry discussion, 56-57
  for multi-talents, 66
  self-analysis of questions, 60-61
  teleological/anthropomorphic, 65-66
  tests for Bloom's taxonomy, 246-55 (see also Tests)
  types of, 58-60, 72-75
  wait-time for responses, 67, 68

Raths, Louis, 116, 120, 126
Reading
  exercises for objectives, 286-87
  interrelationship with other subjects, 290-96
  National Assessment Project objectives in, 282
Recognition, for achievement and multi-talent, 201
Reflexive thinking, 25, 41
Roe, Ann, 208
Rogers, Carl R., 8, 51
Rowe, Mary Budd, 68, 210
Rules
  accepting, 28
  and discipline, 312
  and value clarification, 113

Salinger, Richard, 44-45
Scannell, Dale P., 255
Scheduling, individual instruction, 178
Schools
  extracurricular programs for gifted students, 195

Schools (Continued)
  facilities for individualized instruction, 177
  programs for gifted students in small schools, 197
  surplus equipment for, 195
Schutte, Wand, 323
Science, A Process Approach, 29
Science
  exercises for objectives, 284-86
  interrelationship with other subjects, 291-96
  National Assessment Project objectives in, 282
  student affective behavior toward, 111
  "Summary Description of Grade Nine Science Objectives and Test Items," 247
Science Curriculum Improvement Study at University of California, 29
Science nights/days, 196
Science syllabus, 180-81
Self-concepts (self-esteem)
  of individuals, 8
  of students, 9, 11, 43, 44
Self-determination, 212-13
Self-evaluation inventories, 36-37, 270-72, 361-66
Self-evaluation questions, 14-15
Senior high self-discipline, 317
Shaver, James P., 125, 126-28, 138
Shulman, Lee S., 51
Silberman, Charles, 105
Simon, Sidney, 115-16
Skills development, 90
  acquisitive, 91
  communicative, 92
  creative, 91
  manipulative, 92
  organizational, 91
  rationale for, 92-95
Social issues, teaching methods for, 124-30
Social studies
  National Assessment Project objectives in, 283

Index

Social Studies (Continued)
 syllabus, 181-86
Space (see Time)
Stanford Teacher Competence Appraisal Guide, 353-55
Stillwagen, Walter R., 255
Stimulation
 external, for child, 26
 in preoperational stage, 20
 in sensori-motor stage, 17
Student activities, in inner-city teaching, 170
Student-centered
 discussions, 68-72
 inquiry instruction, 42-43
Students
 individual instruction for slow learner, 198
 in inner city, 165
 in inquiry learning, 45
  self-concepts of, 43-44
 programs for gifted students, 194-98
 relating with teachers, 9-10
 self-evaluation inventories, 271, 272
 understanding secondary students, 310-11
Student teaching
 advantages, 327-29
 and discipline, 340
 the first day, 341
 observation period, 332-37
 preparing a lesson, 338
 and responsibilities, 342
 and supervising teacher, 329-32
 tips for, 343-44
Suchman, J. Richard, theory building approach, 137-40
Summer work experience, 195
Synectics, and creativity, 219-27
 example, 222-27
Syllabuses for individualized instruction
 English, 187-93
 science, 180
 social studies, 181-86
Taba, Hilda, seven inductive approaches, 130-37, 138

Talents, 44 (see also Multiple-talents)
Taylor, Calvin, 10-11, 208
 six talent areas, 107, 108-9
Teacher competencies, 300-5
Teacher-prepared tests, 243
Teachers
 characteristics of a good teacher, 352-55
 checklist for qualities, 304
 how to gain respect, 311
 and individual instruction, 178
 job procurement, 348
  after getting the job, 352
  interview, 351
  letters of application, 350
  placement services, 349-50
 making class exciting, 314-16
 multi-talent approach, 10
 new, in the inner city, 167-68
 professional growth, 356-57
 relating with students, 9-10
 self-evaluation inventory, 361-66
 and student teachers, 329, 32
Teaching
 four major tasks, 300
 humanizing, in inner city, 168-70
 three steps in learning process, 106
Teaching activities, for individual differences, 199-201
Teaching methods
 democratic methods, 124-30
 other inquiry methods, 151-61
 pictorial riddle approach, 140-51
 problem-solving abilities, 123
 Taba's seven inductive approaches, 130-37
 Suchman theory building approach, 137-40
Teaching principles, 7-8
Tests
 completion and matching, 260
 diagrams or pictures, 261
 guidelines to use, 262
 multiple-choice, 259
 a problem test, 261
 questions using Bloom's taxonomy
  analysis, 248-50
  application, 247-48

Tests (Continued)
   comprehension, 246
   evaluation, 251-53
   in mathematics, 253-55
   recall, knowledge, 246
   synthesis, 251
   self-test, 260
   student correction, 262
   true or false, 258
   types of, 243
Term oriented individualized instruction, 175
Thelen, Herbert, investigative group approach, 125-26, 138
Theory (see also Instructional theory)
   Suchman's theory building approach, 137-40
   three fundamental functions, 4
Thinking (see Critical thinking; Thought processes)
Thought processes
   abstraction, 28-29
   facilitating logical thinking, 30-35
   formal thought, 41
   hypothetical-deductive, 27, 32
   not reversible by child, 21
   propositional thinking, 27, 33
   reflexive thinking, 26, 34
   stimulus related, 22-23
Time and space concept, of a child, 22, 24
Torrance, Paul, 205, 207, 239
Trust, 212, 213

UNIPACS, 200
University of Northern Colorado, 331, 343

Value clarification, 112-20
   areas of conflict, 117
   conforming stage, 113, 114
   pre-moral stage, 113-14
   procedures for students, 118
   self-accepting moral stage, 113, 114-15
   strategies, 119, 120
Values
   analyzing, of individuals or groups, 135-36
   defined, 116
   conflicts in social issues, 127-30
Variables, controlling, 28
Verbal level of learning, and inquiry method, 44-45

Wait-time, for responses to questions, 67, 68, 210
Weber, Wilford A., 300
Weil, Marsha, 128
Welch, David, 323
Wolfe, Thomas, 107
Wong, Harry, 106
Writing
   exercises for objectives, 287-88
   National Assessment Project Objectives in, 282

Zwicky, Fritz, 227

DATE DUE			
JUL 2			
GAYLORD			PRINTED IN U.S.A